Marvel Comics'
Civil War

Exploring the Moral Judgment of Captain
America, Iron Man, and Spider-Man

Mark D. White

Published by Ockham Publishing in the United Kingdom

ISBN 978-1-910780-10-7

Cover design by Armend Meha

www.ockham-publishing.com

About the Author

Mark D. White is Professor and Chair of the Department of Philosophy at the College of Staten Island/CUNY, where he teaches courses in philosophy, law, and economics. He is the author of *The Virtues of Captain America: Modern-Day Lessons on Character from a World War II Superhero* (Wiley-Blackwell), *The Manipulation of Choice: Ethics and Libertarian Paternalism* and *The Illusion of Well-Being: Economic Policymaking Based on Respect and Responsiveness* (both from Palgrave Macmillan), and *Kantian Ethics and Economics: Autonomy, Dignity, and Character* (Stanford University Press), as well as over 50 academic journal articles and book chapters on the intersections between economics, philosophy, and law. He has edited or co-edited a number of books on these subjects, including *The Thief of Time: Philosophical Essays on Procrastination* (with Chrisoula Andreou), *Economics and the Virtues: Building a New Moral Foundation* (with Jennifer A. Baker), and *Retributivism: Essays on Theory and Policy* (all from Oxford University Press), and he edits two book series: "Perspectives from Social Economics" (Palgrave Macmillan) and "On Ethics and Economics" (Rowman & Littlefield International).

Mark is also author of the 'A Philosopher Reads…' series on philosophy and comic books with Ockham Publishing, and a frequent contributor and editor in the Blackwell Philosophy and Pop Culture series. He has edited or co-edited volumes on *Batman*, *Watchmen*, *Iron Man*, *Green Lantern*, *the Avengers*, and *Superman*, and contributed to volumes on *Spider-Man*, *X-Men*, *Black Sabbath*, *Metallica*, *South Park*, *The Office*, *Family Guy*, and *Alice in Wonderland*.

You can find more information about Mark's books, articles, and blogs (including his popular Psychology Today blog, "Maybe It's Just Me, But…") at http://www.profmdwhite.com and follow him on Twitter (@profmdwhite).

Acknowledgments

I want to thank Rob Johnson and Ockham Publishing for embracing this project, and I hope we have a long and fruitful publishing relationship. I thank Louise Spencely for an amazing job copyediting the manuscript (as she also did on *The Virtues of Captain America* and *Superman and Philosophy*) as well as providing invaluable and never-ending help with formatting and preparation for publication. I thank S.L. Johnson for providing wonderful insights about publication and promotion. I thank Liam Cooper and Leila Campoli for invaluable advice through the formation of the project. For unending friendship and support, I thank Lauren Hale, Carol Borden, Anita Leirfall, and William Irwin.

I also want to thank all of the brilliant and thoughtful creators at Marvel Comics who participated in *Civil War* and its aftermath, people such as Mark Millar, Steve McNiven, J. Michael Straczynski, Brian Michael Bendis, Paul Jenkins, Christos Gage, Mike Deodato, Jr., Mike McKone, Ron Garney, Ramon Bachs, Matt Fraction, Ed Brubaker, Tom Breevort, and Joe Quesada. This is the storyline that drew me fully into the Marvel Universe, and it remains a high-water mark for thoughtful, suspenseful, and action-packed event comics.

Finally, I want to thank the creators of the three characters on whom I focus here: Stan Lee, Jack Kirby, Steve Ditko, Joe Simon, Larry Lieber, and Don Heck. Without you, comics, movies, and pop culture in general would not be the same—and neither would this simple philosopher.

Table of Contents

Introduction

After a tragedy involving tremendous loss of life, the United States government quickly passes a law that favors security over liberty, and then engages in secretive and questionable methods of detention, with both aimed at preventing a similar tragedy in the future.

Sound familiar? If you were old enough to realize what was happening on September 11, 2001, or have learned about it since, it should. The tragic events of 9/11, as that day has come to be known, made Americans all too aware of a growing threat of terrorism that, until then, seemed to be confined to the rest of the world. Afterwards, the US government scrambled to ensure a similar catastrophe could never happen again, and in the process took actions that ignited a new debate over liberty and security that continues to this day.

But if you're a comic book fan, my description of events also brings forward images of a group of young inexperienced heroes triggering an accident that caused the deaths of hundreds of innocent people (including dozens of schoolchildren), after which the US government passed a law required masked superhumans to register and reveal their identities, culminating in a lengthy battle between heroes—in particular, one with a red, white, and blue shield fighting against another wearing golden armor.

Marvel Comics' *Civil War* was a self-conscious allegory to the events of September 11 and its aftermath (even though the actual events of 9/11 occurred in the world of the Marvel superheroes as well). It cast two of the premier Marvel superheroes as figureheads of the two ideas being debated, with Captain America fighting to preserve liberty and Iron Man struggling to ensure security. Nearly every other hero took sides—the promotional materials for the storyline asked readers, "Whose Side Are *You* On?"—and the most popular Marvel superhero of them all, Spider-Man, was caught in the middle.

In this book, we'll follow the paths of these three heroes through Marvel's Civil War, which took place in 2006 and 2007 in the seven-issue *Civil War* comic book and in about 100 tie-in comics in other titles such as *Captain America*, *Iron Man*, and *The Amazing Spider-Man*. We'll look at the actions and motivations of Cap, Iron Man, and Spidey, in terms of the personal ethics behind their decisions as well as the broader principles of liberty and security at the heart of the Civil

1

War—the same principles that still motivate debates in the real world over controversial issues such as surveillance, detention, and torture.

In the decade since the original series, Marvel Comics has revisited the Civil War several times, in several issues of *What If?* in 2008 and 2009 as well as a new *Civil War* miniseries in 2015, all exploring different ways the conflict could have gone and ended—or, in the case of the miniseries, if it never ended at all. There was also a novelization of the storyline in 2012 and a *Civil War II* miniseries in 2016, the latter coming out around the same time as the feature film *Captain America: Civil War*, which portrays the ideological battle between Captain America and Iron Man on the big screen. The Civil War storyline never seems to go out of style, largely due to the issue at its core: conflicts between important principles, whether the broad societal principles of liberty, privacy, and security, or the more personal principles of duty, loyalty, and care. The way we balance these principles in our personal, public, and political lives is a topic that this philosopher loves to write about, and Civil War gives him the perfect opportunity to discuss them with you.

Whose side are *you* on? Let's see…

Chapter 1: Setting the Stage

> "In everyone's life, Peter, there's an 'it'… your wife leaves you, or you get cancer. There's your life before 'it' and your life after 'it.' 9/11 was an 'it' of national magnitude. And Stamford… is going to be another one."—*Iron Man to Spider-Man*[1]

The world of Marvel Comics, known to fans as the Marvel Universe, has always been more of a mirror of our real world than the world of DC Comics is. While DC has Metropolis (home to Superman), Gotham City (Batman), and Central City (the Flash), the architects of the early Marvel Universe chose to put most of its heroes in or around New York City.[2] This enables readers to connect more closely to the locales in the comics: they see Spider-Man swinging from the Chrysler Building, Daredevil chasing a criminal through the alleys of Hell's Kitchen, and the X-Men training in Professor X's Westchester mansion, all real places they can live in, visit, or see on the news.

This aspect of realism in Marvel Comics also allows the creators to portray real-world events in their stories. Because most Marvel stories are set in New York City, celebrities and political figures often show up, from mayors to talk show hosts like David Letterman. When the president of the United States is shown, he (or, someday, she) is usually the real-world president at the time (although often depicted in shadow to preserve some degree of timelessness in the story). And when something cataclysmic happens, especially in New York City, the comics show that too, as they did with the events of September 11, 2001. A very moving issue of *Amazing Spider-Man* showed various heroes (and a few villains) mourning the death and destruction from that day, and a story arc in *Captain America* modeled the ideal reaction to the tragedy, perfectly balancing sensitivity to Americans of Middle Eastern descent while focusing the military response on the individuals responsible.[3]

While we can assume that the US government in the Marvel Universe reacted in the same way to 9/11 as ours did—they passed the PATRIOT Act, for example—readers had to wait until 2006 to see the Marvel superheroes react to their own tragedy.[4] Even though, unlike 9/11, the incident that launched the Civil War was caused by a handful of inexperienced heroes, following a series of catastrophes involving other heroes, it prompted a similar public outcry and legislative response as occurred in response to 9/11 in the real world. Unique to the comics, however, the tragedy in the Marvel Universe resulted in a wholescale war that posed hero against hero.

If we peel away the superhero façade, under the capes and masks we see the same debates in the Marvel Universe as we do in the real world. These include conflicts between liberty and security in the political realm as well as between defending the right and advancing the good in the personal realm. For these reasons, I call the Marvel Comics Civil War a war of *principle*: on the surface, it's an exciting battle between superheroes, but dig a little deeper, and you find a battle of ideals. And this isn't your ordinary good-versus-evil battle, such as when Captain America protects freedom against the Red Skull's dreams of tyranny. Instead, this battle of principle is amongst the forces of good, where each principle is valid and admirable on its own, such as liberty and security. Yet, as we've seen numerous times since 9/11, these principles are not compatible, and we have to decide which one to favor over the other at any particular time. Rather than choose one principle to favor over others, we must find a way to balance them, and the proper balance will not always be the same—nor will anyone likely agree with anyone else on what the proper balance should be.

The general point I want to make in this book is that these conflicts of principle occur all the time, in both our political and personal lives, and even though we have to prioritize certain principles in particular cases, all of the principles remain important and valuable. Even though we may decide to privilege security or liberty at some point, both of them must still be valued and promoted; we wouldn't choose one and dismiss the other entirely. In terms of personal decision-making, even though some people try to do what's right, according to rules and duties, while others try to promote what's good, in terms of welfare or well-being, they are all advancing important principles of morality. With all due respect to Iron Man, the choices here are not stark ones—they're not about right answers and wrong answers, but about finding the right balance between equally valid principles for a particular situation, and recognizing that different situations require different solutions with their own unique balancing of principles.

In this chapter, we'll summarize the main points of the story and the aspects of it that we'll focus on throughout this book. If you haven't read Civil War yet, I *highly encourage* you to do so now. As they say in the biz, there will be spoilers! There is much, much more in the over one hundred issues of comics in the Civil War storyline than I can include here (although I do try to cram in as much as I can), so this book is no substitute for the real thing. Here, I want to draw out some topics of philosophical interests from Civil War; if you haven't read the original, I'll give you enough information to get the points I'm making, but to enjoy this book to the fullest, it would help to read at least the main Civil War series first. (Wait, don't put this book back! Buy this *and* Civil War. Whew, that was close.)

A Snapshot of the Marvel Universe Before the Civil War

The Civil War did not start out of the blue; events had been leading to it for quite a while. What did the Marvel Universe look like heading into the Civil War? Let's set the stage and see what embers were smoldering before the final match was lit, and also introduce the main characters involved.

One of the most common sights in superhero comics (and blockbuster action movies of any type) is wide-scale destruction, especially in the middle of a major metropolitan area such as New York City. Occasionally comics creators will make note of the damage caused by battles between superheroes and supervillains, and sometimes attention is paid to the clean-up efforts (as in Marvel Comics' *Damage Control* series), but less often to the human costs. We may like to think that no one is seriously hurt when Iron Man fights the Wrecking Crew in the middle of Times Square, and that the resulting harm is "merely" property damage for which victims can be compensated (usually out of Tony Stark's deep pockets). But this stretches even the generous disbelief that readers may engage in to believe that people can fly, shoot energy beams from their eyes, and return from the dead more easily than you return from the dentist.

The Civil War was born out of the realization amongst the ordinary citizens of the Marvel Universe that enough is enough, that they could no longer bear the increasingly frequent, costly, and sometimes deadly catastrophes that resulted from their superheroes mixing it up with their arch-nemeses (or even their fellow heroes). In fact, leading up to the disaster in Stamford, Connecticut, that directly led to the Civil War, a number of lesser disasters had occurred in the Marvel Universe.[5]

> *Genosha*: After an abhorrent history of mutant apartheid, the island nation of Genosha was designated by the United Nations as a mutant sanctuary to be ruled by Magneto, master of magnetism and former head of the Brotherhood of Evil Mutants. Its population numbered over 16 million—about half the mutants on Earth—when the villain Cassandra Nova and her mutant-hunting robot Sentinels destroyed all life on Genosha.[6] The

world of the Marvel Universe, already plagued by anti-mutant prejudice, was now faced with a 21st-century holocaust (directly analogous, of course, to the Jewish Holocaust during World War II).

Avengers Disassembled/House of M: The Scarlet Witch, a long-time Avenger and mutant, suffered a mental breakdown which led to the deaths of several Avengers, including Hawkeye and her ex-husband the Vision, the destruction of the Avengers Mansion, and the (temporary) dissolution of the Avengers.[7] But that wasn't all: even under the care of her father Magneto, now returned to Genosha, the Scarlet Witch's condition continued to deteriorate until she lost control over her reality-warping powers, reforming the world into a mutant paradise in which her father Magneto was ruler and the two children she had lost years ago were still alive.[8] When reality reverted to normal, only the heroes involved remembered the incident—but the three simple words the Scarlet Witch uttered had enormous ramifications for the Marvel Universe going forward: "No more mutants." With these words, the Scarlet Witch robbed nearly all remaining mutants on Earth of their powers, leaving only 198 mutants (give or take) left with their powers.[9]

Nick Fury's Secret War: When Nick Fury, longtime director of SHIELD, uncovered a plot by the prime minister of Latveria, Lucia Von Bardas, to carry out terror attacks in the United States by arming minor villains with advanced technology, the US government refuses to act due to its new diplomatic ties with the country now that Doctor Doom is no longer ruler.[10] Fury then assembles a clandestine group of superheroes, including Captain America and Spider-Man, to attack Latveria; they destroy the seat of government (Doom's castle), only to be brainwashed by Fury afterwards so they retain no memory of the incident. But the heroes start to remember as they're attacked by Von Bardas' villains, and together they (and Von Bardas) strike back on American soil, detonating a massive antimatter bomb in New York City. Fury blames the State Department for what he sees as a repeat of 9/11, and the heroes blame Fury for the extreme measures taken in Latveria and for brainwashing them. As a result, Fury goes underground, and Maria Hill—who will play a significant role in the Civil War—takes over as director of SHIELD.

Philadelphia: The City of Brotherly Love was rocked by a terrorist bombing masterminded by Captain America's arch-foe the Red Skull, who framed Jack Monroe (one-time sidekick to Cap as well as to the 1950s Captain America, William Burnside). To make matters worse, the bombing was carried out by the Winter Soldier, who turned out to be another person associated with Captain America.[11] Regardless of the truth, the public came to associate the deadly bombing with a former superhero.

Las Vegas: Near the jewel of the desert, the Incredible Hulk finds a HYDRA installation with a gamma bomb, which explodes and makes the Hulk even larger, stronger, and more uncontrollable than usual. Two members of the Fantastic Four, the Human Torch and the Thing, fly to Las Vegas and, for three issues, mix it up with the Hulk in Las Vegas, ending only when the Torch uses one of his "nova blasts" to put a halt to the Hulk's rampage, but not until after 26 people were killed.[12]

And following these disasters, where were the main players in the Marvel Universe at the time?

Iron Man (Tony Stark): After going public with his identity as Iron Man, Tony Stark was serving as the United States Secretary of Defense when the Scarlet Witch, in the midst of her breakdown, made him appear drunk and dangerous in front of the United Nations General Assembly.[13] After the destruction of Avengers Mansion and the dissolution of the Avengers, Tony put together a new Avengers team with Captain America, including, for the first time as a regular member, a certain friendly neighborhood Spider-Man.[14] At the same time, he also took the Extremis techno-virus to recover from a fatal beating, which enabled him to reengineer his mind and body to more closely interface with his armor on a cellular level.[15] However, this also subjected his armor to mind-control through him, causing hundreds of deaths and making him realize the danger his armor posed to the general public.[16]

On the side, Tony had been meeting in secret with Reed Richards (Mr. Fantastic of the Fantastic Four), Dr. Stephen Strange (Sorcerer Supreme), Black Bolt (king of the Inhumans), Professor Charles Xavier (mentor to the X-Men), and sometimes Namor (the Sub-Mariner, Prince of Atlantis), a covert brain-trust known to readers as the Illuminati. In a bit of revisionist comics history, the Iluminati were revealed to have been operating behind the scenes of the Marvel Universe to steer the course of history since the days of the Kree/Skrull War, and would play a role in the upcoming Civil War as well.[17]

Captain America (Steve Rogers): Around the same time that he reassembled a new Avengers team with Iron Man, Steve Rogers also discovered that his teenaged partner during World War II, James "Bucky" Barnes, did not die when the rocket he was trapped on exploded, as Cap long thought.[18] Instead, his body was recovered by the Soviets, who replaced his missing arm with a robotic prosthetic, brainwashed him, and retrained him to be the lethal assassin known as the Winter Soldier (who later set the bomb in Philadelphia, mentioned above). Once Cap became aware of the Winter Soldier's identity, he tracked Bucky and managed to break through his retraining, after which Bucky went into hiding.[19] Meanwhile, Cap also reconnected with his longtime love, Sharon Carter, also known as SHIELD Agent 13, as well as his longtime crimefighting partner in the modern world, the Falcon (Sam Wilson).

Spider-Man (Peter Parker): Shortly after being invited into the Avengers by Captain America, a young man with a grudge against Peter Parker burned down the apartment he shared with his wife Mary Jane as well as the home of his devoted Aunt May.[20] The three of them then move into Avengers Tower, where Aunt May is charmed by Captain America (who asked to see pictures of her late husband Ben) and wooed by the Avengers' butler Jarvis.[21] Peter also finds himself working closely with Tony Stark, a fellow scientific mind, who builds Peter a new costume—the technologically advanced "Iron Spidey" suit—and asks him to be his right-hand man as the political climate surround the superhero community begins to deteriorate.

We'll spend a lot more time with these three heroes throughout the rest of this book. Before we forget, however, let's talk about two important Marvel heroes who were conspicuously absent during the Civil War...

> *The Hulk (Bruce Banner)*: Last we saw the Hulk, he had killed 26 people in Las Vegas. The members of the Illuminati, frustrated at their inability to either cure, restrain, or control the Hulk, decide to trick him into a space capsule and launch him into deep space.[22] He landed on a savage planet on which he was enslaved, turned into a gladiator, and fought his way to becoming ruler and marrying, only to have his world inadvertently destroyed—by the Illuminati.[23] The Hulk managed to get back to Earth with some of his new friends, after the Civil War ended, to confront his old chums. If you think the Hulk caused some destruction before, just read the story that could only be titled... *World War Hulk*.[24]

> *Thor (just... Thor)*: Just before the Avengers were disassembled, the gods of Asgard experienced Ragnarok, the End of Days, in which they all died.[25] They would eventually return after the Civil War ended, but for the time being, all that was seen of the Odinson was his hammer, which mysteriously fell to Earth near Broxton, Oklahoma.[26] But in his stead, another wouldst rise, one who wouldst have deadly consequences and turn the tide of the Civil War. (Verily!)

It All Began in Stamford

The incident that started off the Civil War takes all of seven pages in the first issue of the series.[27] The team of young heroes known as the New Warriors were traveling the country filming a reality show when they became aware of four escaped supervillains—and I'm using the term *supervillain* very generously—holed up in a house in Stamford, Connecticut. Hoping for their breakthrough episode, the New Warriors engage the villains, more concerned about mugging for the camera than quickly and safely apprehending them. As Namorita (cousin of Namor) attacks the villain Nitro, he mocks her, claiming to be much more of a threat than they're used to handling, and triggers an explosion, killing over 600 people, sixty of them children playing outside at a nearby school.

Public outcry was immediate, especially considering the growing trend of superhero-related catastrophes over the years leading to Stamford. Talking heads on television began debating the wisdom (or foolishness) of unregulated superhero activity. Miriam Sharpe, whose son was one of the hundreds who died that day, became the public face of the Stamford tragedy and the legislative response: the Superhuman Registration Act (HR 421), or SHRA (not the snappiest acronym, admittedly). The SHRA requires that all super-powered heroes, including those who get their abilities through technology (like Iron Man), register with the federal government and SHIELD, revealing their identities (but not making them public), and submitting to training and being held accountable for their actions. In effect, they become members of a specialized unit of federal or state police, military personnel, or SHIELD, and would be assigned to one of the sanctioned superhero teams in every state in the union under the Fifty-State Initiative.[28] Heroes who refuse to register, as well as anyone aiding and abetting them, would be in violation of the law and subject to arrest and imprisonment. (Exactly where they would be imprisoned will be a major point of emphasis to come.)[29]

As we'll see in chapter 3, self-professed futurist Tony Stark saw this legislation coming and warned his fellow Illuminati about it.[30] He tried to defeat it while still in conference in the US Senate, and having failed at that, decided to take charge of its implementation. With Spider-Man at his side and working with other big brains such as Hank Pym and Reed Richards, Iron Man led a select team of registered Avengers to round up unregistered heroes as well as perform the normal duties of Avengers, such as fighting crime and saving lives (roles that risked being forgotten in the process of fighting over registration). He also engaged in such activities in support of the SHRA that some, both in the Marvel Universe and our own, found questionable, including using a prison in the Negative Zone (an antimatter dimension discovered by Reed Richards) to hold heroes who refused to register, enlisting the aid of confirmed villains to help capture said unregistered heroes, and creating a clone of one of his fellow Avengers that ended up creating a tragedy of his own.

Standing in opposition to registration and Iron Man was Captain America, the Sentinel of Liberty. As we'll see in Part II of this book, Cap argued strongly against the SHRA from the beginning, becoming a fugitive from SHIELD and the US government—not an unfamiliar position for a hero who has always stood for principle over politics.[31] Quickly going underground with his own band of rebels, including the Falcon, Daredevil, and Luke Cage, Cap focused on trying to protect unregistered heroes and rescue those already captured, at the same time that he debated the finer points of liberty and security with Iron Man. (We'll enjoy analyzing several of those debates later in this book.)

Finally, Peter Parker was the Spider-Man in the middle, starting out on Iron Man's side as he tried to prevent and then manage registration, but then gradually coming to agree with Captain America and his arguments against it. More so than for either older hero, registration was personal for Spidey, since he regarded his secret identity as essential to keeping his wife Mary Jane and his beloved Aunt May safe from his many enemies (who had struck out against those close to him in the past). As we'll see in Part III, this gave his decision-making a more grounded flavor; where and with whom he stood on the balance between liberty and security had enormous and potentially devastating consequences for his family.

As seen through the eyes of these three very different characters, we get to look at the ethical principles and ideals of the Civil War at various levels, from Cap and Iron Man's differences over political ideology and personal ethical stance that supports each hero's viewpoint, to Spidey's more personal take that brings the abstract issues down to earth and into his life.

Comparing the Marvel Comics Civil War to the Real World

As I mentioned in the introduction, Civil War was a loose but unrestrained analogue to the events following the attack on the World Trade Towers on September 11, 2001, in particular the PATRIOT Act and the prison at Guantanamo Bay. These aspects of the story were touched on in most of the related books, but were made explicit in *Civil War: Front Line*, a series that looked at registration and the Civil War through the eyes of two citizen journalists.[32] (We'll hear much of them in the chapters that follow.) In this section, we'll briefly discuss the parallels and differences between the world we live in and the one that includes Cap, Iron Man, and the rest of our favorite heroes.[33] (Ah, if only we could choose!)

While there was a tragic inciting event and rushed legislative reaction, as there was in the real world, the issue at the heart of *Civil War* was not terrorism but rather the irresponsible behavior of unaccountable superheroes. While it raised the same issues of liberty and security that the PATRIOT Act did here, the SHRA was more analogous to calls for gun-control legislation after tragedies like that at Sandy Hook Elementary School in December 2012. This was made explicit shortly before Stamford when Tony Stark became a victim of mind control and the man controlling him used his armor to kill hundreds of innocent civilians.[34] When Stark's friend assured him that he bore no responsibility since he was not in control, he responded, "every super hero is a potential gun... and the last time I checked, guns required registration."[35]

However, there are aspects of terrorism present in the story also, particularly in the fact that the combatants did not represent states or breakaway territories, but rather ideological factions. In a sense, Iron Man and the pro-registration heroes fought on behalf of the United States government and the SHRA, while Captain America and the anti-registration heroes were rebels, considering themselves to be freedom fighters, resisting what they saw as an oppressive law. As Captain America told a journalist after the Civil War ended, "I saw the possibility of a registration act as a basic violation of our rights as Americans."[36] The anti-registration forces were not military combatants—with the possible exception of Captain America, whose official military status has always been vague—but nonetheless were called "unregistered combatants" by the government, SHIELD, and Iron Man. Although Cap's forces did have to hide to escape detection and fought for ideological reasons—as terrorists often do—they certainly did not use the usual tools and tactics of terrorism, such as creating fear and targeting civilians. At their heart, the heroes on both sides tried to minimize the harm to civilian lives and property; as we'll see later, both Iron Man and Cap considered their positions to be based on what was best for the people they had sworn to protect.[37]

Despite a few parallels with terrorism, and the more obvious analogues to post-9/11 America, the conflict over registration truly resembles a civil war, with "establishment" forces fighting off a rebellion within its borders, setting citizens against each other over principles and ideals rather than territory or resources. As he stood in front of the Lincoln Memorial in Washington, DC, after testifying in front of Congress against registration, Tony Stark told Peter Parker that he admired Lincoln for knowing that the nation had to survive even if it meant a civil war in which "brother hunted down brother, friend turned against friend. It was terrible. It was bloody. It was necessary. Because at the end, the republic held, and the nation was restored."[38] As is typical for Tony, he saw what was coming better than most, but even he couldn't know everything that the Civil War between heroes would cost them.

The Principles of Liberty and Security and the Importance of Balance

At the heart of the Civil War—and between Captain America and Iron Man in particular—were the dual principles of liberty and security. We'll discuss them in more detail in relation to each hero (and Spider-Man) throughout the rest of the book, but it might be good to preview the major themes before we start.

For Captain America, liberty in this context means the freedom to operate as a superhero in a larger community that polices itself—an autonomous peacekeeping force, in essence—that also enjoys privacy with respect to their secret identities and activities. To Cap, this is a matter of autonomy, personal security, and efficacy. As he tells Sharon Carter, by requiring registration the government is "endangering innocent lives, and destroying the lives of heroes."[39] He explains that because he chose to make his identity public, his friends and neighbors are in constant danger, which he accepts, but "not everybody is willing to risk what I have... Should they be denied the right to make that choice?"[40] In a long conversation with Iron Man in the early days of the Civil War—from which we'll draw much insight in the chapters that follow—Cap acknowledges that the government will be in charge of the heroes' secrets, but argues nonetheless that secrets get out, especially in a world with supervillains who have access to advanced technology and psychic abilities.[41] He combines his concerns for autonomy with a skepticism of politicians and the political process: as he tells Iron Man, "the registration act takes away any freedom we have, any autonomy. You don't know who could get elected, how public sentiment could change," recalling the Japanese-American internment camps during World War II.[42]

On the other side of the coin, Iron Man is concerned, above all, with security. After witnessing the destruction caused by irresponsible superheroes—including himself when under the influence of alcohol—he appreciates the negative impression of superheroes among the public that led to the SHRA. As he tells his best friend Happy Hogan, "in order to protect our role in society, there needs to be some accountability." Like Cap, Iron Man is also distrustful of politicians, which is why he assumed control of registration himself in order to protect his colleagues in the superhero community. "Can you imagine?" he asks Hogan. "Some C-plus-average public-sector schlub in the Department of Redundancy Department riding herd on people like Cap?"[43] During his long conversation with Captain America, Iron Man cited mistakes made by superheroes that might have been prevented had they been better trained, for which no one was often there to stop them or hold them accountable. When Captain America invoked the internment of Japanese Americans, Iron Man argued that Cap's laissez-faire approach "is a lot more likely to get us put in camps than mine."[44]

At the end of their discussion, the conflict over liberty and security came to closely resemble the gun-control debate in the real world. Iron Man says that his support of registration "is predicated on that premise that superheroes make mistakes. And you're Captain America. You don't make mistakes."[45] He tells Cap that if all heroes were like him, the perfect, unshakeable hero, registration would not be necessary—but because they're not, someone needs to make them take responsibility for their actions. This is a clear parallel to gun-control debates: defenders of gun rights emphasize personal responsibility and agency, while supporters of gun control focus on accidents and stolen weapons. Likewise, the examples of superhero malfeasance and poor judgment cited by Iron Man make a similar case for registration and accountability, while Captain America prefers to handle training and accountability on a private basis.

Framed this way, the Civil War in the Marvel Universe—much like many civil wars fought around the world that we live in—was a conflict of principles, wherein one side favored safety and security while the other side favored liberty and privacy. Another way to look at it is that one side favored obeying the law as passed by legitimate democratic processes, while the other side favored standing up for the more general moral principles that laws are supposed to embody. However we want to characterize the ideology of the two sides in the conflict— and whichever side any of us happens to agree with—it's only fair to recognize that each side sincerely fought for a principle that, on its face, is entirely reasonable and supportable.

At the risk of overgeneralizing, everyone wants to feel safe and secure, and everyone wants to be free and enjoy privacy. Hardly anyone would argue that either of these things is bad, even if they would argue for certain limits or qualifications on some of them. And that's the most important point to make here—that conflicts, ranging from disagreements at family dinners, to electoral debates, to civil wars, cannot always be cast in terms of grand dramatic representations of Right and Wrong. As I said before, this is not Captain America versus the Red Skull, democracy versus tyranny, or good versus evil. If you look at the US Civil War as a battle over slavery, it fits the good-versus-evil picture, but if you look at it as a struggle between federal rights and states' rights, aside from the particular rights at issue, it's a different story altogether. Instead, conflicts often arise when one good idea comes into conflict with another good idea, and one or both have to bend. The idea is not to pick one side and reject the other—bending does not imply breaking—but rather to find a balance between them that works for everybody at that point in time.

The United States faced such a situation in the aftermath of September 11, 2001, when we as a nation had to decide how much liberty we were willing to sacrifice for greater security (or at least as much security as we thought we had on September 10). Much like with the SHRA in the Marvel Universe, the US government in the real world passed the PATRIOT Act with uncharacteristic speed, and it effectively reset the national definition of where the trade-off between liberty and security stood. Since then, the acronyms NSA and TSA have become part of our collective language, and many have argued that, after fifteen years without a second major act of international terrorism on American soil, that balance needs to be redefined.[46]

Benjamin Franklin famously wrote that "those who would give up essential Liberty, to purchase a little temporary Safety, deserve neither Liberty nor Safety."[47] While this statement is often used in an absolutist fashion to warn against *any* sacrifice of liberty for *any* degree of security, Franklin was a more subtle thinker and writer than this. He warned only of giving up "essential" liberties to gain "a little temporary" security, not that *some* liberty must *sometimes* be sacrificed to gain *some* security. He questioned the wisdom of a foolish or imprudent trade-off between them, not the idea of a trade-off in general. Again, the question is where the appropriate balance between them lies at any point in time, not whether to endorse an absolute devotion to one or the other.

As we'll see in the next three parts of the book, which describe the judgments regarding these principles made by Iron Man, Captain America, and Spider-Man, all of them questioned the choices they made and the balance they endorsed. Even though they prioritized either liberty or security (or each at different times), all three saw both liberty and security as valuable principles and did not dismiss any of them entirely. They did, however, endorse different ways of balancing them, based on their judgment informed by experience and formed by their basic moral characters. Throughout the rest of the book, we'll examine what made each of these heroes of the Marvel Universe take the side he did, looking at their codes of ethics, the way they made decisions regarding the principles at play in the debate over registration, and the consequences of those decisions—which were tragic for each of our heroes in very different ways.

Some Details about Discussing Comics (Especially without the Pretty Pictures)

Before we delve into this fascinating and timely story, we should probably discuss a few of the sticky details about comics, especially when writing about them in a noncomics format such as this book.

Comic-book dialogue

Because of the way that most comics dialogue is represented, lengthier passages are often broken up into numerous balloons in order to fit in and around the magnificent art, with phrases and even words separated by ellipses or em-dashes, as in "But, Tony... what are you—what are you *saying*?" This makes even relatively short bits of dialogue appear odd when reproduced in continuous prose form. I used my own judgment to break long passages into paragraphs for easier reading, but I did retain the ellipses and em-dashes to retain fidelity to the source material (and simply to reflect my love of the form).

Also, comics dialogue typically shows emphasis using italicized and bold text. Again, while this is accepted as normal in comics, it can look excessive and hyperbolic on the printed page. In this case, I have decided to remove emphasis from the dialogue reproduced here *except* when **absolutely** *necessary*. (See what I mean?) Even when their words are not emphasized with italics or boldface, superheroes use a lot of exclamation points! Often more than one!! Even after every sentence!!! You don't see these as much in modern comics as you did in the 1960s, but they still crop up here and there throughout this book. (You'll pry my extra exclamation points from my dead hands, copyeditor!)

Finally, I do not pretend that the words or dialogue in comics can be represented accurately without the illustrations that are an essential part of the medium. Comics are a visual medium, a melding of words and pictures, and you simply can't do justice to one without the other. At the end of the day, that is a limitation of the prose form within which I must work, and I have tried to do the best I can. But by all means, *go read the comics!!!*

Sources

I have cited all of the comics from which I quote dialogue or draw events, and all of the details about these comics are at the end of the book, including where they can be found in collected volumes. Most of the cited material is from the *Civil War* series and related comics, but I also draw on comics leading into and stemming out of the Civil War (especially in Part IV on the aftermath of the event).

There are several things I should clarify about the references for those of you who are not regular comics readers (yet). You may wonder, for example, why *Iron Man* #13, one of the key *Civil War* tie-in comics, was published in 2006 when Iron Man has had his own title since the 1960s. (Comics publishers can get behind on their publication schedules, but that's ridiculous!) But this is volume 4 of the *Iron Man* comic, which started in 2005 (and ended in 2009). Sometimes, a comic book series is "relaunched" with a new #1 to attract new readers and call attention to a new creative team, a different approach to the character, or even a different person under the mask. (Some publishers, including Marvel Comics, are now emulating the seasons of TV shows, in which a lengthy story is told over a year or two and then the comic is relaunched for the next long story.) Most of the issues of Captain America cited in this book are from volume 5, for instance; even *Amazing Spider-Man* and *Fantastic Four*, which were both in the 500s when the Civil War occurred, have since been relaunched. (Since new volumes of modern comics will probably never reach triple digits again, I chose not to list volume numbers for these high-numbered issues.)

Also, you will no doubt notice that I do not include page numbers when I cite specific pieces of dialogue, citing only the comic title, volume, and issue number. This is an unfortunate omission, especially for a writer and editor who is, shall we say, quite fastidious about bibliographic detail. (In other words, I'm a referencing nerd—don't tell anyone.) But the fact is that very few modern comics or collections include page numbers, and I don't think you or I want to count pages of all the comics I cite in this book when we can better spend our time reading the comics instead.

Unity of character

Have you ever asked yourself, "Who is Captain America?" or "Who is Iron Man?" I don't mean their secret identities, but rather the essence of the character himself. Is it the version of the character presented by the original creators: Joe Simon and Jack Kirby in the case of Captain America, and Stan Lee, Larry Lieber, Don Heck, and Kirby in the case of Iron Man? Or has the character changed over the years as different creators worked on them, so the original version is no longer canon? If the latter, how can we consider the Iron Man and Captain America of 2016 to be same as in 2006—much less 1966?

In all cases of serial fiction in which a character or concept is handled by a series of creators over time, whether it be Captain America or Captain Kirk, these issues arise: who the character is, what elements define the character, and what responsibilities the creators have to maintain those essential aspects of the character. Luckily for us, the people who created the major Marvel Comics superheroes in the 1960s, heroes like Iron Man, Spider-Man, the Hulk, the Fantastic Four—and I'll even include Captain America with them, referring to his revival in 1964—defined their character traits so well from the very beginning that later creators had a clear template to follow, while they continued to develop the characters in new ways consistent with their origins. Tony Stark started "life" as a wealthy, playboy industrialist and inventor whose addictive and indulgent qualities were explored over the years. Peter Parker was a kind-hearted science nerd who felt a responsibility to use his newfound powers for good, even as he struggled in his personal life with finances, romance, and self-doubt—struggles carried through many life changes, such as college, jobs, and marriage. In the 1940s, Steve Rogers was a model of inner strength and integrity even before he was transformed into a specimen of physical perfection; in the 1960s and onward, he struggled to find a life in a time he didn't belong in and in a country that had changed dramatically. Due to the work of creators who respected the work of their predecessors, these characters grew and changed organically over the years, but rarely in conflict with the integral and basic traits that defined them from their beginnings.

In this book, we're not looking at characters over decades of comics—most of the Civil War comics were published in 2006 and 2007. However, a number of different creators wrote and illustrated their adventures over that short time period, especially the main characters, Iron Man and Captain America, and to a lesser extent Spider-Man. There were some criticisms at the time that Iron Man was shown to be humble in one comic but arrogant in another, even though the two comics may have come out the same week, and that some events were represented in different ways in different books. This is the unfortunate but inevitable result of an effort by a publisher and its editors to coordinate a number of creators telling different aspects of the same large-scale story. For the most part, I think the characters were depicted quite consistently across the various comics, again based on the stable template provided by the original creators and their dedicated successors over the years. Three different creative teams could tell three different sides of the same story using Iron Man and portray him as a single character because Iron Man had been portrayed consistently for over forty years at that point. And in any case in which he seemed to be portrayed inconsistently, I will give the creators the benefit of the doubt and assume it's a feature of the story, not a flaw with it. (After all, do *you* act consistently "in character" all the time? That's what I thought.)

---

[1] *Amazing Spider-Man*, vol. 1, #532 (July 2006).

[2] While there aren't many fictional cities in the Marvel Universe, there are fictional countries, such as Wakanda, the technologically advanced African kingdom ruled by the Black Panther; Latveria, the small Baltic country ruled by Doctor Doom; and Genosha, the island country and mutant sanctuary ruled by Magneto. (Wolverine and Alpha Flight hail from Canada, but we're still not sure if that's a real place.)

[3] *Amazing Spider-Man*, vol. 2, #36 (December 2001); *Captain America: The New Deal* (2003).

[4] Tony Stark mentions the PATRIOT Act in *Iron Man*, vol. 4, #13 (December 2006).

[5] For a thorough accounting of all the many reasons the public has to question its heroes—compiled for the president by none other than Tony Stark himself—see the *Civil War Files* one-shot (September 2006).

[6] *New X-Men*, vol. 1, #115 (August 2001).

[7] *Avengers Disassembled* (2006). Recently, it was revealed that the Scarlet Witch and Quicksilver were not, in fact, mutants, nor were they the children of Magneto (*Avengers & X-Men: Axis* #7, February 2015), but the description of events here will reflect the longstanding belief about their species and parentage.

[8] *House of M* (2006).

[9] *Decimation: X-Men—The Day After* (2006) and *Decimation: The 198* (2006); see also *The New Avengers Vol. 4: The Collective* (2007) for SHIELD Director Maria Hill's attempts to find out what happened during the House of M episode.

[10] *Secret War* (2006).

[11] *Captain America*, vol. 5, #6 (June 2005).

[12] *Fantastic Four*, vol. 1, #533–535 (January–April 2006).

[13] *Avengers*, vol. 3, #500 (September 2004).

[14] *New Avengers Vol. 1: Breakout* (2005).

[15] *Iron Man: Extremis* (2007).

[16] *Iron Man: Execute Program* (2007).

[17] The formation of the Illuminati was shown in *New Avengers: Illuminati* one-shot (May 2006), and their history appeared in the collection *New Avengers: Illuminati* (2008). (The Kree/Skrull War is a classic Avengers storyline from the early 1970s, collected most recently in *Avengers: Kree/Skrull War*, 2013.)

[18] *Avengers*, vol. 1, #4 (March 1964).

[19] *Captain America, Vol. 1: Winter Soldier Ultimate Collection* (2010), a storyline echoed in the 2014 film *Captain America: Winter Soldier*.

[20] *Amazing Spider-Man Vol. 9: Skin Deep* (2005).

[21] *Amazing Spider-Man Vol. 10: New Avengers* (2005).

[22] *New Avengers: Illuminati* one-shot and *Hulk: Planet Hulk Prelude* (2010).

[23] *Hulk: Planet Hulk* (2007).

[24] *World War Hulk* (2008).

[25] *Avengers Disassembled: Thor* (2004).

[26] *Fantastic Four* #536–537 (May–June 2006), as echoed in the post-credits scene in the 2010 film *Iron Man 2* and the 2011 film *Thor*. (Thor and the rest of the Asgardians return to Earth in *Thor by J. Michael Straczynski Vol. 1*, 2008.)

[27] *Civil War* #1 (July 2006).

[28] *Civil War* #7 (January 2007), continuing on into *Avengers: The Initiative Vol. 1—Basic Training* (2007).

[29] International reaction to the US legislative response was ambivalent; this is explored primarily in *Black Panther: Civil War* (2007) as the Black Panther and Storm (from the X-Men), king and queen of Wakanda, tour the world, along the way surveying international sentiment.

[30] *New Avengers: Illuminati* one-shot.

[31] See chapter 6 in my book *The Virtues of Captain America: Modern-Day Lessons on Character from a World War II Superhero* (Hoboken, NJ: Wiley Blackwell, 2014).

[32] *Civil War: Front Line Book 1* and *Book 2* (both 2007).

[33] For deeper analysis of the political comparisons between the Civil War and post-9/11 America, see Kevin Michael Scott (ed.), *Marvel Comics' Civil War and the Age of Terror: Critical Essays on the Comic Saga* (Jefferson, NC: McFarland, 2015).

[34] *Iron Man: Execute Program*.

[35] *Iron Man*, vol. 4, #12 (November 2006).

[36] *Civil War: Front Line* #11 (April 2007).

---

[37] For a summary of terrorism from the point of view of philosophers, see Igor Primoratz, "Terrorism," *Stanford Encyclopedia of Philosophy*, February 23, 2015, at http://plato.stanford.edu/entries/terrorism/.

[38] *Amazing Spider-Man* #531 (June 2006).

[39] *Captain America*, vol. 5, #22 (November 2006).

[40] *Captain America*, vol. 5, #22.

[41] *Iron Man/Captain America: Casualties of War* one-shot (February 2007).

[42] *Iron Man/Captain America: Casualties of War* one-shot. He also expressed this sentiment to Sharon Carter: "The registration act is another step toward government control. And while I love my country, I don't trust many politicians. Not when they're having their strings pulled by corporate donors" (*Captain America*, vol. 5, #22).

[43] *Iron Man*, vol. 4, #13 (December 2006).

[44] *Iron Man/Captain America: Casualties of War* one-shot.

[45] *Iron Man/Captain America: Casualties of War* one-shot.

[46] Without implying any difference in importance or impact, I use the term "international terrorism" to differentiate from the tragic acts of domestic terrorism we have seen recently, such as the shootings in the Emanuel African Methodist Episcopal Church in Charleston, South Carolina, in June 2015.

[47] Benjamin Franklin, "Pennsylvania Assembly: Reply to the Governor," November 11, 1755, in *Votes and Proceedings of the House of Representatives*, 1755–1756 (Philadelphia, 1756), pp. 19–21, available at http://franklinpapers.org/franklin/framedVolumes.jsp?vol=6&page=238a. For the source of this quote, as well as interesting analysis, see Benjamin Wittes, "What Ben Franklin Really Said," *Lawfare* (blog), July 15, 2011, http://www.lawfareblog.com/2011/07/what-ben-franklin-really-said/.

Part I: Iron Man—On the Side of Security

As I write this, Marvel Comics has just announced its "All-New, All-Different" character line-up starting in fall 2015 and proclaimed Iron Man as their flagship character, replacing Spider-Man as the standard-bearer for the company. This is an incredible development for a character who, before his breakout 2008 film, was considered by many to be a B-list player in the Marvel Universe, on a distinctly lower level from Spidey, the Hulk, and the Astonishingly Popular X-Men. Of course, that film, fueled by Robert Downey Jr.'s pitch-perfect performance as Tony Stark, as well as brilliant scripting, directing, and acting by all involved, launched the Marvel Cinematic Universe, an interconnected series of films that echoes the tightly woven tapestry of the Marvel Comics Universe begun by Stan Lee, Jack Kirby, Steve Ditko, and others in the early 1960s.

Even though he was never as popular as Spider-Man or Wolverine until recently, Iron Man has been a significant figure in the Marvel Universe almost since his introduction in *Tales of Suspense* #39 in March 1963. Later that year, he appeared as a charter member of the Avengers in the first issue of their book (*Avengers*, vol. 1, #1, September 1963), both as a member and, in secret, as their wealthy patron, Tony Stark. As all Avengers did, from time to time Iron Man would leave the team only to return later, but overall he was one of the most stable members; he was even anointed one of the "Avengers Prime" along with fellow charter member Thor and the "new kid," Captain America, who didn't join until the fourth issue in March 1964. Furthermore, as founder of the secretive Illuminati, Iron Man embedded himself firmly in the Marvel Universe, pulling strings behind the scenes that would not come to light for years.

It wasn't until the build-up to the Civil War, however, that Iron Man took his largest and most public leadership role, not just spearheading the registration effort but replacing Maria Hill (who replaced Nick Fury) as director of SHIELD after the conflict ended. Not everybody was happy with Tony Stark's ascension, however, including many people in the Marvel Universe as well as those in the real world reading about him. Some disagreed with his goals, other with his motivation, and still others with his tactics—and not a few took issue with all three!

In this chapter, we'll delve into the character of Tony Stark, the Invincible Iron Man, and his actions leading up to, during, and after the Civil War. What moral philosophy stands behind his support of registration as well as the means he took to pursue it? What circumstances in his life made him particularly sympathetic to those concerned with the unregulated behavior of superheroes? And what is it about his moral code that makes him so controversial to the other heroes, one star-spangled one in particular?

Armor up—we're going in.

Chapter 2: Introducing Utilitarianism

If you've read any of his comics or seen his movies, you'll know that Tony Stark is the picture of an imperfect hero, as all heroes in the Marvel Universe are imperfect (even Captain America). But as Thor would say, Tony is a hero true—verily—and as a hero, he follows a certain code of ethics. In this first chapter focusing on the Armored Avenger, we'll look at *utilitarianism*, one of three classical schools of ethics, alongside deontology and virtue ethics (both of which we'll see in the next part of the book), and the one Tony exemplifies in many ways. We'll start by defining utilitarianism, focusing on the three aspects of it that separate it from a general ethics based on consequences. Next we'll look at the crucial role that judgment plays when putting utilitarianism into action, and we'll finish by looking at some shortcomings of utilitarianism from the viewpoints of other major ethical systems as well as common moral intuition.

What Is Utilitarianism?

Simply put, utilitarianism asks us to take actions that are likely to achieve the greatest happiness for the greatest number of people. If people's well-being is one of the things you consider when weighing a moral decision—especially if you try to consider all of the people affected by your actions, not just those close to you—then to some extent you are thinking like a utilitarian.

Even though philosophers have long endorsed increasing the good in one way or another—there's a bit of that in every ethical system—utilitarianism is usually dated back to Jeremy Bentham and John Stuart Mill.[1] Bentham was more interested in implementing social and legal reform than advising people on personal matters of ethics, but his straightforward utilitarianism has become tremendously influential in both areas—and this makes him very relevant to Iron Man, registration, and the Civil War. Bentham recommended that governments and individuals take those actions that maximize the excess of pleasure over pain, or positive effects on well-being (or "utility") over negative effects. In his words, an action is ethical "when the tendency it has to augment the happiness of the community is greater than any it has to diminish it"—and the action that does this the most, that maximizes utility, is the required action.[2]

While Bentham saw utility in terms of pleasure and pain, Mill's utilitarianism was more nuanced, recognizing that there can be different kinds of pleasure or utility. As he famously wrote, "it is better to be a human being dissatisfied than a pig satisfied; better to be Socrates dissatisfied than a fool satisfied."[3] This may sound elitist or snobbish today, but Mill believed that the higher pleasure that came from education and culture was intrinsically better than the "base" pleasure of a pig rolling in the mud. We don't have to endorse Mill's particular value judgment regarding what the higher and lower pleasures are to appreciate his more general point that pleasure or utility comes in different forms or kinds that may not be directly comparable (and, despite Mill's emphasis on higher pleasures, need not be ranked as better or worse). After all, how can we compare the joy of hearing a great song, meeting your baby niece for the first time, finishing writing a book—or eating a perfect Chicago-style hot dog? For most people, each of these would involve more pleasure than pain, but they are distinctly different kinds of pleasure, and we would be very hard pressed to say that one of them definitely created more excess pleasure than another.[4]

While utilitarianism seems fairly general, it is actually a specific form of *consequentialism*, which holds that the consequences of an act—however they might be defined—determine its moral status.[5] Consequentialism is often contrasted with *deontology*, which maintains that there is something inherent in an act itself that makes it moral or immoral, regardless of its consequences. (We'll talk more about deontology in Part II of this book.) An example would be lying: a consequentialist would say that lying is bad because it usually results in negative outcomes, but a deontologist might say that lying is wrong because it uses people as a means to an end or fails to give them appropriate respect. Utilitarianism would be more specific than consequentialism and say that lying is bad because it causes more pain than pleasure on the whole to those affected; it often hurts those who are lied to, and can also backfire on the liar.

There are three ways we can distinguish utilitarianism from consequentialism in general. First, it specifies the consequences that are of moral concern; as we've seen, it focuses on *utility*, which is usually some measure of what's good for a person, whether we define it as pleasure, happiness, well-being, or the fulfillment of desires. For this reason, we usually say that utilitarianism is a theory of *the good*, with the understanding that the good is something that can be measured and influenced (hopefully for the better!).

Second, utilitarianism requires that we consider the effect of an action on the utility of *everyone* affected by an action in order to determine whether an act raises or lowers total utility. Obviously, this stops a person from doing something to benefit himself without first considering the impact on others. More generally, it should inspire even those trying to do good for others to make sure there are no significant negative side-effects (or unintended consequences) to what they are planning. Before Iron Man redirects the flow of a river to a drought-affected area, he must consider what will happen to the people downstream from where the river originally flowed, as well as other effects on the natural environment that will have an impact on people. This makes utilitarianism difficult to put into practice well, especially in the case of large-scale actions such as laws or policies that potentially affect millions of people, but this is the responsibility assumed by the utilitarian decision-maker (and the primary concern of Jeremy Bentham).

Finally, when the utilitarian adds up the effects of her actions on various people, those effects must be weighted *equally*. In other words, everyone's utility counts the same; no one person's utility counts for any more than any other person's. The equal moral status accorded to every person is perhaps the noblest aspect of utilitarianism; even those who disagree with the focus on utility can appreciate the egalitarian core of utilitarianism. This emphasis on moral equality forces even generally altruistic people to consider the effect of their actions not just on those they care about, but also on those they may never have even thought about. This is a particular focus of Peter Singer, perhaps the most well-known modern utilitarian, who stresses the obligation of those of us in wealthy countries to give aid to those in poor countries.[6] Furthermore, if we consider utilitarianism's demands for moral equality in historical terms, we realize that Bentham and Mill were well ahead of their times. When class divisions were much more strict than they are today, and protections for women and racial, ethnic, and religious minorities were all but nonexistent, their bold proclamations of moral equality were shocking and courageous—and just as important to keep in mind even today.

Why Is Judgment So Important?

Utilitarianism seems very straightforward on the surface: after all, what could be simpler than trying to make people better off and trying not to make them worse off? However, as with most things, the devil is in the details. Specifically, under the surface of utilitarianism lies a significant amount of uncertainty and vagueness, which requires the diligent utilitarian, in golden armor or not, to use *judgment*, an undervalued talent in ethics in general, but especially in utilitarianism. While the final step in utilitarian decision-making is basic arithmetic—adding and subtracting utility—there is a tremendous amount of judgment required to obtain those utilities in the first place.

For starters, you need to use judgment to determine how much utility will be gained or lost by every person affected by an action. It is difficult enough to know how much better off something will make *you*: psychologists and philosophers have written volumes on how poorly we understand our own happiness and well-being and how events and things will change them.[7] This problem is magnified tremendously when trying to estimate how much better or worse off your actions will make other people. To some extent, this isn't that important: if you have a chance to give someone a hand, it would be a nice thing to do, and it really doesn't matter if you know exactly how much this will help them! But if you have a chance to help several different people in different situations—such as when you want to donate some money but can't decide which charity or cause to help—you might want to decide where your help will do the most good, and for that you need to make some degree of comparison based on some knowledge of other people's circumstances. This doesn't speak against utilitarianism, but merely points out that some judgment is necessary to determine what people's utilities are before you can use that information to decide what to do to make them better off. Also, given that you literally cannot imagine *every* person affected by your actions as they ripple out into the world, you need to use judgment to decide how far out to track the effects of what you plan to do.

Wait, it gets more complicated: even if you think you know how much various actions will affect people's well-being, those effects are often to some extent uncertain. If you help your elderly neighbor clean a foot of snow off of his car, you can be fairly certain that will help him out. But if you're considering a more wide-ranging act, such as starting a business, campaigning for a political cause, or even taking a job in a new city, there are not only more people to consider, but many possibilities of how that decision can play out and affect each of them. You may have found this out when you tried to list the pros and cons of a big decision, which is a simple utilitarian exercise, but one that grows very complicated the deeper you get into it. Any of the choices I mentioned above will affect various people in different ways with probabilities that are impossible to know for certain, all branching out and expanding in influence the farther you look into time. Again, no one can possibly determine all the probabilities of the change in utility of each person potentially affected by a decision—a perfect utilitarian could and should, but no real person can. Judgment is necessary to estimate all of these utilities and probabilities—as well as to decide how far to go in trying.

Ironically, the complexity of utilitarian decision-making, taking into account all of the utilities and probabilities you need to estimate and compute, may imply that the process itself is too costly to be recommended by utilitarianism! If we tried to do this, we might all be frozen when faced by any decision, trying to consider every little tiny effect of each action—this effort and sincerity may be admirable in a way, but it's self-defeating if it means we never actually come to a decision.[8] For that reason, some philosophers recommend *rule utilitarianism*, as opposed to the *act utilitarianism* we've been describing. In rule utilitarianism, a person follows certain rules of thumb, such as "do not lie," that improve total utility on the average. Even though there might be cases in which lying does good overall, it may not be worth trying to figure out when those cases arise, and you'll do more good over time if you simply follow a rule that prohibits lying.

Rule utilitarianism seems to solve many of the problems with the tremendous burdens placed on judgment when practicing act utilitarianism. But what if you *really* think a particular case justifies breaking the rule? Shouldn't you look into that, in the interests of increasing utility even more than you would by simply following the rule? And how do you know when you have a case that merits looking into? Is there a rule for that? Rule utilitarianism may save a lot of effort in simple cases, but unless you're willing to follow the rules all of the time, it does not completely eliminate the need for judgment. Also, it is not useful in unique decision-making circumstances in which no general rules can be developed, such as deciding whether to get married, start a new career—or take charge of superhero registration.

In the end, utilitarianism should be taken for what it is: a reminder of what is morally important in a situation and a framework to help figure out what to do with it. For a lot of moral problems, the utilitarian decision-making process does not depend on accurately determining utilities and estimating probabilities. In practice it's much easier than that: utilitarianism simply wants you to consider how your actions affect the people around you, to value those people and their utilities equally, and to take those effects into account when choosing an action. If the pros and cons are so close in a particular situation that the "right answer" depends on precisely how you calculated the various utilities or probabilities, then it's a close call anyway and the action you end up choosing likely won't make a huge difference either way. But in most cases, just some quick back-of-the-envelope thinking tells us whether an action does more harm than good. You don't need a high-powered computer and a crystal ball to be a utilitarian—you just need to think things through and in the right way, specifically the way that recognizes each person as equally valuable.

Are There Any Problems with Utilitarianism?

As I said before, the difficulties of making ideal utilitarian decisions do not speak against utilitarianism as a system of ethics; no ethical system is perfect, and none is guaranteed to lead us to perfectly moral choices in every case. But there are some deeper ethical problems with utilitarianism that conflict with our basic moral intuitions and feelings. Of course, sometimes our moral intuitions can be proven wrong by a system of ethics, but most ethical systems correspond to some aspect of our moral sentiments and simply state them in formal academic language. If an ethical system implies something that is totally out of whack with our basic moral impulses—such as justifying bald-faced lies or opportunistic murder, for example—that would give us a good reason to at least question it, if not reject it. (Very few people believe in ethical egoism, for instance, which is little more than a fancy name for selfishness.)

The most basic objections to utilitarianism would be with the focus on utility (or consequences in general) that defines the system. As we saw above, deontologists would certainly make this argument, believing instead that there is something intrinsic in an act itself that makes it right or wrong. A deontologist might say, for example, that lying is wrong because it takes advantage of people by deceiving them, regardless of whether it has good or bad consequences. At its core, this represents a fundamental difference between these two systems of ethics, a disagreement that cannot be resolved simply by referring to one or the other. The deontologist would need to argue why the intrinsic nature of lying is more important ethically than consequences are, and the utilitarian would have to argue the opposite. Neither is "obviously" correct, which is why such arguments usually appeal to our basic moral intuitions: which ethical approach "feels" right to any of us.

A more specific and frequent criticism that stems from common moral intuitions is that utilitarianism endorses the belief that "the ends justify the means." This is a simple implication of utilitarianism, and sometimes it's natural and harmless. For instance, increasing total utility sometimes involves small decreases in utility to some people in order to generate larger increases in utility to others. As the saying goes, you can't make an omelet without breaking some eggs. One example of this is taxing the rich to help the poor: if we assume, as economists usually do, that the rich get less utility from an extra dollar than do the poor, then redistributing some income from the rich to the poor hurts the former less than it helps the latter. (By the same token, a policy that funnels money from the poor to the rich would be seen as lowering overall utility.) Another example is the small business owner who truly cares for her employees but, in a bad economic climate, may have to lay some of them off in order to keep her company running and the rest of her workers employed.

It would be a simplistic form of utilitarianism indeed that required that every single act, small or large, must increase utility.[9] Instead, utilitarianism usually endorses instrumental choices that, in and of themselves, lower utility, if they contribute to raising utility in the larger scheme of things. This becomes a serious issue only if those that lose out always seem to be the same people, namely the disadvantaged in society who get the short end of the stick more often than the rest. If we are going to accept small losses in utility for the purpose of greater gains overall, we should make sure those losses are spread out fairly equally and not borne by the same people every time, which betrays the spirit of moral equality at the heart of utilitarianism.

The more serious objection to thinking that the ends justify the means is when those means do not simply lower utility but are also considered morally wrong in a more intrinsic (or deontological) sense. It isn't difficult to imagine examples because these situations arise all the time in our lives. A college student considers cheating on an exam so he can get into law school to provide legal services for underprivileged defendants. The CEO of a drug company fakes experimental results to get a life-saving drug to the market faster. A politician lies to the public to get legislation passed that she sincerely thinks will benefit her constituents. All three of these people could claim that their short-term actions were justified by the long-term gain, but others could argue that they did something *wrong* in the process, a wrong that isn't as easily offset by the long-term gains as short-term losses in utility are.

Of course, it's possible that even in purely utilitarianism terms these actions aren't justified either: for example, bypassing experimental checks during the development a new drug could increase the chances of deadly side-effects. But even if things did turn out for the better in all of these cases, the people involved still did things along the way that many consider morally wrong and are not justified by even the most admirable ends. This implicitly places deontological concerns with right and wrong above utilitarian concerns with good and bad, limiting the pursuit of the good to methods that are not wrong. But as we shall see throughout this book, such conflicts arise often—in real life as well as in epic superhero tales—and they generate very difficult choices that we need to use judgment to resolve.

Other criticisms of utilitarianism stem, ironically, from its moral core: its emphasis on moral equality as reflected by its equal weighting on every person's utility. One problem with counting everyone's utility equally is that some people naturally experience greater changes in utility than others. We all know someone who goes into a state of bliss at seeing a beautiful flower, or an extreme state of melancholy at finding out the movie he wanted to see is sold out. Philosophers call these people "utility monsters" because they "consume" more utility (positive and negative) than the average person does.[10] At the same time, some other people seem more stoic than the average, not experiencing the great highs and lows in the same way as most, but keeping an even keel (or "stiff upper lip," for our friends across the pond).

Outside of utilitarianism, these utility "reactions" would be mere psychological quirks, of concern only to the people experiencing them (and perhaps the people who live or work with them). But to a utilitarian, these different responses influence moral decisions in both the personal and policy realms. Let's say Tony Stark really likes expensive Italian sports cars—really, *really* likes them—while his erstwhile assistant Pepper Potts likes her small, humble compact. If the government wants to subsidize one type of car in order to maximize total utility, then it would have to take into account that Tony would likely get a huge boost in utility from having another Ferrari, while Pepper would not derive anywhere near as much extra utility from another Fiat. But does Tony deserve preferential treatment just because he happens to enjoy his car more than Pepper does? Or think of a simpler example, such as allocating food to the hungry. If one person gets enormous pleasure from eating, even after he's had more than enough to feed anyone else, then utilitarianism would say he should still get more food even if others have had not nearly as much (or nearly enough). Even though each person's amount of utility is considered equally under utilitarianism, everyone has a different capacity for experiencing utility, which can skew moral decisions in ways that seem unfair (compared to everyone getting equal shares of food, or granting auto subsidies based on safety or environmental factors).

Another issue with equal treatment under utilitarianism is that, due to their behavior or actions, some people may not be considered to deserve equal treatment. A burglar may get more utility from the huge plasma television set that he steals from Tony's Malibu mansion than Tony would—after all, he probably has three others—but we wouldn't usually include the criminal's utility when deciding whether his act is wrong. The burglar is still a person and a member of society, but the wrongfulness of his actions would seem to disqualify him from equal consideration in a utilitarian judgment of his actions. ("I really enjoyed it" is rarely an effective criminal defense.) Neither is his utility a consideration when he is punished for his crime; punishment is *intended* to lower utility, so it doesn't make sense for the effects on a criminal's utility to be an argument against his punishment.[11] In general, we might not want to consider a person's utility equally with the utilities of others if that person derives his or her utility from something that we consider wrong—another instance of holding deontological concepts of right and wrong above utilitarian considerations of good and bad.

~~~~~

Thus ends our brief survey of utilitarianism. In the next chapter, we'll turn to Tony Stark himself to see how he puts utilitarianism into practice in his role as Iron Man, and how certain aspects of his personalities influence how good a utilitarian he is.

---

[1] See Jeremy Bentham, *The Principles of Morals and Legislation*, and John Stuart Mill, *Utilitarianism*, both widely and freely available online. For an excellent discussion of the pros and cons of utilitarianism, see J.J.C. Smart and Bernard Williams, *Utilitarianism: For and Against* (Cambridge: Cambridge University Press, 1973).

[2] Bentham, *Principles*, chapter 1, paragraph 7. (I cite this way so you can refer to any version, in print or online.)

[3] Mill, *Utilitarianism*, chapter 2, paragraph 6.

[4] Make it two Chicago-style hot dogs, and the choice becomes much easier.

[5] For more on the varieties of consequentialism, see Walter Sinnott-Armstrong's "Consequentialism," *Stanford Encyclopedia of Philosophy*, October 22, 2015, at http://plato.stanford.edu/entries/consequentialism/.

[6] See Peter Singer, "Famine, Affluence, and Morality," *Philosophy and Public Affairs* 1 (1972): 229–243, available at http://www.utilitarian.net/singer/by/1972---.htm.

[7] See, for instance, Daniel Gilbert, *Stumbling on Happiness* (New York: Vintage, 2005), starting with chapter 4.

[8] Outside of ethics, this complexity leads to the theory of *satisficing* (as opposed to "optimizing"). Whereas most philosophers and economists assume that we seek out and incorporate each and every relevant piece of information in order to make the very best decision we can, satisficing recommends that we try only to make a "good enough" decision to save on the costs of decision-making itself. See Herbert

Simon, "Rational Choice and the Structure of the Environment," collected in his book *Models of Thought* (New Haven, CT: Yale University Press, 1979), chapter 2.

[9] This is actually one way of stating the *Pareto improvement* criterion for policy used in economics and philosophy, which requires that a policy change make at least one person better off while making *no one* worse off. It is widely regarded as idealistic and dismissed in favor of a maximizing framework like the one described in the text.

[10] Utility monsters were first suggested by Robert Nozick, a strident critic of utilitarianism, in *Anarchy, State, and Utopia* (New York: Basic Books, 1974), p. 41.

[11] Some scholars have started to consider whether the experience of convicted criminals should count in the length or severity of their punishment. After all, if we want to give the same punishment to two criminals convicted of the same crime, but one suffers from prison much more than the other (not unlike a utility monster), are they really punished to the same degree for their crimes? See Adam J. Kolber, "The Subjective Experience of Punishment," *Columbia Law Review* 109 (2009): 182–236.

Chapter 3: Tony Stark, the Utilitarian Iron Man

In the last chapter we introduced the idea of utilitarianism, wrapping up with some criticisms of the system. Perhaps the greatest argument against utilitarianism, however, is Tony Stark himself, who doesn't always make utilitarianism look good. He was generally seen as the "villain" of the Civil War, among his fellow heroes in the Marvel Universe as well as a majority of fans in the real world.[1]

But is this fair? How does one "represent" utilitarianism, anyway? In this chapter, we'll turn our attention from utilitarianism as an abstract ethical system to Tony Stark as an individual who generally makes decisions using utilitarian reasoning. We'll see particular aspects of his personality and character that interact with and inform his decision-making—for better and for worse.

What Makes Tony Stark Tick (Besides the Glowing Thing in His Chest)?

It is easy to say that Tony Stark is best described as a utilitarian, based on his goal-oriented ethical thinking and his willingness to do whatever it takes to achieve his goal—often exemplifying the "ends-justify-the-means" reasoning we discussed in the last chapter. But we must be careful not to identify him as "just" a utilitarian, or lump all utilitarians in with Tony Stark. (Some might not appreciate that!)

All utilitarians are not created equal, for several reasons. For one, nobody's perfect, and a more specific version of this profound observation is that nobody's a perfect utilitarian. Utilitarians, like anyone else, make mistakes, and Tony has made his share, as he knows all too well. Of course, there are mistakes and there are *mistakes*. Some are based on poor information and sloppy decision-making, two problems that Tony Stark does not have often. If he makes a mistake, it's usually not a "dumb" one. Instead, it's more often a matter of *weakness of will*, knowing what the best action is but failing to carry through with it. Tony's alcoholism provides the easiest example; not only was he weak when it came to succumbing to alcohol, but when drunk he would make bad decisions or carry out decisions sloppily. Anyone who's had too much to drink does this, of course, but Tony would be drunk while he was operating the Iron Man armor, fighting supervillains while trying not to hurt anybody, which as we shall see did not always turn out well.[2]

Mistakes aside, however, even utilitarians who do not make dumb mistakes or experience weakness of will—"perfect" utilitarians, if you will—will not necessarily make identical decisions in the same situations. In the last chapter we saw that, while the basic idea of utilitarianism is very simple, the practice of utilitarianism is much more difficult, requiring judgment to estimate utilities and probabilities as well as deciding whose utilities deserve to be counted at all. Two equally skilled and knowledgeable decision-makers are going to exercise their judgment differently based on their individual experiences and core values. What's more, one decision-maker may change his mind on an issue, not because of new information or aspects that come to light, but because reexamination of the problem leads to a different judgment. This leads to doubt—as we'll see, even the brilliant and arrogant Tony Stark had doubts throughout the Civil War about supporting registration—but doubt is good if it indicates that someone reflects on the wisdom of his decisions.

The more general point is that no ethical system leads to definite answers in any but the simplest moral dilemmas. Instead, they offer only frameworks or rules of thumb, which give a person a place to start deliberating the ethics of a situation. Should I lie to my boss to get out of work to see the new Captain America movie? If I were a utilitarian, I would probably start by thinking that lying is generally bad because it leads to bad outcomes. Might there be especially good outcomes in this case? Sure, you'll probably love the movie, especially if you're a utility monster (or a Marvel Zombie like me), but you would love the movie whenever you see it, and you presumably have many other opportunities. Also, you would make trouble for your boss and your company, and may be putting your continued employment in danger. Overall, this case of lying is probably not a good idea. Things might be different if you're planning to take your niece to the movie the day before she goes into the hospital for major surgery; I'm not saying that necessarily justifies this lie, but it might be a relevant ethical factor in support of it.

Like any system of ethics, utilitarianism only gives you a way to think about the moral issues in a decision-making situation, not the answer. For that, you need judgment. Put judgment and willpower together, and you get *character*, the unique aspects of a person's faculty of choice that distinguish that person from all others. Take any two "perfect" utilitarians and they will have two different levels of willpower and two different ways they exercise their judgment. This is why equally devoted, passionate, and intelligent people, using the same basic moral framework, can still disagree over what to do in a major choice situation—because despite all they have in common, they are still two different people.

So what is it about Tony Stark that makes him who he is and defines his character? In one episode during the Civil War, Sue Richards—the Invisible Woman of the Fantastic Four—shadows Tony for a day. She narrates the issue with her observations, including this assessment:

> Flippant, self-deprecating when he needs to be… asking all the right questions… always listening, carefully considering all his options… Distilling, calculating, calling shots… Always on the move… Relentlessly pursuing his agenda… Playing the visionary… Obsessed with victory… by any means necessary…[3]

Not a simple guy, our Tony. But everything that Sue mentions about him supports his self-assigned role as the guiding light of the Marvel Universe, the one person that knows where it should go—and is willing to do whatever it takes to get it there. We'll focus on three aspects of the man of iron: his role as futurist, his determination to take charge, and his inherent pragmatism.

Futurist

Most important to understanding Tony's behavior and choices is his claim to be a futurist. As he told the Illuminati (graciously referencing Reed Richards in the process),

> I'm a futurist. The way my mind works—the way Reed's mind works—we can intuit the future. That why we're such successful inventors. We know what people will need before people even know they're going to need it. And now I'm going to tell you the future.[4]

He believes he knows what's going to happen in the world, not by virtue of any supernatural powers of prognostication, or even mathematical or computational modeling as is done in economic forecasting (or Isaac Asimov's "psychohistory" from his *Foundation* novels), but due to his prodigious intelligence and superior grasp of all information vegetable, animal, and mineral.

As he tells his Illuminati colleagues before Stamford, "I'm telling you: this is happening. Right now. House of M, Nick Fury's Secret War, the 198, the attack on Avengers Mansion… it's all come to this. An environment of fear has been created where this can not only exist but will pass." Then, he launched into a classic speech (also known as "Starksplaining"), outlining what he predicts will happen and why.[5]

> A hero, probably a young one... one of the Young Avengers, or those kids in Los Angeles... some carefree, happy-go-lucky, well-meaning young person, with the best of intentions, will do something wrong. He'll be trying save someone—do something heroic—but he'll make a mistake. Turn to the left instead of the right—and people will be hurt or killed because of it.
>
> And it'll either happen on live TV, or it'll be recorded... and, like Rodney King, it'll play over and over and over... all over the world. Until... the unrest that is already bubbling will boil over... and every politician looking to make a name for himself will run right on TV and they'll tell America how they are going to save the world from these out-of-control costumed characters who think the law doesn't apply to them.
>
> And half of us will go along with it and half of us won't. And because of this mini-rebellion, our lawmakers will be forced to make an example of someone. Someone like our friend Spider-Man. Someone that they can make a real spectacle of. Someone they can unmask on TV, destroy his marriage and family and pin a crime or two on! All for the whole world to see.
>
> And the country will rupture. Sides will be taken and people will get hurt. Friend against friend. People who used to be adversaries finding themselves teamed up against a common cause. Friends dying at the hands of a former ally or teammate. That is what will happen.

Based on this prediction, Tony pled with the rest of the Illuminati to help him get ahead of registration, to "diffuse" the situation before it went as far as he predicted, but only Reed agreed with him; Namor, Dr. Strange, and Black Bolt all walked out.

After the Civil War ended, Tony explains to a fellow hero how he saw the conflict coming, starting with a time-travel adventure in which he teamed with King Arthur to fight Doctor Doom and Morgana le Fey.[6] (Comics!) It was during that battle that "I saw it as a clear as day. I saw us. At war." Next, just in case we forgot, he reminds us that

> I'm an inventor. I can envision the future. I can see what the
> world will look like. And I can see what the world will need to
> make that future worth living for. I see what we will need and I
> invent the thing that will help us get there. That's how I invented
> my armor. That's how the Avengers were born. That's how eve-
> ry idea I've ever had in the world has come to be. I invent a solu-
> tion. I knew there would be a war of heroes. I knew it.[7]

He didn't know what the war would be about or when it would happen, but as he
said, "I knew I'd know it when I saw it." So he tried to motivate the Illuminati to
help coordinate the world's superheroes, to avoid conflicts between heroes and
focus on fighting evil, crime, and disaster, but they didn't listen.

Tony even notices the shift in ordinary people's attitude toward superheroes:

> They started taking us for granted. They started seeing us as fa-
> miliar. They started relying on us to help them instead of hoping
> we would. They didn't know they were doing it, but they were—
> they were taking it all for granted. And with familiarity—
> contempt.[8]

As he tells Peter Parker later, after discussing the Stamford situation with the
president, "You don't need a Richter scale to know there's been a tectonic shift in
the way the country sees us, Peter. You can feel it. The whole country just
shuddered."[9] Nonetheless, he failed to see the actual legislation coming, but once
Nick Fury showed him an early draft of the SHRA, "I knew what it meant. I knew
it would pass. I knew exactly who would fall on what side of the issue. … I knew
my feelings. I knew your feelings. I knew this was it."[10]

Having the skills of a futurist is valuable for a utilitarian, who has to be able to
forecast the future to some extent in order to increase utility reliably. Remember
that being able to imagine future states of the world, as well as estimating their
likelihoods, is essential to make decisions that will be most likely to increase total
utility in whichever state of the world actually occurs. This doesn't require that the
powers of prediction have to be perfect, of course, but the better a person is at
"knowing" the future, the better his or her actions will be to promote higher utility
in the future. It also makes it less likely that a person like Tony will resort to rule
utilitarianism, because he will usually feel he is better suited to make precise,
specialized judgments in each situation. Tony may have his issues, but cognitive
limitations are not among them (or, at least, not that he would acknowledge
them).

Despite his much-vaunted arrogance and confidence, Tony Stark is all too aware of human fallibility and the danger it represents, especially when a fallible human has superpowers or a suit of armor. Especially pertinent to Tony in this regard is his alcoholism, which he mentions to Captain America as one argument for registration. "You know how dangerous a drunk is behind the wheel of a car?" he asks Cap. "Imagine one piloting the world's most sophisticated battle armor."[11] He tells Cap about an incident, much earlier in his career, when he fought Machine Man (an android superhero) while inebriated and nearly injured two of his own employees.[12] Cap argues that registration wouldn't necessarily have prevented that from happening, especially if no one knew of his problem (or even if they did, as Cap remembers trying in vain to help Tony when he hit rock bottom soon thereafter).[13] Tony counters that at least there would have been some accountability, and that he would have been prosecuted and sent to jail if appropriate. Cap argues for self-policing among superheroes, but Tony thinks he's minimizing the problem of fallibility. Tony's perspective is "predicated on the premise that super heroes make mistakes. And you're Captain America. You don't make mistakes. … If everyone were like you, we wouldn't need registration. But they're not."[14] In Tony's view, registration will do more than protect ordinary people from fallible superheroes—it will protect those heroes from themselves.

Because Tony realizes he is not perfect, he has his doubts, like anyone else. The night before registration takes effect, he tells his best friend Happy Hogan, "Oh, God. Please let us be doing the right thing here. …"[15] Soon after registration passes, another old friend tells a conflicted Tony, "you're not nearly as sure about this as you're going to need to be to see it through."[16] Later, at the funeral of Goliath, who died at the hands of a clone of Thor created by Reed, Tony, and Hank Pym, a shaken Tony received reassurance from Miriam Sharpe, public symbol of the Stamford tragedy, who gives him her son's favorite toy, an Iron Man action figure, "just to remind you why you're doing this."[17] And as we'll see in the next chapter, Tony was full of doubts even after the Civil War was over, asserting that he did the right thing but that it wasn't worth it, given the tremendous costs that he and the world suffered. Tony's doubts are admirable, given his outsized confidence, and appropriate, given the frequent scale of his actions and the magnitude of the possible consequences.

So, Tony has all this knowledge, all this foresight, all this capacity for invention and making things better, confidence that he was right despite all-too-human doubts, and no one would listen… what's a genius to do? Take charge. And he did.

Taking Charge

One aspect of utilitarianism that often goes unrecognized or underappreciated is the responsibility that comes with it, especially for a futurist such as Tony Stark. It's one thing for a less intellectually gifted hero—such as the Human Torch (sorry, Johnny)—to see the writing on the wall and wonder what he can do, but for someone endowed with the mental gifts of Tony Stark, standing on the sidelines is not enough. If you're a utilitarian devoted to the cause of increasing human well-being, and you're confident that you have both the knowledge and the ability to do something toward that end, it would be unethical not to—especially when no one will listen to your warning of impending doom. After all, the Illuminati ignored his warnings early on when he called for more cooperation among the superhero community, as well as when he brought SHRA to them: "You should have listened to me then, and I'm begging you to listen to me now."[18] After the Civil War ended, he said to a friend, "I told you. I told anyone who would listen. ..."[19]

Besides urging the rest of the Illuminati to get ahead of registration and suggest tighter self-policing amongst the superhero community, Tony talked to the president of the United States about the coming legislation, and then testified in front of the Senate Select Committee on Superhuman Relations against the act.[20] As he said to Captain America during their debate early in the conflict, "It was coming anyway. I always thought it was inevitable, though I did try to delay it. But after Stamford there was no stopping it."[21] Accepting it as an inevitability, Tony adjusted his strategy to the new circumstances—like a good utilitarian—and decided he had to spearhead the efforts himself. After Cap surrendered and the Civil War was over, he asked Tony, "I want to know what the hell made you think this was your job to do? Who made you the moral compass of us?"[22] As Tony told him later, "I knew that I would be put in the position of taking charge of things. Because if not me, who? Who else was there? No one. So I sucked it up. I did what you do. I committed."[23]

Tony regards himself as being in a unique position to head the registration efforts for a number of reasons, starting with the fact that, as we saw above, he saw it coming and therefore had time to prepare. He also felt a responsibility to his colleagues in the superhero community—he couldn't stop this from happening, so he was going to make sure the negative effects on his friends were minimized. For instance, soon after registration went through, he was complaining to Happy about the pushback from some in the hero community:

This isn't gonna go away, Hap. Registration was inevitable. It had to happen sooner or later. I'm just trying to keep it from getting out of hand. Can you imagine? Some C-plus-average public-sector schlub in the Department of Redundancy Department riding herd on people like Cap? Why can't they see that I'm trying protect them?[24]

Similarly, he tells Peter Parker early on that "I have to take the lead in making the other powers register. If I don't, someone worse will."[25] Finally, as he told Miriam Sharpe after the war ended, "the super hero community just found the greatest friend they'll ever have."[26]

Certainly, there are other very smart people in the Marvel Universe, such as Reed Richards and Hank Pym, but they're scientists at heart, brilliant researchers and innovators, but lacking in the strategic management skills that Tony gained through years of running his company, chairing the Avengers, and serving as Secretary of Defense. As all of his meetings with the president show, Tony's political acumen was just as valuable as his scientific knowledge in shepherding the registration efforts. As the Mad Thinker, one of the Fantastic Four's regular foes, tells Reed Richards after seeing his social dynamics equations predicting the outcome of the Civil War,

> Stark doesn't have the mind to appreciate the subtleties of your equations. But he does have the gut instincts of a futurist and the political sense to know that his actions would make him reviled among his former friends in the super hero community. And he's man enough to do what needs to be done.[27]

Even a Mad Thinker can recognize and admire Tony's commitment.

Nonetheless, Tony also had doubts about his leadership of the registration efforts. After he complained to Happy about the reactions of his fellow heroes, Happy asks, "So that's what this is all about, ain't it?" When Tony asks what he meant, Happy explains:

> You said "they." "Why can't they see?" You're thinkin' just cuz you didn't get bit by a radioactive cockroach or bombarded with some kinda whammo-ray, who are you to be makin' the rules? You're thinkin' maybe you don't have the right. Well that's crap, and here's why… You, my friend, are the only cape in the bunch

that's both one of us and one of them. Who else can see both
sides the way you do? Who else can make sure things are fair?

Tony's response? "You know something, Hap? You're the only guy I've ever met
who can make me feel like a moron."[28] Even with his doubts, all it took was a
regular joe to convince Tony that his decision to spearhead the registration effort
was the right one, and not only because he's a futurist. (He *did* mention that,
right?)

Pragmatism

As we said above, Tony adapts to changing circumstances, always trying to
maximize the good within the parameters of the situation at the time. Recall that
at first he opposed registration and argued against it before Congress. After the
disaster at Stamford, the president told him the SHRA would be passed and
signed as soon as possible, and Tony shifted because he realized that continued
resistance would be ineffective and counterproductive. Instead, he decided to get
behind registration and manage it, minimizing the harm and maximizing any
good effects that might come from it. When Peter Parker argues that he shouldn't
be forced to register because he had nothing to do with Stamford, Tony simply
said, "Doesn't matter. The world where that made a difference just ended. The
rules have changed, and once the president signs that act, those rules become law.
Here's how it's going to work from this day on, Peter," and proceeded to lay out
his new plan.[29] And not only did his strategy adapt to the new circumstances, but
so did his opinion on registration: "Frankly," he told Peter, "I think it's the right
thing to do at this point." Captain America picked up on this too, telling Tony
that Stamford really seemed to change his mind. When Tony tried to explain it
was just the "inevitability," Cap argued, "but you're not just bowing to the tide of
history, Tony. You truly believe in this. I can tell."[30] He may not have believed in it
before Stamford, but as he told Peter, that tragedy changed the world they lived in,
and in that new world, Tony believed that registration was the best option
available.

Here, Tony illustrates an important point about utilitarianism: the ideal or
perfect outcome is not always possible, so you have to do the best you can within
your circumstances. In other words, you have to be pragmatic.[31] As he prepared to
face the Hulk, who was very angry about being exiled by the Illuminati, Tony
thought to himself,

> I'd hoped this wouldn't prove necessary... and if it did, that I'd
> have more time. But I know better than anyone that things rare-
> ly turn out the way you hope. So you do the best you can with
> what you have... in whatever time you have... with whatever
> help you can get.[32]

As an engineer, Tony knows this well: his visions and plans in general are constrained by available technology (including the new technologies he can develop with it) and the materials at hand and acquirable. We see this in the gradual development of his Iron Man armor, starting with the crude, rudimentary suit he built to escape his captors in his origin (both in the comics and the first *Iron Man* film), which became more complex with each iteration as the available technology advanced.[33] And just when we think Tony's become spoiled with access to the world's most scientifically advanced equipment, we see him reduced to simple tools, such as when he worked in Harley's garage in the 2013 film *Iron Man 3*.

This ability to adapt and adjust to circumstances applies not only to Tony's engineering efforts, of course, but also his grander plans, including registration. He acknowledges throughout the storyline that the game has changed, and supporting registration is the best way to play it going forward. This perspective is most clear during an argument with Captain America, in which he comes out and asks Cap if he had any idea what the alternatives to registration were.

> I do. I saw the plans. When I was Secretary of Defense. Have you
> ever heard of Project Wideawake? Imagine a sky full of [robot]
> Sentinels hunting us down. Forcibly implanted inhibitor circuits
> in our brains, taking away our powers. Genetic testing of the en-
> tire population so any potential superhumans are under gov-
> ernment control before they're even born.[34]

Cap says it would never happen, that they'd fight it, to which Tony responds angrily, "What do you think I'm trying to do? From day one, I've been trying to keep this from getting as bad as I know it can be."[35] Tony nails it here: he's not trying to make a perfect world but, acknowledging the limitations of the situation, he's making it the best it can be.

An encounter with a mysterious stranger after the Civil War ended also drove this point home. Tony unloads, arguing the inevitability of registration and saying "one of us had to be on the inside. Running the show. Why couldn't Steve see that?" The stranger—actually Uatu the Watcher, cosmic chronicler—answers, "perhaps because, for all his virtues... Steve Rogers was never a pragmatist. He was not one to be comfortable with the lesser of two evils."[36] Tony wasn't comfortable with it either, but his utilitarian nature made him see that when neither option was good, he had to work toward the one that was less bad—or, as Reed Richards put it, "the lesser [sic] of thirty-one evils. Each more horrible than the next."[37]

No matter how often Tony proclaims himself a futurist, no one knows for sure what is going to happen, and no one can be certain how his or her actions will influence the world. As they say, hindsight is 20–20, but utilitarians can't make decisions with a rearview mirror. The best Tony can do is do the right thing at the time given the circumstances, the information at hand, and his best judgment, and only time will tell if he made the right decision. The better question would be: was Tony justified in his confidence regarding his foresight? Did he actually know well enough what was going to happen to justify the actions he took? Perhaps a little humility would have changed his behavior—and perhaps his course would have been firmly set all the same.

Tony Stark's Motivation

Like almost all of the Marvel superheroes, who were designed from the beginning to have recognizable human flaws, Tony Stark is an imperfect man. Well known are his problems with alcohol and his penchant for womanizing (the latter played up more in the movies than in the comics), but there are also the arrogance, presumption, and narcissism that stem from his intelligence, foresight, and success. Sue Richards' assessment of him quoted above was fairly positive, and all the traits she mentioned fed into and support his general utilitarian nature. But others' opinions have been less generous—in particular, those of Captain America, who admires and appreciates Tony's heroism and vision but nonetheless disagrees with him on fundamental matters of ethics and motivation, which have emerged on numerous occasions over their history together as Avengers.

During Civil War, these disagreements came out most clearly in the one-shot comic, *Iron Man/Captain America: Casualties of War*, from which I've drawn quite a bit already. After the death of Goliath at the hands of the clone of Thor, Cap and Tony meet at the ruins of Avengers Mansion for a talk, during which they reminisce, argue, and fight. (Of course they fight.) The portion of their long discussion (*avant le combat*) that is relevant here is when Cap questions Tony's motives for his taking charge of a previous incident:

CAP: You're a good man at heart, Tony, but you've always thought you knew best by virtue of your genius. And once you decide, that's it.

TONY: I was the one best qualified to—

CAP: It was also what you wanted. And when you get down to it, what you want has always come first.[38]

Cap goes on to cite many examples, including the time that he gave up the "title" of Captain America in protest of the government's attempts to control his actions, and instead adopted the (completely different) name of "The Captain."[39] Tony offered him a new shield, which, according to Cap, was conveniently timed to secure Cap's gratitude while Tony was breaking laws trying to get his old armors back from parties who had acquired them, whether criminal or legitimate, and even took down Cap from behind.[40] Cap concluded this trip down memory lane by saying, "you can be the nicest guy in the world, Tony... the bravest hero, the staunchest ally... but at the end of the day, what you want trumps everything else."[41]

This illustrates a frequent issue with motivation: what we *should* do, and what we *want* to do, do not always match up. In most of the examples Cap cites, including the episode during his time as the Captain, he implies that Tony's selfishness got in the way of his heroism, which is obviously a problem. However, cases in which he *does* want to do what he should do are also problematic, albeit in a different way. At first glance, it seems just a coincidence of motivations would be great, with the ethical and the self-interested reinforcing each other. Certainly, we usually think of a hero wanting to help people as well as feeling moral obligated to do so. However, many ethical systems—with the notable exception of utilitarianism—put a lot of weight on the importance of having the proper motivation, doing the right thing because it's the right thing and not because you want to do it for other reasons. Immanuel Kant, a deontological philosopher we'll talk about more in the next chapter, wrote that a man who is naturally disposed to help the needy is not truly moral unless he does so out of the knowledge that he *should* do so.[42] We don't have to go quite that far to recognize that a selfish motivation causes us to question the moral value of an act: a woman saving a drowning child from a pool is doing a good thing, but we admire her less if it comes out that she only did it in the hope of getting famous on YouTube.

One way that Kant identified to help determine whether a person's motivation was truly moral—although, as he recognized, we can never be sure, even about our own motivations—is to ask if the behavior was in the person's selfish interests at all. We may question the motives of the woman who saves a drowning child if her friend happens to be there taking a video on his phone, but not if she did it while no one was around, and even less so if she endured some sacrifice for it (such as missing an important appointment). Based on this, we can ask if his support for registration served Tony's own interests, or did it cost him more than it helped him? Was it a decision made solely to help the superhero community from a worse fate, or was it an excuse for Tony to exert his influence and control over the future? Or... both?

It's clear that Tony did suffer some enormous costs from Civil War, some foreseeable and others not. He lost a colleague, Goliath, at the hands of a cloned Asgardian god that he helped create. He lost his best friend Happy Hogan, who had been a supporting character in the Iron Man stories, along with Pepper Potts, since Tony's very first appearance. (This was a tremendous loss to Iron Man fans as well.) And, of course, he lost much more when you take into account everything that happened as a consequence of the Civil War (including a very poignant loss to Tony, the superhero community, and the world).

Of course, the costs of the Civil War were not all for Tony to bear on his own. No one doubts that most of these costs were borne primarily by those who died and their loved ones, as well as those who lost their homes and businesses to the devastation of the final battle in New York City. And, because he's a futurist, Tony foresaw many of these costs. As he and Peter Parker walked by the Lincoln Memorial in Washington DC after the Senate hearings were over, Tony said,

> I've always admired Lincoln. When the South began going its own way, he knew that taking a position against them would lead to civil war. But he did it anyway, because he understood something... understood it more perhaps than anyone else in that time. He knew that a house divided against itself cannot stand... nation cannot be divided and survive. Under his administration, brother hunted down brother, friend turned against friend. It was terrible. It was bloody. It was necessary. Because at the end, the republic held, and the nation was restored.[43]

Tony concluded by saying, "I sometimes wonder if I would have had the courage to do as he did." (Peter adds he hopes that won't be necessary because it didn't turn out that well for Lincoln).

Another cost that Tony bore was the loss of respect and friendship among his fellow superheroes; recall that even the Mad Thinker realized that "his actions would make him reviled among his former friends in the super hero community." As the final battle neared, Miriam Sharpe thanked Tony for his support of registration, saying, "I hate how much it's cost you personally. I never would have asked if I'd known your lives would get torn apart like this." Tony did not deny the cost, but justified it, perhaps to himself as much as to Sharpe, when he said, "There's no shame in making enemies if it means making people safer."44 Reporter Sally Floyd, no fan of Tony Stark, told him after the Civil War had ended that "you sacrificed your status as a friend, colleague and hero for the greater good of this country. You alone understood the ramifications of such a course of action."45

Because he disregarded the personal costs of his actions in favor of what he perceived as the good of all, Tony's motivation for leading the registration effort seems, on this standard, to be moral. But we also have to look at what he might have gained—after all, he may have endured all of those costs in order to reap greater benefits. First, we can imagine that he simply likes being in charge, knowing that only he can do the job right, based on his foresight and intelligence. Also, despite scaling down the defense-related aspects of his business over the years, Stark Enterprises still provided services to the government and the military. In the middle of the storyline, as Peter Parker is starting to doubt his allegiance with Iron Man, he hears a news report that Stark Enterprises and Fantastic Four, Inc., received no-bid contracts worth two billion dollars to build superhuman holding facilities like the one in the Negative Zone, "a huge boost to Stark's position on the stock market, making him one of the wealthiest men in the country."46 When Peter asks Tony about this, telling him that it "looks like you're set to make a killing. On the stock market, that is," Tony dismisses his concern, saying he hadn't noticed. It is at this point that Peter demands to see the prison holding unregistered heroes and hears for the first time that it's in the Negative Zone, which also increases his concerns about Tony's agenda as well as his motivation. This concern is only heightened after Peter and journalist Ben Urich (a regular character in the Daredevil comics and Netflix series) hack into Tony's computers and uncover suspicious financial activity just two days before the SHRA was announced and other pivotal events during the Civil War (on which more later).47

We'll discuss Peter's concerns and his see-saw ethical journey through the Civil War more in Part III of this book, but let's put our focus back on Tony Stark. Even if he benefitted in financial terms from registration, does that imply that this was a motivation for him to support it? It's possible, of course, but it would be cynical simply to assume it. He did try to prevent registration from becoming law, after all, engaging in the same type of manipulation to stop it as he did later to support it (including hiring the Titanium Man to attack Spider-Man to reinforce the value of superheroes to the Senate committee).[48] Furthermore, the Negative Zone prison was built by Reed Richards before any of this began, and even Tony couldn't foresee how many heroes would refuse to register—he'd hoped to convince them all—so any financial windfall from registration was uncertain at best.[49] As Ben said to Peter after uncovering his financial irregularities, "I don't get it, Peter. Tony Stark was never that way. He's just not the kind to play with people's lives for personal gain—it goes against everything I know about the man."[50] And as it turns out, an investigation by Sarah Floyd and Ben showed that Tony diverted his profits from the Civil War into charities helping police officers, firefighters, registered heroes, and their families.[51] Just because someone seems to benefit from events he set in motion doesn't imply that he was motivated by those benefits, although it is clearly a possibility, or even that the apparent benefits were realized (at least for the person involved).

But let's say that Tony was indeed motivated by financial gain—why would that be a problem if his motivations were also partly altruistic? The practical concern with coinciding motivations is this: what happens when the person no longer wants to do the right thing, or the right thing no longer coincides with the person's interests? A naturally helpful person is a very nice person to know, of course, until he changes his mind, whereas a person who helps because he feels he should is less likely to change his behavior on a whim. Even more serious is when a person's self-interest comes to dominate his judgment regarding the right thing to do. Captain America suspects this with respect to Tony's support of registration, which "just happens" to let him take charge and run the show, implementing all of his technocratic visions in the process. In an incident just before Stamford, Iron Man defeated the Crimson Dynamo by stopping his heart and immediately reviving him. Cap criticized him, arguing that "You could have handled the situation without stopping the man's heart! I can think of at least four ways—" Tony interrupted, "—and I can think of seven. But this one was the most expedient." Cap asked, "Expedient, Tony? Or interesting?"[52] Rather than using the safest and fastest method possible, Tony chose flash and dazzle over effectiveness, playing the showman more than the hero. When all was said and done, he got the job done and saved the day, but he also made sure he looked good doing it—a definite conflict of motivation from Cap's point of view.

In the end, despite all of the suggestions of financial gain and personal power that Tony gained by throwing his weight behind registration and enduring the Civil War, he remained a hero. This is demonstrated by many of the extreme measures of self-sacrifice that he took around and during this same period that his power increased, both physically (because of the Extremis virus) and politically (being appointed director of SHIELD after the war ended). For example, as we mentioned before, a young man took control of Tony's mind and armor and killed 200 people (which Defense Secretary Kooning later said would have kicked off registration had Stamford never happened).[53] To prevent any more deaths using his tech, Tony literally killed himself with a 10,000-volt shock—the same tactic he uses on the Crimson Dynamo at the beginning of the storyline—to disable the mental link to his armor. After he was revived, Kooning remarked that "the only thing that I can't believe is that a guy as narcissistic as Tony Stark would kill himself to save someone else."[54] This may be the most obvious case of moral motivation for a heroic act (with no word from Cap about whether this was "interesting" rather than expedient).[55]

Regarding his heroic motivation, perhaps Tony said it best as he flew into space to face the Hulk upon his return from exile by the Illuminati, for which he assumed sole responsibility:

> This is Tony Stark. Iron Man. Director of S.H.I.E.L.D. And yes, I fired the Hulk into space. So if you need to blame someone for his return… blame me. But everything I've done… everything I'll do today… everything I'll ever do… I do to protect this world. Someone once told me that with great power comes great responsibility. … When I put on this armor, I took on more power than any human was ever intended to have… and maybe more responsibility than my heart can truly bear. But today… I will do my job. I will protect you… no matter what it takes.[56]

Tony's not perfect, but as Captain America told him, he's a "good man at heart." Some would say it's easy for a perfect person to be a hero, but more admirable for an imperfect person to find it in himself or herself to rise to the occasion. If that's true, then Tony may be the greatest hero of them all.

~~~~~

But before we hold a parade for Saint Anthony based on his heroic goals, motivations, and self-sacrifice during the Civil War, we need to look at the actions he took during the conflict—which may take some of the shine off of that golden armor.

---

[1] For more on Tony's image as a villain during the Civil War—and its accuracy—see Joseph Darowski, "'I Would Be the Bad Guy': Tony Stark as Villain of Marvel's *Civil War*," in Joseph Darowski (ed.), *The Ages of Iron Man: Essays on the Armored Avenger in Changing Times* (Jefferson, NC: McFarland, 2015), pp. 181–191.

[2] For a closer look at Tony's alcoholism and weakness of will, see my chapter "Does Tony Stark Have an Iron Will?" in my edited book, *Iron Man and Philosophy: Facing the Stark Reality* (Hoboken, NJ: Wiley Blackwell, 2010), pp. 172–185. For an in-depth philosophical treatment of weakness of will, see Sarah Stroud and Christine Tappolet (eds), *Weakness of Will and Practical Irrationality* (Oxford: Oxford University Press, 2003).

[3] *Iron Man*, vol. 4, #14 (January 2007).

[4] *New Avengers: Illuminati* one-shot (May 2006), through Tony's big speech.

[5] I can't take credit for "Starksplaining"—Tony himself uses the term in *Iron Man*, vol. 5, #18 (January 2014).

[6] This adventure took place in *Iron Man*, vol. 1, #149–150 (August–September 1981). As for the identity of Iron Man's "friend"... I don't want to give away too much at this point.

[7] *Civil War: The Confession* one-shot (May 2007).

[8] *Civil War: The Confession* one-shot. This is really a topic for another book, but the way ordinary people see superheroes is a key difference between the universes of Marvel Comics and DC Comics. In Marvel, superheroes were always "among" the people, who looked at them with both awe and trepidation (as seen in 2004's *Marvels*), while in DC they were revered and admired. This contrast is well depicted in the crossover event *JLA/Avengers* (2008), where the Avengers traveled to the DC Universe and saw the monuments and museums erected in honor of members of the Justice League, whereas the Marvel heroes were used to suspicion and protests from the beginning. For traces of this in *Fantastic Four* in the earliest days of the Marvel Universe, see Colin Smith, "What's to Be Done With the Fantastic Four?," *Too Busy Thinking About My Comics*, March 18, 2014, at http://toobusythinkingboutcomics.blogspot.com/2014/03/whats-to-be-done-with-fantastic-four_18.html.

[9] *Amazing Spider-Man* #532 (July 2006).

[10] *Civil War: The Confession* one-shot.

[11] *Iron Man/Captain America: Casualties of War* one-shot (February 2007).

[12] *Iron Man*, vol. 1, #168 (March 1983).

[13] *Iron Man*, vol. 1, #172 (July 1983).

[14] *Iron Man/Captain America: Casualties of War* one-shot.

[15] *Civil War* #2 (August 2006).

[16] *Iron Man*, vol. 4, #13 (December 2006).

[17] *Civil War* #4 (October 2006).

[18] *New Avengers: Illuminati* one-shot.

[19] *Civil War: The Confession* one-shot.

[20] *Amazing Spider-Man* #530–531 (May–June 2006).

[21] *Iron Man/Captain America: Casualties of War* one-shot.

[22] *Civil War: The Confession* one-shot.

[23] *Civil War: The Confession* one-shot. Wait, was that his "friend"? Hey, look, a squirrel!

[24] *Iron Man*, vol. 4, #13.

[25] *Amazing Spider-Man* #532 (July 2006).

[26] *Civil War* #7 (January 2007).

[27] *Fantastic Four* #542 (March 2007).

[28] *Iron Man*, vol. 4, #13.

[29] *Amazing Spider-Man* #532.

[30] *Iron Man/Captain America: Casualties of War* one-shot.

[31] Here, I am using the word "pragmatic" in the familiar, common-sense way; I am not referring to the American philosophical tradition known as *pragmatism*, as exemplified by John Dewey, William James, and Charles Sanders Pearce. For more, see Christopher Hookway, "Pragmatism," *Stanford Encyclopedia of Philosophy*, October 7, 2013, at http://plato.stanford.edu/entries/pragmatism/.

[32] *Iron Man*, vol. 4, #19 (August 2007).

[33] *Iron Man: The Many Armors of Iron Man* (2008).

[34] *Iron Man/Captain America: Casualties of War* one-shot.

[35] *Iron Man/Captain America: Casualties of War* one-shot.

[36] *What If? Civil War* one-shot (February 2008), "The Stranger." Gee, this certainly makes it sound as if Cap were… nah.

[37] *Fantastic Four*, vol. 1, #542.

[38] *Iron Man/Captain America: Casualties of War* one-shot.

[39] *Captain America: The Captain* (2011).

[40] *Captain America*, vol. 1, #339–340 (March–April 1988) and *Iron Man*, vol. 1, #228 (March 1988).

[41] *Iron Man/Captain America: Casualties of War* one-shot.

[42] Immanuel Kant, *Grounding for the Metaphysics of Morals*, trans. James W. Ellington (Indianapolis, IN: Hackett), p. 421.

[43] *Amazing Spider-Man* #531 (June 2006).

[44] *Civil War* #6 (December 2006).

[45] *Civil War: Front Line* #11 (April 2007).

[46] *Amazing Spider-Man* #535 (November 2006). This is a clear parallel to similar contracts given during the Iraq War to Halliburton, a company for which Dick Cheney once served as CEO before being elected vice president under George W. Bush. (Halliburton is also mentioned in the comics as a frequent beneficiary of military activity.)

[47] *Civil War: Front Line* #9 (December 2006), "Embedded Part 9." Another company that benefited from the Civil War—specifically, the superhero-caused destruction—was Damage Control, which specialized in clean-up and reconstruction. As Wolverine uncovered, Damage Control did manipulate the events of the Civil War; most notably, its CEO Walter Declun provided Nitro with mutant growth hormone to boost his explosive powers, making the tragedy at Stamford much worse than it otherwise would have been (*Civil War: Wolverine*, 2007).

[48] *Amazing Spider-Man* #530–531.

[49] *Fantastic Four: Foes* (2005). When Reed explained his plans to catch *all* of their foes, but complained that there was no prison suitable to hold them, Sue said "Sounds like we'll just have to build a better prison" (*Fantastic Four: Foes* #2, April 2005). She just didn't say where!

[50] *Civil War: Front Line* #9, "Embedded Part 9."

[51] *Civil War: Front Line* #11.

[52] *Iron Man*, vol. 4, #7 (2006).

[53] *Iron Man*, vol. 4, #13 (referring to events in *Iron Man: Execute Program*).

[54] *Iron Man*, vol. 4, #12 (November 2006).

[55] Tony does a similar thing after the Civil War when a giant, genetically engineered neoplastic tumor consumes the SHIELD helicarrier: he removes his armor and lets the cancer consume him, trusting the Extremis in his system to fight it off (*Iron Man*, vol. 4, #18, July 2007).

[56] *Iron Man*, vol. 4, #19 and *World War Hulk* #1 (August 2007). In the former, we see Spider-Man listening, and when he hears Tony repeat his famous "with great power" line, he says, "well, whaddaya know. He was listening."

Chapter 4: Do the Ends Justify the Iron Man?

When we introduced utilitarianism in chapter 4, we talked about the "ends justifying the means," which is a problem when actions considered immoral by common intuitions (or deontological ethics) are taken to further the goal of increasing utility. After the tragedy in Stamford, the change in the sentiment among the people and the government regarding superheroes, and his own experiences with human fallibility, Tony Stark definitely feels that registration will lead to more security, renewed faith in heroes, and higher utility in general. But some of the actions he took before and during the Civil War were, to say the least, morally questionable when considered outside of a strict utilitarian perspective—and it turns out that no one knew this more than Tony Stark himself.

In this chapter we'll look at some of the things Tony did in the service of registration that might have skirted the line of ethics. First, we'll examine how Tony manipulated people, even those close to him, to further his goals. Then we'll turn to the specific actions he took during the Civil War, such as using the prison in the Negative Zone to hold unregistered heroes, and how they were treated while they were there (a direct analog to the prison in our real-world Guantanamo Bay in which terror suspects have been held). We'll finish by stepping back from what Tony did and why, to ask "was it worth it?"

Manipulation

Tony Stark is a charming man and he put his charms to good use in "convincing" other heroes to join him in his cause. No one fell under the sway of Stark more than Peter Parker, the Amazing Spider-Man. It started when he joined the Avengers: having worked with the team over the years and flirted with the idea of joining, Spidey finally signed on formally in Tony and Cap's reassembled team following the "Avengers Disassembled" storyline.[1] After both Peter and his wife Mary Jane's apartment and his Aunt May's house were destroyed, Tony invited all three to move into the new Avengers Tower, where May met many of the Avengers for the first time, taking an immediate liking to their butler Jarvis (and a strong distaste for Wolverine).[2]

We can't fault Tony for opening his skyscraper to the Parkers Three (keeping in mind the possibility of mixed motivation). However, having a good idea about the impending conflict—he *is* a futurist, if he didn't mention that before—Tony started buttering Peter up as soon as he was caught in Tony's web. He began by making Peter a new costume, the "Iron Spidey" armor, that incorporated Stark's advanced electronics (and red and gold color scheme) into a light and flexible costume, soon to be augmented with robotic arms (but, much to Peter's disappointment, no rocket boots).[3] Naturally, Peter is suspicious of Tony's motives, and asks him, point blank, "why?" After prevaricating, Tony says that

> More than anyone else here, you and I have a great deal in common, Peter. We're both scientists, levelheaded, practical… we don't just react, we evaluate. We have similar temperaments, and we speak the same language. … The language of common sense.
>
> There are some potentially… difficult times coming, Peter. I'm hoping those times can be avoided, but in case I'm wrong— it would be good to have someone at my side that I can depend on.

The kicker was when he said, "Peter, I've taken a special interest in you from the day I invited you to come here. You, and MJ, and May, you're like family to me."

Next he asked Peter to be "my second, my protégé… someone I can trust implicitly to back me up. Not to put too fine a point on it… I need your help, and your word, that you'll stick with me through what's coming, no matter what." When Peter tells him that sounds like a blood oath, Tony agrees, saying "that's exactly what it is, Peter," and he makes Peter promise not to tell any of the other Avengers—not even Captain America.

Peter responded as you'd expect Peter to respond: unequivocally.

> Look, Tony, I—you've been good to us, especially to May, and MJ, and… and I owe you a lot. You've put yourself on the line for me again and again. I trust you. I took a vow a long time ago to help people who needed me… and to be there for the people who have always been there for me. No questions asked, no quarter given. Whatever it takes, whatever it costs, in time or in blood—I'm there. You've got your blood oath.

Tony then handed him the letter from the president summoning him to Washington, and in the next issue they were off.

Peter's words "whatever it costs, in time or in blood" could not have been more prophetic, given the consequences of his unmasking on television, revealing his real identity to the world for the first time, all of which we'll discuss at length in Parts III and IV of this book. After Peter switched sides to ally with Cap and his anti-registration forces, Iron Man told him, "I'm disappointed in you, Peter," "I trusted you, Peter! I took you under my wing! Is this how you repay me?" and later, "I trusted you, Pete. I was relying on your support. You let me down. You let us all down."[4] It was loyalty that drew Peter to Tony's side in the first place, and it was loyalty that Tony used to get him back—or punish him. (Take your pick.)

In addition to manipulating him with praise and support, Tony also threatened Peter, especially with the safety of Mary Jane and May—ironically the same people that Tony promised to protect if Peter signed on and later agreed to unmask. As Tony told him,

> If you don't unmask, you'll be just like the other powers who defy the law. Wanted criminals. Hunted. Jailed. Not just you, but MJ and your aunt, because they'd be considered accomplices. If you turn against the law, I can't have you with me. I won't be able to protect you… or your family.[5]

But later, in their first big fight after Spidey decided to join Cap—so important that it was detailed in two different comics—Tony told him, "Don't be a fool! You really think you can just go back to your old life now that everyone knows who you are? This isn't just about you anymore! What about May? What about Mary Jane?"[6] Like a movie mobster who puts small business owners in danger and then extorts protection money from them, Tony made Peter unmask, putting his family in danger, and then holds that very same danger over Peter's head.

Tony's manipulation involved playing on Peter's specific emotional needs and his moral virtues to gain his trust, gratitude, and loyalty. As Captain America told Tony during their long conversation early on in the conflict, "what you did to Spider-Man was unconscionable. He wears his need for a father figure on his sleeve, and you played the role to the hilt to make him do what you asked."[7] Tony argued that Peter made his own decisions, but that's true only on the surface. Manipulation differs from coercion in that it doesn't force certain decisions or behavior, but it does involve steering them, sometimes very subtly, in the direction the manipulator favors. It can take advantage of emotions and ethics to steer people's decisions away from what they would have chosen otherwise. In the words of Immanuel Kant, it makes the other person a "tool" to serve the ends of the manipulator, who should instead be treating that person as in end in himself or herself. The manipulated person does make his or her own choice, but based on a decision-making structure that the manipulator sets up. Tony took Peter and his family in, flattered him, treated him like a partner and confidante, and assured his family's safety if he signed up. How could anyone say no to that?

Spider-Man is the most obvious target of Tony Stark's manipulation but he's hardly the only one. Tony tried to convince Emma Frost, the White Queen of the X-Men, to lead her team in cooperation with him, arguing that it was to their political advantage (as well as subtly suggesting blackmail with regard to a continued "arrangement" between them). After she refuses, he tells his best friend Happy Hogan to continue with the plans to contain and neutralize them.[8] On a much more personal level, Sue Richards accused Tony of manipulating her husband Reed, otherwise known as Mr. Fantastic:

> SUSAN: I've been shadowing you all day, just trying to get a chance to talk to you, to make you understand… to stop this insanity. The things you're doing… the things you're making Reed do…
> TONY: Reed's a big boy.
> SUE: No! Reed's not a big boy! Not around you! He idolizes you! It's disgusting how much he looks up to you, how eager he is to please you!
> TONY: Oh yeah! That's me! The puppet master! Has it ever occurred to you that he might just agree with me? Or is that too much for your ego to handle?[9]

In this case, Tony's manipulation may not have been as conscious as it was with Peter, but he may still be responsible for it to the extent that he should have been aware of it.

Several times throughout the Civil War story we hear of Reed's admiration for Tony's grand vision and political acumen. As the registration act headed toward passage and Reed began to make plans with Tony and Hank Pym, he raved to Sue:

> Tony's big plan for the superhuman community is the most exciting thing we've ever worked on, Sue. He wasn't kidding when he said he'd revolutionize every meta-human in America. I haven't been this excited since I saw my first black hole. … You should hear the ideas he and Hank Pym have been tossing around. They're like concept machines.[10]

Reed even boasted about the plan to T'Challa, the Black Panther, after Spider-Man's unmasking, and demonstrated his characteristic cluelessness about Tony's skill at manipulation, telling T'Challa that Peter "unmasked voluntarily, because Iron Man explained the gravity of our situation."[11] If Reed couldn't see how Tony had mesmerized Peter, he certainly wouldn't have realized how Tony did it to him—just as he couldn't see how this conflict was affecting his wife and brother-in-law, who joined Cap's team after the clone of Thor that Reed helped develop killed Goliath.[12]

Manipulation is just one tool in service to Tony's utilitarian nature, one way on which he believes that "the ends justify the means." And while personal manipulation of his friends and colleagues may be the most offensive example, due to the lack of respect and betrayal of loyalty it reflects, he also manipulated events during the Civil War—and even before it started. As we know, during the Congressional hearings he hired the Titanium Man to mount an attack in an attempt to sway the committee. Peter immediately suspected Tony was responsible, and all but asked him about it, but Tony denied it, outright lying.[13] And remember Peter's shiny new Iron Spidey armor? Tony programmed a kill code into it so he could disable it if (and when) he needed to, saying, "I'm a technocrat, Peter. And what kind of techie would I be... to hand over a suit as powerful as that one without building in safeguards to make sure it couldn't be used against me?"[14] It gets worse: Tony used the armor to study Peter's neurophysiology, enabling him to fool his "Spidey sense" into not alerting him to danger and to give him false positives, not to mention duplicating it to use on his own.[15]

Excessive Tactics

Of course, manipulation is the only the most subtle of the means Tony used to support registration and fight the Civil War. Many of the others we've mentioned already, so we can be brief here.

One controversial tool that Tony used was enlisting the aid of convicted supervillains to round up unregistered heroes. After Goliath's funeral, Tony and Reed explain to Janet van Dyne (the winsome Wasp) and Happy Hogan that as more of their people defect to join Captain America's team, they need more recruits. Janet proposes getting the Fifty-State Initiative up and running, but Reed says it not ready, saying instead that "we need to move and we need people with experience in superhuman combat"—which leaves supervillains, in the form of a new Thunderbolts team assembled for the sole purpose of helping round up unregistered heroes.[16]

The Thunderbolts are traditionally a team of supervillains who cooperate with the government to reduce their sentences, earning their freedom by proving they can be heroes (and not just for one day). As Tony told Miriam Sharpe, "giving offenders a second chance is something we tried to do as far as back as the original Avengers."[17] A little over a year into the Avengers' existence, most of the team left and Captain America assembled his "kooky quartet," made up of himself and three former villains—Hawkeye, Quicksilver, and the Scarlet Witch.[18] More would join later, including the Black Widow and the Vision (which makes you wonder which Avengers were good to begin with!). In fact, Hawkeye even left the Avengers to lead the Thunderbolts for several years, with the rationale that no one could reform a group of villains better than a reformed villain himself.[19]

But the last page of *Civil War* #4, featuring psychopathic murderer Bullseye and a half-dozen other vicious criminals, does not fill the reader with confidence that the new team of Thunderbolts will be easily controlled or restrained (despite nanites injected into their bloodstreams for precisely that purpose). In fact, once Spider-Man goes rogue, two of them chase Peter down, drug him, and nearly beat him to death. Only the lethal intervention of the Punisher saves Peter's life, and leads them both to offer their services to Cap's team. After he brings Peter in, the Falcon asks "since when were you on this team?" to which the Punisher responds, "Since the other guys started enlisting known thieves and multiple killers."[20] In this case, Tony's extreme action to support registration may have actually hurt his cause insomuch as it only energized the anti-registration forces who became hunted by people they once imprisoned and who were now officially sanctioned by the US government.

But even before Tony engaged the Thunderbolts, another one of his initiatives had fatal consequences (as well as driving more heroes to the other side). As we know, the clone of Thor created by Tony, Reed, and Hank killed Bill Foster, the hero known as Goliath. As Hank explained to Janet, the clone was created using a strand of Thor's hair that Tony had kept from the very first Avengers meeting: "What kind of man combs his furniture for hair follicles and skin cells?" ("A guy with a lot of foresight I guess," Janet answered.)[21] The clone was activated during the first large battle between the two sides in the Civil War after Tony drew out Captain America's forces with a false emergency call. But the clone went renegade during his first outing, savaging the anti-registration heroes with a viciousness that matched his strength, and finally shooting a bolt of lightning through Goliath's chest. Cap's forces regrouped to escape, but just before the clone's lightning could hit them, Sue Richards protected them with a force bubble, told them to leave ("now"), and at the end of the issue she and her brother joined them.

Not only did Sue and Johnny leave after Goliath's death, but it was at that point that Peter Parker began to have serious doubts regarding the path he had chosen. Tony actually defended the Thor clone to Peter, arguing that he "reacted like a police officer would."[22] But it affected Hank and Reed more deeply, instilling doubts in Tony's two closest allies. As Hank told Peter after the incident, "I just watched a new superhuman I helped create blow a hole through one of my oldest friends. Do you really think I'm so remote—so detached—that this wouldn't have some kind of impact on me?"[23] Later, as they watched Daredevil be led off in shackles to the Negative Zone prison, Reed told She-Hulk that

> Sometimes I wish we'd never gotten involved. Do you ever stop to think how much easier things would be if we hadn't spliced Thor's DNA with Hank Pym's cyber-tech? If we didn't have this final battle planned with all those Thunderbolt lunatics? Hank wouldn't be doped-up on antidepressants and my darling Sue would never have left. …[24]

It's a testament to the creators at Marvel that they portrayed the three individuals at the forefront of superhero registration as conflicted about their mission and methods at the same time that they're resolute in carrying them out. (Otherwise, I wouldn't be writing this book!)

Out of all of Tony's questionable tactics during the Civil War, the one most relevant to events in the real world is the Negative Zone prison itself, constructed earlier by Reed Richards to hold supervillains who ritually broke out of even the highest-security prisons on Earth (for example, in the mass breakout that led Tony and Cap to assemble their "New Avengers").[25] Once the registration act was signed, this prison was repurposed to hold unregistered heroes and named 42 because, as Tony told Miriam Sharpe, "it was number forty-two of a hundred ideas Reed, Hank and I wrote down the night your son was killed. A hundred ideas for a safer world."[26] After the war ended, the public was told about the prison, and as Reed told Sue in a letter,

> Even our controversial prison in the Negative Zone was met with rapturous applause when we finally went public. How frightening the world must have seemed before this: vigilantes, amateurs, super-villains brooding in cells that never seemed to

hold them. The only surprise is that we were tolerated for as long as we were.[27]

(Note how Reed lumps in vigilantes and amateurs with super-villains—with friends like Reed...)

The parallels with the prison on Guantánamo Bay where terror suspects were held (and, at the time of this writing, are still held) following 9/11 are striking. When Peter demanded to see the prison and learned that it was in the Negative Zone, Tony simply said "There's no safe place on Earth to hold them, Peter. We had no choice. No choice at all."[28] When one "occupant" (as the prisoners are called) pleads his innocence, Tony says, "They all say pretty much the same thing." He goes on to claim that "We do all we can to make them comfortable during their stay. We even provide virtual reality systems for those who don't represent a tech-threat. This way, even though they're inside—they can feel as if they're outside" (as a prisoner moans "help me... please... help me..."), recalling the 1999 film *The Matrix* and Robert Nozick's experience machine.[29] After they walk by one prisoner bound like a mummy and held in a massive metal restraint, Tony tells Peter—with no sense of irony—"so if you had notions of some kind of inhumane gulag, or a dark, dark prison dripping sludge and human misery... you were mistaken." These, of course, were the claims of the US government with regard to Guantanamo Bay, claims that lawyers for the terror suspects imprisoned there contest strongly.

Peter seems to accept this as an interim or temporary solution—which, in fact, is how Tony represents it to him later when he asks, "What do you suggest we do with the unregistered super-people? Lock them up with regular prisoners? This is only a temporary measure, Peter. Lock them up in Rykers and they'll be out again in five minutes."[30] But during the grand tour, Tony seems more forthright, offering the same justification but asserting that "this isn't temporary, Peter. This isn't interim. This is permanent. Get with the program."[31] He goes on, showing his impatience:

> You can't put an atomic bomb on probation! You can't put somebody who flies under house arrest! It's real simple, Peter! They either sign up, or they stay here until they do sign up! And if they never sign up then they stay here for the rest of their natural lives! Do you get it, Peter? Do you see it now?

Tony says he hates this, "every minute of it," but "we have no choice. We have to follow the law." Peter replies that "following the law means these people get a trial before you send them away to be imprisoned for the rest of their lives! You can't just lock people away...," but Tony interjects, "Yes, we can, and we have. And that's the end of it."

Finally, as if the parallel to Guantanamo Bay weren't clear enough at this point, Peter mentions Jennifer Walter, lawyer and She-Hulk, ostensibly on the side of registration, but also "in court, every day, defending these guys, making motions—." But Tony dismisses that too, interrupting Peter to offer yet another argument made in the real world:

> She can make all the motions she wants. This is outside the jurisdiction of local and federal courts. This is an act of Congress, signed by the president. Only the Supreme Court can intervene, and I happen to know they won't. This place is not on American soil. American laws don't touch here. American lawyers don't come here. Once non-registrants come here, they're legal nonentities. Occupants. Prisoners. Them... and those who give them aid and support.

With the last part, and the way he looks at Peter, Tony not so subtly suggests that Peter will end up there too if he doesn't keep in line. But that didn't deter Peter, and after that visit to the Negative Zone prison, Peter finally decided to break with Tony and side with Captain America (on which more in chapters 9 and 10).

After the Civil War ended, journalists Sally Floyd and Ben Urich accused Tony of different motives for the Negative Zone prison, maintaining gulag-like conditions to provide incentive for heroes to register, and trumping up the Civil War to test their new superprison with the unregistered heroes so they could use it for supervillains later.[32] That wasn't all they accused Tony of, though. While the Civil War was raging, the forces of Atlantis were threatening an invasion of the surface world in retaliation for the death of Namorita, one of the New Warriors who died in Stamford, and cousin of Namor, the Sub-Mariner. The invasion started with the activation of "sleeper cells," Atlanteans living in the United States disguised as humans (with parallels to undercover terrorist agents in the real world).[33]

While the US government tried to defuse tensions with Atlantis, Norman Osborn—Spider-Man's archnemesis the Green Goblin and a member of the new Thunderbolts team recruited to help round up unregistered heroes—broke loose from his programming and shot an Atlantean ambassador at a high-profile, public diplomacy event.[34] People within the pro-registration camp, as well as Ben and

Sally, looked into who compromised the nanites that were supposed to control Osborn (as they did the other cooperative villains). Tony simply told his colleagues that the "traitor" had been identified and dealt with, which angered those who resented Tony's secrecy.[35] Carol Danvers, the current Captain Marvel then operating under her original codename Ms. Marvel, snuck information about the nanites to Sally, who managed to put together the true story with Ben—then they took it to Tony.[36]

To make a long story short, Sally and Ben fingered Tony as the traitor (and more). They traced the financial dealings that Ben and Peter Parker discovered to events such as Osborn's attack on the Atlantean ambassador, events that only the person responsible would have known about. They deduced that rather than modifying Osborn's nanites to let him loose, Tony made them more effective so he could control Osborn's actions, forcing him to provoke the Atlanteans. Furthermore, Osborn was not punished but instead installed as the leader of the new Thunderbolts, now the official superhero team of Colorado under the 50-State Initiative.[37]

Tony calls it a nice story that doesn't make sense, and Ben agrees, asking "Why would anyone be crazy enough to coerce the Green Goblin into attacking a foreign delegation on a diplomatic mission? Why push us to the brink of yet another war?" Then Ben answers his own question with a perfect description of Tony's utilitarian decision-making process and justification for his actions: "Unless you were so smart that you'd already weighed the pros and cons, and calculated what the outcome was going to be?" The outcome that Tony predicted, according to Sally and Ben, was that the threat of war with Atlantis, heightened by Osborn's attack, would boost registration and unite the superhero community "against a common foe." It's ironic that a "warmonger" such as Tony would risk a second war he never planned to fight in order to stop the first one he never wanted to. Nonetheless, the risk Tony took here eclipses any of his actions leading up to or during the Civil War itself, and illustrates the capacity of both his sense of responsibility to do whatever he could to make things better, and his unparalleled confidence in his judgment that enabled him to do it.

Was It Worth It?

After months (at least in the real world), the massive battle over registration was over, Captain America surrendered, and the Civil War ended. But the great blow to the Marvel Universe was still to come. On the way to his arraignment, Captain America was fatally shot outside the courtroom. The killer was originally thought to be have been his longtime foe Crossbones, but later it was discovered to have been SHIELD agent (and Cap's longtime romantic partner) Sharon Carter, acting under the mind control of two more of Cap's enemies, Dr. Faustus and the Red Skull.[38] While it would be difficult to hold Tony directly responsible for the death of Captain America—although many did, including Cap's sidekick Bucky Barnes—Tony feels responsible for it nonetheless, perhaps wondering if he shouldn't have supported registration so resolutely, or if he should have tried harder to convince Cap to join him.

There were tremendous costs to many people from the Civil War itself. Among the hero community itself, the most obvious cost was the death of Goliath at the hands of the clone of Thor. This was also a symbolic turning point in the Civil War in that it showed not only the extraordinary lengths Tony Stark and his allies were willing to go to in supporting registration, but also highlighted what happened when their overzealousness went horribly wrong. In general, roughly half of Marvel's heroes were driven underground and made criminals, and many of them stayed there after the war ended, including Spider-Man and Luke Cage (whose adventures continued in the *New Avengers* comic after the Civil War ended). Speaking of our favorite wallcrawler, Spider-Man found out what happens when his worst enemies find out who he is under the mask. (More on that in chapter 11.) Reed and Sue Richards' marriage was severely tested, although it survived after Reed risked his life to save Sue during the final battle.[39] This is not even to mention countless injuries and general demoralization in the superhero community as a whole for years to come.

Ultimately, however, the heroes did not suffer the brunt of the costs of the Civil War. After the final battle ended, a television news anchor said, "when measuring the cost of this conflict, what dollar figure do we give to lives lost, careers destroyed, relationships torn apart and wounds that will never truly heal?"[40] As Ben Urich asked himself early on, "you know who's going to pay for all of this? We are," by which we meant the ordinary people in the Marvel Universe, not the ones who fly overhead.[41] These ordinary people are the ones that Captain America realized, at the end, were being harmed, after which he called for a stop to the fighting and surrendered (as we'll see in chapter 7). After emerging from the subway tunnel where she and Urich hid during the final battle, Floyd surveyed the destruction and muttered, "You stupid, selfish idiots. What have you done?"[42] At other times she waxed more philosophical; before the final battle, she thought to herself that the registration act resulted in "the fracturing of our society, the seeding of paranoia and the fostering of mistrust that only a police state like the Soviet Union could perfect," and afterwards that "America's problems came into focus, no longer shrouded by the fogs of war. Opinions were sharply divided."[43] When she meets Captain America after his surrender, she tells him that he's broken the country and asks him, "What are you gonna do to fix it?"[44] (I don't have to tell *you* how many people are asking similar questions in the real world right now.)

If registration and the Civil War were motivated by utilitarian reasoning, it is only natural to ask, after it ended, if it was worth it. Were the costs justified by the benefits—did the ends justify the means? The problem with such assessments, however, is that they're based on counterfactual thinking: we need to imagine what the Marvel Universe would have looked like if Stamford happened but the SHRA was never passed, or if Tony and his team took different, less aggressive steps to enforce it. That's a great topic for an issue of *What If?*, Marvel Comics' long-running comics series exploring different ways famous events could have played out.[45] But even those stories are presented as merely one possible way things might have turned out if something had gone differently. In the two issues of *What If?* related to the Civil War, a number of different scenarios were considered, all of them ending up much worse than the actual events did.[46] But that doesn't mean there aren't an infinite number of alternative possibilities, with no way to know which one "would" have happened if things had gone differently.

But one person did ask himself if it was worth it, the person chiefly responsible for the way that registration was handled: Tony Stark himself. In public, he seemed very pleased with the way things turned out on the whole. Before the final battle, he tells Reed that crime rates are down to levels not seen "since Eisenhower was in office," and it was only going to get better once the new heroes-in-training were good to go.[47] He likely agreed with Reed when he wrote to his wife Sue that "on the whole our experiment has been an enormous success. What once seemed like our darkest hour has been transformed into our greatest opportunity."[48] And Tony himself was jubilant when talking to Miriam Sharpe at the very end of the *Civil War* series, telling her that he, Reed, and Hank Pym have, "a hundred ideas for a safer world and we aren't even at number fifty yet. Doesn't that sound exciting to you?" After Miriam tells him he's a good man and that "I truly believe you've given people heroes they can believe in again," he says, "Oh, the best is yet to come."[49] He even gloated and taunted Captain America following his surrender, declaring victory and calling him a sore loser.[50]

That was before the assassination of Captain America, however. During his confession in front of Cap's corpse, Tony recounted his decisions and his justifications for them. In tears, he concluded by summarizing the things he did that he wasn't proud of, as well as his final assessment:

It was!! It was the right thing to do! And—and—and I was willing to get in bed with people we despise to get this done. And I knew the world favors the underdog and that I would be the bad guy. I knew this and I said I was OK with it. And—and even though I said… even though I said I was willing to go all the way with it… I wasn't.

And—and I know this because the worst has happened. The thing I can't live with… has happened. And for all our back and forth—and all the things we've said and done to each other… for all the hard questions I've had to ask, and terrible lies I've had to tell…. . There's one thing I won't be able to tell anyone now. Not my friends or my co-workers or my president… the one thing! The one thing I should have told you. But now I can't…

It wasn't worth it.[51]

Granted, Tony only seemed to have arrived at this epiphany after his fellow Avenger and personal idol died—before that, he seemed quite happy with things. Sometimes it takes just one tragic event to make us see past events and choices in a different light.

Even now, however, he seems untroubled by the choices he made, the corners he cut, the otherwise immoral activities he engaged in to further his goals. In one of their arguments long before the Civil War ever began, Tony defended some extreme measures to Captain America, arguing that "I knew you could never understand that—you don't believe that the ends justify the means."[52] Despite the final costs, he still believes that his decisions were proper, and they may very well have been proper from the point of view of utilitarianism. But at the same time, that point of view is subject to criticism, which we discussed in chapter 2, mostly from the point of view of deontological ethics and basic moral intuitions. Like Cap, some people do not believe that ends always justify the means, and those people are always going to have a problem with people like Tony Stark.

Whether we agree with registration, with Tony's role in it and his actions to promote it, or with utilitarianism in general, we should acknowledge that Tony did step up when he felt someone had to, and he made choices that no one else was willing to make. As Tony explained in the next large conflict when the Hulk returned from exile, "every day I choose between courses of action that could affect millions, even billions of lives. With stakes that high, how dare I decide? But at this point, doing nothing is a decision in and of itself."[53] As Sally Floyd said to

Tony when she and Ben presented their conclusions about his manipulations during the conflict with Atlantis:

> You controlled the entire event, Mister Stark. You weighed the possibility of war with Atlantis against the inevitability of costumed individuals tearing this country apart, and you did what had to be done. You knew how unpopular the act would be. You were the only one prepared to take the biggest gamble in history because you knew it would pay off. ... You knew this would happen all along. You sacrificed your status as a friend, colleague and hero for the greater good of the country. You alone understood the ramifications of such a course of action. And for that act of courage I truly and honestly applaud you.

If Tony saw something coming, some harm that could be prevented or at least lessened by his intervention, choosing not to act would still be a choice, and to a utilitarian it would be an unethical one. As he told Cap's corpse, he stepped up and he committed, which is what someone in his position and with his moral code was obligated to do.

Furthermore, Tony also realizes that he is responsible for the consequences of his choices, even though he felt he had no choice but to make them. We see this in another example from the Hulk's return. While flying to confront the Hulk, Tony thinks to himself,

> some people avoid hard choices. As a CEO, as an Avenger, as Director of S.H.I.E.L.D., as a recovering alcoholic, I make them on a daily basis. Some days, it's as simple as not having a drink. On others, millions of lives hang in the balance. I do what I think best. What I think is right. I make no apologies for that. But I do make one promise: that I'll face the consequences. I make the decision... and I pay the price.[54]

Of course, other people also pay the price, but we can give Tony the benefit of the doubt and assume he takes those costs into account as well and feels them as though they were his own. (OK, that may be a lot of benefit of the doubt, but I did argue Tony's general heroism in the last chapter, so bear with me.)

All in all, a utilitarian like Tony who feels he has the knowledge, judgment, and ability to intervene in the world to make it a better place can only make the best choice possible, at the time it has to be made, with the information at hand.

When the decision has played itself out and the consequences are clear, he or anyone else can assess whether the choice was a good one or the best one, and whether "it was worth it." To be fair, though, we can't criticize the original choice based on what happened after it (even if Tony does claim to be a futurist). If people are going to criticize Tony's choices—as many did, most obviously Captain America—then they have to put themselves in the position he was in and identify where he went wrong in his decision-making. That still leaves a lot to criticize, from his assumptions regarding the future path of events, to his judgment regarding the outcomes and probabilities, to the utility values he implicitly assigned to various outcomes. But it's difficult to criticize him for doing something when he truly felt something needed to be done—and when no one else was willing to stand up.

~~~~~

We only have half the picture at this point, and we'll get the other half in the next part when we discuss Captain America, his arguments against registration, and the source of those deontological principles that he stands for, and which are essential to criticizing Tony's "ends justify the means" reasoning. We'll also ask if Captain America ever compromises his principles, and if he does, what that implies about his integrity.

---

[1] Spidey became an official Avenger in *New Avengers Vol. 1: Breakout* (2005); his earlier adventures with the team are collected in *Spider-Man: Am I an Avenger?* (2011).

[2] *Amazing Spider-Man* #518–519 (May–June 2005).

[3] *Amazing Spider-Man* #529 (April 2006), through Peter's speech to Tony.

[4] *Civil War* #5 (November 2006); *Amazing Spider-Man* #536 (November 2006); *Iron Man*, vol. 4, #14 (January 2007).

[5] *Amazing Spider-Man* #532 (July 2006).

[6] *Civil War* #5.

[7] *Iron Man/Captain America: Casualties of War* one-shot (February 2007). Peter even sarcastically calls Tony "Dad," such as in *Amazing Spider-Man* #535 (November 2006) when Tony catches Peter leaving Stark Tower to join Cap.

[8] *Civil War* #3 (September 2006). Emma told fellow X-Man Storm that mutants "don't need any more image problems" after the Scarlet Witch lost control, and that the Civil War had actually taken the heat off of them for a moment (*Black Panther*, vol. 4, #22, January 2007). Nonetheless, three mutants did join Tony: Bishop, Sabra, and Micromax (*Civil War: X-Men* #1, September 2007), and as Tony told Wolverine, the 198 remaining mutants after the House of M incident were already in a government database and therefore *de facto* registered (*Wolverine*, vol. 3, #43, August 2006). For more on the X-Men's activities during the Civil War, see *Civil War: X-Men*, *Civil War: Wolverine*, and *Civil War: X-Men Universe* (all 2007).

[9] *Iron Man*, vol. 4, #14 (January 2007). Space prohibits me from detailing the experiences of the Fantastic Four, but be sure to check out *Civil War: Fantastic Four* (2007) and *Fantastic Four: The New Fantastic Four* (2008) to see the effects the Civil War had on the First Family on comics.

[10] *Civil War* #2 (August 2006).

[11] *Civil War* #3.

[12] *Civil War* #4 (October 2006).

[13] *Amazing Spider-Man* #530–531 (May–June 2006).

[14] *Amazing Spider-Man* #536 (November 2006). Peter surprised him, though, reactivating the suit, and saying, "And what kind of techie would I be, not to figure out you've built in an override... boss!"

[15] *Iron Man*, vol. 4, #14.

[16] *Civil War* #4. Meanwhile, the regular Thunderbolts team, under the leadership of Captain America foe Baron Zemo, was also engaged by Iron Man, Reed Richards, and Hank Pym, not to round up unregistered superheroes but rather to help control the rest of the supervillains (and recruit them to the cause) (*Civil War: Thunderbolts*, 2007). In the final battle of the Civil War, however, members of both Thunderbolts teams fought on Iron Man's side.

[17] *Civil War* #7 (January 2007).

[18] *Avengers*, vol. 1, #16 (May 1965).

[19] Hawkeye leaves the Avengers in *Avengers*, vol. 3, #9 (October 1998) and first joins up with the T-Bolts in *Thunderbolts*, vol. 1, #21 (December 1998), staying with them for several years.

[20] *Civil War* #5. Yes, the irony of this was noted (by Misty Knight).

[21] *Civil War* #4.

[22] *Civil War* #5. (Those words take on a distinctly different meaning as I write this, with the death of Sandra Bland currently in the news and the memory of Eric Garner still fresh.)

[23] *Civil War* #4.

[24] *Civil War* #5. Two notes about identities: the Daredevil we see during the Civil War was not Matt Murdock, who was in jail at the time, but rather Danny Rand, otherwise known as Iron Fist. (See *Civil War: Choosing Sides*, December 2006, "Choosing Sides.") Also, we find out later (in *Mighty Avengers*, vol. 1, #15, August 2008) that "Hank Pym" was actually an imposter, a member of the Skrulls, an alien race of shapeshifters that invaded Earth after the Civil War, and "he" intentionally made the Thor clone more violent than planned. (See chapter 12 for more on the Skrulls' "Secret Invasion.")

[25] *Fantastic Four: Foes* (2005); *New Avengers, Vol. 1: Breakout.*

[26] *Civil War* #7.

[27] *Civil War* #7.

[28] *Amazing Spider-Man* #535 (as are all the quotes in this paragraph).

[29] This idea may have been Reed's too; see *Fantastic Four: Foes* #2 (April 2005). On the experience machine, see Robert Nozick, *Anarchy, State, and Utopia* (New York: Basic, 1974), pp. 42–45, or *The Examined Life: Philosophical Meditations* (New York: Simon & Schuster, 1989), pp. 104–108. On the philosophy of *The Matrix*, see William Irwin (ed.), *The Matrix and Philosophy: Welcome to the Desert of the Real* (Chicago: Open Court, 2002).

[30] *Civil War* #5.

[31] *Amazing Spider-Man* #535 (as are the rest of the quotes in this and the next paragraph).

[32] *Civil War: Front Line* #11 (April 2007).

[33] The story started in *Civil War: Front Line* #3 (September 2006), "Sleeper Cell Part One," and continued through most of the rest of the *Civil War: Front Line* series. (It was not mentioned in the main *Civil War* series.)

[34] *Civil War: Front Line* #8 (January 2007), "Sleeper Cell Part Six."

[35] *Civil War: Front Line* #10 (March 2007), "Embedded Part 10."

[36] *Civil War: Front Line* #11 (through the rest of this section).

[37] From there he would go on to greater things, as we'll see in chapter 12.

[38] *Captain America*, vol. 5, #25 (April 2007).

[39] *Civil War* #7.

[40] *Amazing Spider-Man* #538 (January 2007).

[41] *Civil War: Front Line* #2 (August 2006), "Embedded Part Two."

[42] *Civil War: Front Line* #11.

[43] *Civil War: Front Line* #7 (December 2006), "Embedded Part Seven"; *Civil War: Front Line* #11.

[44] *Front Line* #11; we'll see much more of this conversation in the next chapter.

[45] Such explorations included what if the Avengers had never formed (*What If*, vol. 1, #3, June 1977) and what if Jane Foster had found the hammer of Thor (*What If*, vol. 1, #10, August 1978)—which actually happened a quarter century later in *Thor*, vol. 4, #1 (December 2014).

[46] The one-shots *What If? Civil War* (February 2008), with the stories "What If Captain America Led All the Heroes Against Registration?" and "What If Iron Man Lost the Civil War?", and *What If? Fallen Son* (February 2009), which asked "What If... Iron Man Had Died?" (instead of Cap).

[47] *Civil War* #6 (December 2006).

[48] *Civil War* #7.

[49] *Civil War* #7.

[50] *Civil War: The Confession* one-shot (May 2007).

[51] *Civil War: The Confession* one-shot.

[52] *Captain America*, vol. 1, #401 (June 1992).

[53] *World War Hulk* #4 (November 2007).

[54] *Iron Man*, vol. 4, #19 (August 2007).

Mark D. White

Part II: Captain America—On the Side of Liberty

Unlike his friend the Armored Avenger, Captain America is one of the original superheroes of Marvel Comics—or rather Timely Comics, as it was known in the 1940s. Introduced in *Captain America Comics* #1 in March, 1941, delivering a right hook to Adolf Hitler, Captain America and his young sidekick Bucky joined other Timely heroes such as the Human Torch and Namor in an early version of the Marvel Universe. Less than a year later, Japanese pilots attacked Pearl Harbor, and soon the United States entered World War II, after which Captain America's mission of patriotic reassurance and fundraising lasted until the fighting stopped in 1945. Cap and the other heroes hung on a while longer until their comics were cancelled at the end of the decade, and despite several unsuccessful revivals in the mid-1950s, Captain America was all but dead to the world.

But you just can't keep a good Sentinel of Liberty down. In November 1961, the Marvel Universe as we know it came to life with the publication of *Fantastic Four*, vol. 1, #1, soon followed by comics featuring Spider-Man, Ant-Man and Wasp, Thor, Iron Man, and the Hulk, with storylines weaving through the growing line of books, which had never been seen in comics before. Before long, the last five of these heroes would come together in *Avengers*, vol. 1, #1 in September 1963 to fight threats no hero could face alone. In *Avengers*, vol. 1, #4 (March 1964), with the help of Namor—who had appeared for the first time in the modern Marvel Universe in *Fantastic Four*, vol. 1, #4 (May 1962)—our heroes discovered Captain America, frozen in an iceberg after a battle at the end of World War II that cost the life of his young sidekick Bucky.

Ever since that fateful day, Captain America has been a central force in the Marvel Universe, providing a moral center against which every other hero is compared and with which many have disagreed—none more than Iron Man. Cap is a frequent leader of the Avengers, and even when other heroes take the lead, they can't help but compare their leadership to his. His devotion to principle over policy grants him a personal integrity that has been reflected in several conflicts with his own government, when its elected leaders headed down a path that does not sit well with the foundational ideals of the country that Cap was sworn to protect.

His natural leadership, inspiration, and integrity were tested more than ever when the Civil War began, a situation which cast him against his fellow heroes, his

71

own government, and the American people, who largely supported registration. In the next three chapters we'll go behind the shield and see why Captain America opposed registration. How can we best describe his moral code, and in what ways does it contrast with Iron Man's? Which specific principles led him to feel so strongly against registration and take the action he did in opposition to it (and to Tony)? Does Captain America always put his principles above any consideration of welfare or utility—and if he doesn't, what does that imply about his character and integrity?

Chapter 5: Introducing Deontology

As we hinted in the last part of the book, Captain America does not think much of Iron Man's pragmatic utilitarianism—in fact, we just heard Tony tell him, in defense of killing an alien leader to prevent an intergalactic war, "you don't believe that the ends justify the means."[1] In one of the classic team-ups, Iron Man used a villain's mind-altering technology to make the world forget about his secret identity, after which Cap told him that "your ends didn't justify your means as neatly as you say," questioning his judgment as well as his basic morality.[2] Cap disagrees with many of Tony's choices, not on the basis that they wouldn't increase utility, but because there is something intrinsically wrong about them *even though* they may increase utility. It makes sense that someone like Cap would oppose murder and mind control aside from their effect on utility, but exactly what type of morality does this kind of thinking represent?

In this sense, Captain America's moral code most closely resembles *deontology*, which is often contrasted directly with utilitarianism (or consequentialism in general). While there is no one accepted definition, it's fair to say that deontologists in general maintain that the moral status of an action is not determined solely by its consequences, but also depends on something inherent in the act itself.[3] This "something" makes the act right or wrong, regardless of whether it helps further the good or increases the bad, and is usually based on some conception of rights or duties; in other words, an act that violates someone's right, such as assaulting them, is wrong regardless of whether it promotes the greater good. For this reason, at the risk of oversimplifying matters, deontology is usually associated with the "right," while consequentialism and utilitarianism are associated with the "good."[4]

It would be all too easy to say deontology is just "anti-consequentialism"; even though for some purposes that works, it's a little too quick and easy for us. As I said above, deontology does not deny that consequences have some moral worth in some cases—it does deny, however, that *only* consequences have moral worth in *all* cases. Typically, if no rights or duties are at stake in a given choice, then consequences are all that's left to determine the outcome. If you're deciding which charity to donate $100 to, and you owe no special obligation to any particular charity (based, for instance, on an earlier promise), then the ethical thing to do may be to donate the money to the charity you think will do the most good with it. But if you did make a promise to donate to one of them, then that promise may give you a good duty-based reason to donate to that charity *even if* it's not the one you think will do the most good. In the end, all deontology says, in its mildest form, is that sometimes rights and duties "trump" considerations of utility, which is the opposite of consequentialism only in the literal sense that consequentialism says consequences are the only thing that matter.

But this only brings us back to the question: if consequences or utility are not all that matters, then what else does? And this is what makes deontology more difficult to define than utilitarianism. Utilitarianism is defined in terms of the one thing it does consider morally worthy: utility. But deontology is defined in terms of the one thing it *doesn't* always consider morally worthy: again, utility. In other words, deontology is defined in terms of what *isn't*, not what it *is*, so we still need to determine what it is. That leaves a big hole that can be filled by many things, such as rights and duties, as defined in different ways by different philosophers. To be fair, utility has been defined in different ways by different philosophers also, but we were able to discuss utilitarianism easily without getting into the specifics of any one precise definition of it. With deontology, however, we need to choose one version of it; we simply Kant do it any other way. (Such is philosophy humor, sorry.)

Kant, Duty, and the Categorical Imperative

Immanuel Kant, whom we met several times already, is usually regarded as the most important deontologist philosopher, and his duty-based ethics are taken by many to define deontology itself. Even though I wouldn't argue that Captain America follows Kantian ethics in particular, nonetheless it's worthwhile to introduce the basic outline of Kant's system, which represents one influential example of where duties come from, how people should work them into their lives, and how they interact with consequences.[5]

For Kant, everything starts with *autonomy*, the capacity of every person to make moral decisions without undue influence from external forces, such as authority or peer pressure, and internal ones, such as desires and drives. In other words, we have the ability to make the right choice even if it conflicts with what other people tell us to do or what we really want to do. Resisting authority and social pressures is what we usually think of when we think of independence or autonomy—forging our own path and following our conscience—but to Kant it was just as important that we be able to make the right choices even when they go against what *we* want. Furthermore, both parts of autonomy apply to our usual conceptions of a hero (super or not). Heroes do what they believe is right, regardless of what others say they should do—even, sometimes, the law or government—and more important, they usually make some personal sacrifice to do so. In fact, sacrifice is usually taken to be the critical aspect of heroism, and because it is so difficult to put one's own interests aside to help others, it is a very highly valued and regarded quality in a person. This explains why we hold heroes such as Captain America and Spider-Man in such high esteem—and why we tolerate Tony Stark at all!

Autonomy sounds like an impossible ideal. After all, all of us are weak from time to time, and we give into our own desires, as well as pressure from other people, even when we know we shouldn't. Kant realized this, and wrote that no one has perfect autonomy except God and the angels, because we are all physical beings as well as rational ones. But simply having the capacity for autonomy, a capacity which we are responsible to develop and nurture, grants human beings *dignity*, an incomparable and incalculable worth that separates us from mere things. We should emphasize that *all* human beings have dignity, no one more than any other, implying that all persons are of equal moral status and are deserving of equal respect and consideration—the same principle, as we saw in chapter 2 that grounded utilitarianism, although Kant draws very different conclusions from it. (And to be fair, Kant said it first.)

Based on the two concepts of autonomy and dignity, and the moral equality of all persons that is implied by them, Kant developed his *categorical imperative*, the bane of so many Philosophy 101 students. The categorical imperative, which can be stated in several different "formulae," was Kant's attempt to formalize what he considered "the moral law," which he believed most people followed implicitly without ever thinking about it in the way that philosophers do.

This is the way you use the categorical imperative: let's say you're contemplating an action which you suspect is morally questionable, such as telling your annoying superhero partner you're not patrolling tonight so you can have a night of crimefighting to yourself (and maybe happen to run into the cute superhero who just moved into the neighborhood). Generally speaking, that is an example of lying for your own advantage, which we can call our *maxim* or plan of action. We then submit our maxim to the categorical imperative test: if it passes the test, acting on the maxim is permissible, but if it fails the test, acting on the maxim is forbidden. Specifically, if the maxim is rejected by the categorical imperative, we have a duty not to engage in that behavior; in this case, if our maxim of lying for our advantage were rejected, we would have a duty not to lie for own advantage (which covers a *lot* of lies). This duty also has a right associated with it: a duty not to lie implies a right not to be lied to, just as a duty not to steal implies a right to be secure in one's property, and so on. In this sense, rights can be considered deontological concepts as well.[6]

How does the categorical imperative do this? The most widely known version of the categorical imperative is based on universalization: "act only according to that maxim whereby you can at the same time will that it should become a universal law."[7] In other words, if you want to follow a maxim, you must consider what would happen if everybody were allowed to follow that maxim too. By this logic, lying fails the universalization formula because if you want permission to lie, you have to consider that everyone will be given this permission. But if everyone lied whenever they wanted to, no one would believe anything anybody said, which defeats the purpose of lying in the first place. Therefore, a maxim of lying contradicts itself if we universalize it, generating a duty not to lie.

Even though Kant proposed this as the most straightforward version of the categorical imperative for people to apply to moral decisions, there is a lot of ambiguity in it. For instance, if you define it narrowly enough, almost any maxim can be universalized; lying to gain advantage may be contradictory, because people are likely to exercise that permission fairly often, but lying to save someone tremendous anguish may not be, because it doesn't arise often enough to lead to widespread disbelief and mistrust. (Consider a doctor falsely telling the family of a recently deceased patient that she passed on painlessly.[8]) This points to another practical problem with this formula: it requires some idea of how much lying is necessary to generate widespread disbelief. Clearly, people do lie, but generally we trust many of the people we interact with to tell us the truth. The fact that we can distinguish between those we trust to be truthful and those we don't shows that the relationship between lying and trust is not as simple as the categorical imperative would make it seem.

Also, the universalization formula seems to be ethically sterile, focusing on logical noncontradiction to the exclusion of anything explicitly moral. Are we supposed to believe that lying is wrong simply because thinking of everyone lying generates a logical dilemma? Actually, yes and no. The moral content of this version of the categorical imperative cannot be found in universalization itself, but in the reason *why* we universalize in the first place. I can't simply carve out special moral exceptions for myself; because of the equal moral status of all persons, if I give permission to myself to do something, I have to be willing to give the same permission to everyone else. If doing that leads to a contradiction, that means I can't legitimately give myself that permission because it would make me "more equal" than others. Underneath its logical façade, it turns out that the universalization formula is actually based on equality and reciprocity, which gives it a profoundly moral foundation.

Nonetheless, the issues with defining maxims and predicting the effects of universalization do threaten to make this formula unwieldy. Luckily, there is another version of the categorical imperative that wears its moral essence on its sleeve, often called the formula of respect: "act in such a way that you treat humanity, whether in your own person or in the person of another, always at the same time as an end and never simply as a means."[9] This boils down to the requirement that we not use other people as tools toward achieving our own ends without at the same time treating them as full persons—or, as Kant would say, as *ends-in-themselves*.

Again, it would be all too easy just to say "do not use people." We use other people all the time: we use the workers at supermarkets and restaurants to get food, we use bus drivers to get around town, and we use superheroes to get our kittens out of trees. But when we use these people, ideally we treat them with respect as persons with dignity, meaning that we don't lie, manipulate, or force them into doing what we want. Kant identifies deceit and coercion as the two methods by which we treat other people simply as means and not at the same time as ends, because they deny people the ability to contribute voluntarily to what we are trying to accomplish. Instead, employing deceit or coercion fools people or forces them into doing something, using them as tools in the same way that a carpenter uses a hammer to drive in a nail. (Kant actually used the world "tool," or the German equivalent—he wasn't being flip. Kant was many things, but he was rarely flip.)

Judgment Is Just as Important Here

As the name suggests, we don't have to dig deep into the formula of respect to find its moral basis in equality and dignity. However, it is no more precise than the universalization formula is, because it is difficult to draw the line between using people the right way and the wrong way. This practical shortcoming of both formulae of the categorical imperative we discussed is not as big a deal as it may seem, though. The categorical imperative was not meant be used as an everyday decision-making tool, like a calculator you whip out whenever you have to figure a tip (which, by the way, is a good example of treating servers as ends-in-themselves!). Instead, the categorical imperative focuses our attention on the most important moral aspects of a problem—in much the same way that utilitarianism does, as we saw in chapter 2. The categorical imperative tells us to pay attention to what we owe each other based on our equal moral dignity, while utilitarianism leads us to consider how our actions affect other people (also based on moral equality). Neither ethical system gives precise answers, but each does provide us with a framework for ethical deliberation that leaves the final decision up to our most important moral faculty: *judgment*.

As we saw in chapter 2, judgment is of critical importance if you're a utilitarian like Tony Stark, and it's no less important if you're a deontologist like Captain America (even a Kantian one specifically). We already saw one area in which judgment is necessary: using the categorical imperative itself. Remember the logic behind the universalization formula's rejection of a maxim of lying: if everyone were allowed to lie, there would be so much lying that no one would believe anything, defeating the purpose of lying. But as we said above, this relies on assuming two things about human behavior: that people *would* lie often if they were allowed to, and that this much lying would lead to widespread disbelief. Neither is obviously true, but depends on human psychology, cultural factors, and more. For this very reason, Kant wrote an entire book on human nature and its imperfections (what he called "anthropology" at the time), both of which play a critical but undervalued role in his ethics.[10]

Judgment isn't necessary only for Kant's version of deontology, however, but for other versions of deontology, such as that of W.D. Ross.[11] Ross had no precise method for deriving duties, but regarded them as intuitive: everyone "just knows" that activities like lying, theft, and murder are wrong. The more important issue, according to Ross, was what to do when more than one duty applies in a given situation and you can't follow all of them at the same time. We'll see that Captain America encountered this sort of dilemma when he was faced with obeying a law passed by valid democratic processes while he disagreed with the moral basis of the law itself. In his mind, he had a duty to obey and enforce the law, and he also had a duty to oppose what he saw as an unjust law. But these two duties are mutually exclusive; he can't follow both, so he was forced to choose one.

This is where judgment becomes essential to deontology: no matter how you derive your duties, and even if they're clearly defined, if more than one duty comes into conflict in a given situation, you will need to use judgment to choose between them. Kant was adamant that you must do your duty—and do it for the right reason, as we'll see later—but if you seem to have more than one duty, he was less helpful with choosing between them. When you're faced on conflicting obligations, all he said was that your one true duty is determined by which obligation has the "strongest ground," and he left it at that.[12]

Scholars disagree on exactly what he meant by this, but it's reasonable to assume that judgment must play a role at this point—especially because he never said that any duty, in general, was more important than any other, and he never wrote of any "higher" duties to help us choose between lesser ones. Also, Kant has a great respect for judgment, which he regarded as above rules and formulae:

> though understanding is capable of being instructed... judgment is a peculiar talent which can be practiced only, and cannot be taught. It is the specific quality of so-called mother-wit; and its lack no school can make good.[13]

In the context of a real-world decision, then, a person must use judgment to determine which obligation is more important. Presumably, Captain America would take an obligation to confront the Red Skull to be more important than fulfilling a promise to meet Tony for shawarma. While Kant's derivation of duties can seem methodical, judgment between conflicting obligations brings his ethics closer to that of W.D. Ross, who explicitly recommends choosing between conflicting duties according to an intuitive sense of importance.

If Deontology's So Great...

Deontology has its critics, of course. The obvious one, from the utilitarian in the front row, is that deontology ignores well-being in favor of duties and rights; in other words, it substitutes respect for concern. This is the fundamental difference between the two systems, the positions each takes to be primary and foundational, so to some extent they must agree to disagree (or appeal to common moral intuitions, as we saw in chapter 2). Where the deontologist accuses the utilitarian of believing the ends justify the means, the utilitarian counters with the deontologist's attitude of the ends don't justify anything; the ends are irrelevant to the deontologist if the means to achieving them are unethical. At its most extreme, this is summed up in the Latin statement *Fiat iustitia, ruat coelum*, "let justice be done, even if the skies fall." Even if consequences do sometimes matter, for deontologists there must be at least one case in which duty or right is held above them, and indeed the skies would fall before they would compromise those principles. For this reason, deontology is often seen as extreme and unyielding in its demands (as well as misguided in the basis of those demands themselves).

Just as there are no atheists in foxholes, there are few extreme deontologists in times of crisis when following duty and respecting rights lead to enormous and tragic consequences. Most deontologists would admit that there is some level or degree of cost high enough that even their most deeply held principles may have to bend. There are, however, several ways deontology can be modified to account for this. One is *threshold deontology*, which maintains that duties and rules must be followed until the costs of doing so reach some catastrophic level—the threshold—after which those costs drive the ethical decision-making.[14] This is the basis for "ticking bomb" arguments for justifying or excusing torture: torture is wrong and must not be practiced *unless* the stakes in possible loss of human life are high enough, in which case an exception can (or must) be made. Issues still arise regarding how to determine the threshold and what happens in the immediate neighborhood of it; for instance, if the threshold is one million lives lost, then why aren't 999,999 lives enough? And if we make the threshold a vague range, such as "around one million lives," we lose the value of having a precise threshold, and the debate turns to whether 900,000 is "around" a million.

An easier way for a deontologist to acknowledge these type of consequences is to think of the principles that support them. For instance, the argument for allowing torture in the face of extreme loss of life is not simply a case of consequences trumping what's right. Saving lives can also be conceptualized as a principle which must be balanced against the duty not to torture, and obviously the more lives at stake, the more importance that principle takes on.[15] Even saving money, often sneered at as a crass justification for compromising a duty or principle, may be valid depending on what the money would otherwise be used for, especially if it supports another principle. No one likes cutting money from budgets for fire or police departments, both of which perform valuable services in the interest of safety and security, but if the money saved is rerouted to education, that's a different matter. Consequences need not be thought of simply in terms of utility, and if we consider what consequences truly represent, we may find they are more compatible with deontology than ordinarily thought.

As we get farther away from rules based on utility and duty and frame moral issues in terms of general principles and judgment, we get closer to *virtue ethics*, a third school in moral philosophy that is usually contrasted with both utilitarianism and deontology. Dating back to the ancient Greeks and Romans, usually to Aristotle in particular, virtue ethics can be distinguished from the other schools of ethics in that it focuses, not on actions, but on the person performing them and the character traits that lead her to do it. In terms of virtue ethics, a person is a hero not because she does heroic things, but because she has heroic traits, such as courage, honesty, and kindness, that lead her to do heroic things.[16]

As with utilitarianism and deontology, there are many different versions of virtue ethics—it's even harder to nail down than deontology. But one thing that most versions of virtue ethics have in common is the emphasis on a person's good character traits, dispositions, or *virtues*, and the judgment she must use to translate them into moral action. Since there are no rules or formulae in most versions of virtue ethics, no "don't do this" or "maximize that," people have to rely on judgment to apply their virtuous character traits to specific situations. If you're generally an honest person, you don't need a rule saying "do not lie" or a belief that lying rarely ends well; you just need to be honest in situations that merit it, which will be most situations except those where other virtues are called into play (similar to contrasting obligations in deontology). Remember the example of the doctor lying to a family that their loved one died peacefully: this doctor may be a very honest person, but he judges kindness to be the more important virtue to act on in that case. In virtue ethics, judgment is even more important than it is in utilitarianism and deontology, and a person's character becomes key to describing and evaluating her actions.

~~~~~

In some ways, virtue ethics is the best way to analyze a hero's character, especially in the case of Captain America (and, to some extent, Spider-Man, as we'll see later).[17] But deontology provides more details regarding principles and duties, so we'll continue along that path as we look at Captain America's actions during the Civil War in the next chapter.

---

[1] *Captain America*, vol. 1, #401 (June 1992).

[2] *Iron Man/Captain America Annual 1998* (January 1999). She-Hulk brought this incident up in court when interrogating Iron Man in a case on the part of two of New Warriors who weren't involved in the Stamford incident but were subject to death threats spread on a website (*She-Hulk*, vol. 2, #8, July 2006).

[3] For a good overview, Gerald Gaus, "What Is Deontology? Part One: Orthodox Views," *Journal of Value Inquiry* 35 (2001): 27–42; and "What Is Deontology? Part Two: Reasons to Act," *Journal of Value Inquiry* 35 (2001): 179–193.

[4] For example, philosopher W.D. Ross wrote a book titled *The Right and the Good* (Oxford: Oxford University Press, 1930/2003) in which he contrasted deontology and consequentialism. (If only he'd had Iron Man and Captain America to use as examples.)

[5] Kant lays out his moral system mostly in three books: *Grounding for the Metaphysics of Morals* (1785), *Critique of Practical Reason* (1788), and *The Metaphysics of Morals* (1797), all available in different editions and translations from several publishers. For a brief but comprehensive introduction to Kant's ethics, I recommend Roger J. Sullivan's *An Introduction to Kant's Ethics* (Cambridge: Cambridge University Press, 1994), which I've used in class.

[6] This doesn't work for all duties, however. Some duties are more general, such as the duty to help others (which Kant called an *imperfect duty*). Since this duty doesn't require any definite action or inaction, however, no one can have a right to it (although they may reasonably expect it in certain circumstances).

[7] Kant, *Grounding for the Metaphysics of Morals*, trans. James W. Ellington (Indianapolis: Hackett), p. 421.

[8] Cases like this are considered by Thomas Hill in "Autonomy and Benevolent Lies," included in his book *Autonomy and Self-Respect* (Cambridge: Cambridge University Press, 1991), pp. 25–42.

[9] Kant, *Grounding*, p. 429.

[10] *Anthropology from a Pragmatic Point of View* (1798).

[11] Ross, *The Right and the Good*.

[12] Kant, *The Metaphysics of Morals*, trans. and ed. Mary J. Gregor (Cambridge: Cambridge University Press, 1797/1996), p. 224.

[13] Immanuel Kant, *Critique of Pure Reason*, trans. Paul Guyer and Allen W. Wood (Cambridge: Cambridge University Press, 1998), A133/B172. (Most modern editions of this book are combinations of the 1781 and 1787 editions, signified by A and B, respectively. This quote appeared in both editions, hence the dual page numbering.)

[14] Michael S. Moore, "Torture and the Balance of Evils," in *Placing Blame: A Theory of the Criminal Law* (Oxford: Oxford University Press, 1997), pp. 669–736.

[15] This is not to say, of course, that these are the only issues in the debate over torture. For instance, the efficacy of torture itself, whether it results in useful information, is highly questionable; also, the matter of national integrity is paramount. (We'll come back to each later.)

[16] For a brief survey of virtue ethics, see Rosalind Hursthouse, "Virtue Ethics," *Stanford Encyclopedia of Philosophy*, March 8, 2012, at http://plato.stanford.edu/entries/ethics-virtue/.

[17] This is why I titled my previous book *The Virtues of Captain America: Modern-Day Lessons on Character from a World War II Superhero* (Hoboken, NJ: Wiley Blackwell, 2014).

Chapter 6: The Principles of Captain America

Very early in their superhero partnership, Iron Man said to Captain America, "I applaud your devotion to your principles."[1] Over the years, though, Cap's principles would clash with Iron Man's pragmatic utilitarianism time and time again. This conflict comes to a head during the Civil War, after which Cap told Tony, "We maintained the principles we swore to defend and protect. You sold your principles."[2]

Can we really say, however, that Captain America has principles while Iron Man doesn't? That wouldn't be quite fair, though there is a kernel of truth to it. As we see throughout this book, principles often stand in the way of the pursuit of utility or consequences. As Cap thinks to himself early in the Civil War, "freedom isn't a commodity," by which he likely meant that principles such as freedom are immeasurable ideals while goals like safety and security are concepts that can be quantified, maximized, and more easily traded off for other such goals.[3] Again, principles are to utility as "the right" is to "the good," and never was this dichotomy shown more dramatically than in the Civil War.

However, the point of utilitarianism itself—promoting human well-being— that Iron Man believes in so strongly can itself be understood as a principle, and quantifying and maximizing utility is one way of following that principle. It's not the only way: we saw in chapter 2 that following rules such as "do not lie" may be a more effective way of furthering well-being on the average than calculating the best action on a case-by-case basis. Utilitarianism can be seen as specifying the final goal of maximizing utility, which serves as its guiding principle, but does not specify how we further that goal, whether by following other principles or not. When you look at it this way, Iron Man may not be acting according to Captain America's principles when he makes decisions with utilitarian reasoning, but he is acting in service of the general principle that grounds utilitarianism: making people better off.

So, if Iron Man really is a man of principle (in a general sense), what are the principles that Captain America accuses him of "selling"? In this chapter, we'll take a closer look at the principles that Captain America supports. We'll also see how he acts when the very people elected to promote and protect those principles betray them. Finally, we'll find out how Captain America justifies disobeying the registration act, even when it represents "the will of the people."

Principles of Liberty and Privacy

As Captain America told Iron Man early on in the Civil War, "the registration act takes any freedom we have, any autonomy."[4] It should come as no surprise that perhaps the most important principle to a man known as the Sentinel of Liberty would be freedom. The concepts of freedom and liberty are complex ones, and philosophers have written on them at length, but we'll be discussing them here fairly simply.[5] Captain America believes in the ideal that all people should be free to live their lives as they choose, as long as they don't interfere with anyone else's right to do the same. This ideal has firm deontological roots, for instance in the thought of Immanuel Kant himself. In Kant's view, government was held to the same moral standards as were individuals, as we can see in the main guiding principle for public action, the Universal Principle of Right: "any action is right if it can coexist with everyone's freedom in accordance with a universal law, or if on its maxim the freedom of choice of each can coexist with everyone's freedom in accordance with a universal law."[6] Kant believed in the *classical liberal* position that government was needed to protect the people's freedom from interference from each other, but not to interfere in what people did with regard to their own interests.

These ideas are not only deontological, however; they have firm utilitarian support as well. If you believe that people are best situated to look after their own well-being, then a certain degree of freedom to do so—limited only by the same consideration for others—is likely to maximize total utility. This idea was stated well by John Stuart Mill, whom we met in chapter 2 as one of the founders of utilitarianism, and who was also a forceful voice for classical liberalism on utilitarian grounds. In what has come to be known as the *Harm Principle*, Mill wrote that the only justification for government interference in people's activities was to prevent them from harming others, not out of concern for their own well-being.[7] Here, Mill wrote primarily against paternalism, limiting a government's ability to decide what people should do in their own interests, but also provided a firm statement for what came to be known as *liberal neutrality*, the idea that governments should not promote one version of the "good life" over others, instead allowing their citizens to make that choice for themselves (as well as giving them responsibility for the consequences).[8]

Captain America's support of the principle of liberty sits naturally with his opposition to any authority that tries to limit freedom without good reason (such as protecting the interests of others). In his comics tales we see a pervasive theme of fighting tyranny that was most obvious in his World War II adventures but also carried forward into the modern day in his battles against the Red Skull and others. For instance, early in his days with the Avengers, he fought Baron Zemo, the last enemy he faced during World War II before plunging into the frozen waters. As they battled, he said (in typically dramatic fashion):

> I still remembered how you sneered at democracy... how you called Americans soft... timid... too spoiled to fight for free-dom! You mocked free men! You boasted of your contempt for liberty! Feel my grip, Zemo! It's the grip of a free man! Look into my eyes, tyrant! They're the eyes of a man who would die for liberty! The world must never again make the fatal error of mis-taking compassion for weakness!! And while I live, it won't!!![9]

Years later, after the leader of HYDRA mocked his principles, Cap retorted,

> You're glib—but so was Hitler. Like every other tyrant, your lust for power masks your true motive—fear of a free society! For, with freedom, man has pride, dignity and a sense of destiny! Your fear causes you to arrogantly mock those concepts! You seek to reduce mankind to your own level! But against every despot there has always arisen a champion of liberty! That is why I exist—and why men like me shall always win![10]

I could spend the rest of this book quoting Cap's eloquent speeches defending liberty and opposing tyranny, but we need to turn back to the Civil War and why he felt these principles were in danger from the registration act (and the man in the golden armor who enforced it).

In terms of registration, Captain America's concerns about liberty were focused primarily on his fellow members of the superhero community; as he bluntly said to journalists Sally Floyd and Ben Urich after his surrender, "I saw the possibility of a registration act as a basic violation of our rights as Americans."[11] Specifically, liberty in the context of superheroes is closely linked with privacy, in that Cap wants to protect the right of his fellow superheroes to operate without their real identities known to all. This sense of privacy was supported by a concern for safety also, because heroes who maintain secret identities—such as Spider-

Man, as we'll see in the next part of the book—do so for their own safety and even more for the safety of their loved ones. We see the linkage of these issues from the beginning of the Civil War, when SHIELD Director Maria Hill fought with Captain America over whether he would help round up unregistered heroes when the SHRA became law. "Forget about it," he told her. "You're asking me to arrest people who risk their lives for this country every day of the week."[12]

Soon thereafter, Cap and Sharon Carter (Agent 13 of SHIELD) had a long conversation about registration, during which she challenged his hard opposition to the plan. As he told her, "they're endangering innocent lives. And destroying the lives of heroes. Men who have bled to make this world a better and safer place."[13] He then emphasized the safety concerns and basic rights of heroes themselves:

> My identity is public, and what has that meant? People in my life have been targeted, some have been killed, just for knowing me. I couldn't live in a normal apartment, because it was too dangerous for my neighbors. I accept these things, not gladly, but I accept them, because Captain America is who I am... and I understand what comes with that. But not everyone is like me. Not everyone is willing to risk what I have... should they be denied the right to make that choice?[14]

Sharon answers, "Maybe... yes. Because they're risking other people's lives every time they jump into a firefight."

Sharon and Cap move onto another issue and leave this one open, which is unfortunate because it's a very important point, speaking to one of the most basic justifications for limitations on freedom—the safety of others—in the spirit of which the SHRA was passed. As we saw in an earlier chapter, Cap believes that superheroes can police themselves, such as when Hank Pym (as Yellowjacket) and Carol Danvers (under the name Warbird at the time) were court-martialed by the Avengers.[15] During Pym's hearing in particular, Cap was forceful regarding heroes' responsibility of self-regulation:

> One "error" by one of us can cost thousands of lives! We don't dare allow ourselves to think it's ever right to make a mistake. Our responsibility is overwhelming! We've got to judge ourselves harshly! I recommend for Yellowjacket, as I would for myself, the severest possible penalty![16]

As this shows, Cap's disagreement with the accountability aspect of registration is not a failure to recognize the tremendous responsibility heroes take on. Instead, it's a general skepticism regarding those would hold them accountable, given his previous experiences with politicians and appointed bureaucrats.

Captain America and Politics Don't Mix

We see the political and cynical aspect of Captain America's opposition to registration more clearly when he speaks with Urich and Floyd after his surrender:

> I believe in the fundamental freedoms accorded us by our Con-
> stitution, Ben. I believe we have a right to bear arms, a right to
> defend and a right to choose. I have sworn an oath to defend
> America from external forces, and from within. If that means
> standing against my own government, rejecting a bogus law
> passed by my own superiors, then I suppose that's what it
> means.[17]

When Cap says "within," he's referring to the instances of government corruption he has struggled with often since his return to the land of the living in the 1960s. For example, during the Watergate era in the 1970s, Cap was the target of a smear campaign by the "Secret Empire," whose leadership he traced all the way to the United States presidency, an incident that led him to abandon the identity of Captain America for Nomad, befitting a "man without a country."[18] In the 1980s, a special task force within the federal government known simply as the Commission demanded that Cap submit to direct government orders under the contract he signed in 1941. Cap refused, again shunning the name of Captain America, and watched as another took his place, someone more eager to follow orders and do as he was told (and particularly violently at that). After Steve Rogers adopted the identity of "The Captain" (as we saw in chapter 3), he discovered that the Commission was a front for the Red Skull, who was trying to ruin the good name of Captain America in his latest offensive against freedom and democracy.[19]

These were just two prominent examples of Captain America fighting corruption within the US government, but there are other lesser examples, including corruption in the electoral process and in the military.[20] Nor was Captain America shocked by these developments; as writer Roger Stern explained, "Steve is a patriot and an idealist, but he's no starry-eyed fool. As he grew up, he saw corruption, bigotry, and hypocrisy first hand—none of that is new or unique."[21] This helps explain Cap's general stance for principles over politics (as well as politicians), and why he was so skeptical about how registration would be implemented and distorted by those put in control of it.

From the beginning, Captain America saw the possibility for corruption in the SHRA. As he told Maria Hill during their initial standoff in the SHIELD helicarrier, after she invoked the will of the people, "Don't play politics with me, Hill. Superheroes need to stay above that stuff or Washington starts telling us who the supervillains are."[22] When Cap and Falcon tried to enlist Hank Pym to their side only to discover that he'd already joined up with Iron Man in support of registration, Pym lamented that Cap wouldn't "play ball." Cap exploded in response, "Play ball? Who are we playing ball with? Who are we playing ball for? Why can't anyone answer that one simple question?" Cap reinforced his true loyalties when he told Pym, "We worked for no one but those who needed us. And you're throwing it all away."[23]

During his subsequent discussion with Sharon Carter (mentioned above), he struck a new chord: the financial side of government corruption. As he told Sharon,

> The registration act is another step toward government control. And, while I love my country, I don't trust many politicians. Not when they're having their strings pulled by corporate donors. And not when they're willing to trade freedom for security.[24]

This theme is reiterated in Cap's internal dialogue around the same time, questioning the public sentiment that lead to registration:

> They want superheroes to be controlled by the government. They want us to be puppets to a corporate shill structure, like their politicians and everything else on the planet. They don't see that we're all that's left keeping them truly protected and free.[25]

Finally, during Cap and Iron Man's long discussion in the middle of the Civil War, Cap brings up the danger posed by turnover in the government, even if the people who began the push for registration are well-intentioned and honorable: "Governments change, administrations come and go. ... You don't know who could get elected, how public sentiment might change."[26]

Civil Disobedience and the Rule of Law

This leads us to a significant difference between Captain America's previous experience with government corruption and his current opposition to the registration act: the SHRA was implemented and passed by duly elected representatives by ordinary legislative processes (albeit rushed after Stamford). This wasn't an effort by corrupt politicians, or supervillains who had infiltrated the government, but a legitimate expression of, as Maria Hill put it, the "will of the American people."[27] When Cap (in disguise) lured Sally Floyd into the anti-registration forces' hideout—to talk with, as she thought to herself, "the very personification of the American way gone rogue"—she asked him, "What's happened to turn you against the very people you've always been allied with?" He responded (more cynically than ever), "I didn't turn against them. ... This is no longer the country I vowed to defend, Miss Floyd. We're becoming swaths of red and blue on an election-night map. Welcome to the Divided States of America."[28]

This sounds more like what you'd likely hear on cable news than what you'd expect from Captain America, who so often proclaims that he represents and protects the American people. But we see this esteemed regard cracking early in the story once the registration act receives widespread popular support, such as in the quote above about the American people wanting heroes "to be puppets to a corporate shill structure." As Cap continued to muse at the time,

> What do you expect from a society that gets all its news from late-night comedy shows? Of course they don't care! Everything is a punchline. Everything is just—no. That's not true. They care. They just care about themselves more than about the world they live in. They want to comfortable, not safe.[29]

Cap had drawn public scorn in the past, to be sure, such as when he killed an armed terrorist to prevent him from killing hundreds of innocent people.[30] Even though no one was harder on Cap after that than Cap himself, the American people started to wonder what kind of hero he was, and there was even talk of a trial in international criminal court. But registration was different: it wasn't in response to Cap or anything he did, but instead it was an attack on the core principles he was sworn to protect.

Furthermore, it is sometimes legitimate—some would say necessary—to oppose laws and policies passed by standard democratic processes and supported by a majority of the electorate. In his book *On Liberty*, John Stuart Mill warned that tyranny came not only from undemocratic governments but also from democratic ones, particularly when the majority votes to limit essential rights of the minority.[31] No mere theoretical possibility, the tyranny of the majority applies to the denial of equal rights to women, African Americans, and other minorities throughout American history.[32] Whenever Cap mentions the danger that registration poses to the rights of superheroes, such as he did to Urich and Floyd in their post-surrender interview, as well as to Hank Pym when trying to get him to join the resistance, he is implying that the registration act, duly passed by the elected representatives of the people, unjustly limits the rights of the minority— the superhuman community.[33] As such, even the fact that the SHRA was passed legitimately is not enough to compel Cap to comply with it. During their long discussion, Sharon says heroes should be registered not just because they're putting innocent people in danger, but also because, simply put, "it's against the law. And the rule of law is what this country is founded on." Cap disagrees, saying "No… it was founded on breaking the law. Because the law was wrong."[34]

Captain America's language invokes not only the founding of the United States but, more generally, the issue of *civil disobedience*, on which one of the most eloquent writers was Dr. Martin Luther King, Jr. In 1963, King published his "Letter from Birmingham Jail," written while incarcerated for his role in peaceful demonstrations for civil rights, and which is now considered a key statement of the principles and justifications of civil disobedience.[35] In response to fellow clergy who objected to the actions that landed him in jail, King wrote:

> One may well ask: "How can you advocate breaking some laws and obeying others?" The answer lies in the fact that there are two types of laws: just and unjust. I would be the first to advocate obeying just laws. One has not only a legal but a moral responsibility to obey just laws. Conversely, one has a moral responsibility to disobey unjust laws. I would agree with St. Augustine that "an unjust law is no law at all."

Here King quotes the early philosopher and theologian St. Augustine, a proponent of *natural law*, his version of which maintained that civil law should not conflict with moral law (which he held to be divine law).[36]

King provides excellent examples of unjust laws—the state-mandated segregation and laws prohibiting peaceful demonstration against which he and his allies were demonstrating—and explains it in a way that illustrates not only Augustine's position on just and unjust laws, but also Kant's Universal Principle of Right and

Mill's tyranny of the majority, both of which emphasize the importance of equal moral status and the rights that derive from it:

> Let us consider a more concrete example of just and unjust laws. An unjust law is a code that a numerical or power majority group compels a minority group to obey but does not make binding on itself. This is difference made legal. By the same token, a just law is a code that a majority compels a minority to follow and that it is willing to follow itself. This is sameness made legal. Let me give another explanation. A law is unjust if it is inflicted on a minority that, as a result of being denied the right to vote, had no part in enacting or devising the law. Who can say that the legislature of Alabama which set up that state's segregation laws was democratically elected? Throughout Alabama all sorts of devious methods are used to prevent Negroes from becoming registered voters, and there are some counties in which, even though Negroes constitute a majority of the population, not a single Negro is registered. Can any law enacted under such circumstances be considered democratically structured?

Rather than drawing on Scripture, though, King takes as his moral foundation the statement that "all men were created equal" as presented in the Declaration of Independence, and holds up the laws of Alabama (and similar states) to that self-professed standard (one that the United States still struggles to live up to). This is a matter of national integrity, which we'll return to in the next chapter.

Note that civil disobedience does not imply complete disregard for the law or a preference for anarchy, but an action focused on the unjust law in question. As King wrote:

> One who breaks an unjust law must do so openly, lovingly, and with a willingness to accept the penalty. I submit that an individual who breaks a law that conscience tells him is unjust, and who willingly accepts the penalty of imprisonment in order to arouse the conscience of the community over its injustice, is in reality expressing the highest respect for law.

I don't want to exaggerate the parallels here; Captain America's resistance to registration and his battles with Iron Man were definitely not peaceful, and his surrender at the end of the Civil War was not intended primarily to draw attention to the cause or show respect for the law. Nonetheless, his civil disobedience was focused on registration specifically, and any other illegal or immoral activity he engaged in at the time came at a cost to his integrity (as we'll see in the next chapter).

Furthermore, while Captain America is well-known for putting principle over policy and criticizing specific public actions as well as persons within the government, he is not against government in general. In fact, there are many examples in the comics in which Cap expresses his support for proper governance and his admiration and respect for public officials who uphold the basic ideals of the country and execute the duties of their office with honor. For example, when operating as The Captain, Thor raged at his fellow Avenger's treatment by the government, proclaiming that he would "journey to Washington—and overthrow these madmen!" But Cap stopped him, saying that "even though I wouldn't let the current administration use me for a pawn, I still can't allow you to topple it. ... I still believe in and respect the American system of democracy!"[37] Another time, Cap told a group of citizens who wanted him to run for president that "the presidency is one the most important jobs in the world."[38] He explained that elected representatives are forced to make compromises on a day-to-day basis—compromises that were necessary but not his strong suit. (Compare this to Iron Man's thoughts, discussed in previous chapters, about having to make tough decisions.)

Captain America's conflict over the principles and practice of politics was well expressed in two incidents in particular. In one, when deadly chemical weapons were unleashed from Mount Rushmore, the Avengers raced to the scene only to discover that the gas had been developed by the US government. "I'm not shocked," Cap said. "Just disappointed. The system. I believe in it. I believe out government can work. And has. But sometimes it just takes one idiot at the top—hiding somewhere—to make the dominoes fall."[39] In a second, after he and Thor subdued a murderous activist for Native American rights, Cap thought to himself:

> This government can be wrong. Our politics can be flawed. We are, after all, a complex system run by human beings. But the country is good and though it's no longer easy—I still feel pride in her. I still love her and will fight to the death to protect her and keep her safe—so others can—as I know they will—make her right again—most of the time.[40]

Cap's words echo those of James Madison, who wrote in *The Federalist No. 51*: "If men were angels, no government would be necessary. If angels were to govern men, neither external nor internal controls on government would be necessary."[41]

Cap recognizes that the role of government encompasses managing the interactions of not only its citizens, but also the persons working within government itself, and in turn requires the vigilance of the citizens and the press to "watch the Watchmen," as it were. Captain America took on the role of government watchdog himself after the chemical weapons incident (which was masterminded by—guess who—the Red Skull, who had infiltrated the government as the secretary of defense). After he asked the president to make sure that any other chemical weapons operations were found and discontinued, the president asked Cap to actively monitor any other mistakes the government might make.[42] The media is also instrumental in this, as we've seen in Ben Urich and Sally Floyd's investigation of Tony Stark's activities during the Civil War (discussed in the last chapter). Government may be necessary, but it's not perfect, and needs constant oversight—especially when people such as Tony Stark are put in charge. (And wait until you see who came next!)

Who Decides?

As eloquently as Dr. King may have argued for civil disobedience, especially in his careful qualification and limitation of it, there is still the looming issue of who gets to decide what laws are unjust. Captain America certainly has done this himself many times, and in many ways become an exemplar for supporting ideals over policy. At the same time, Cap faced many other people who took it on themselves to regard laws as unjust or unnecessary and practice their own civil disobedience. As one of them asked Cap, "How many times have you placed principle over orders? Ideals over government? Are you the only one who gets to do that? Do we get to defy our government in defense of freedom only if you agree with it? Where is that line, and who gets to draw it?"[43]

The simple answer is that anybody who thinks a law is unjust can defy that law—assuming, as Dr. King wrote, that he or she is willing to accept the consequences of that defiance out of respect for the law as a whole. No one can simply refuse to obey a law and then claim exemption from the penalty for doing so. The more important question is *how* one decides that a law is unjust and should be resisted—and it should come as no surprise that this comes down to judgment, balancing the general principle that laws should be obeyed with the specific principle that one unjust law in particular should not be obeyed. During their long discussion, Sharon Carter told Cap, "The registration act is law. If Captain America doesn't follow the law, then who does?" Cap relied, "That's why I can't. The issue isn't black and white, and those are the only colors that law can see."[44] To be effective, laws have to be straightforward and simple, declaring some actions right and others wrong, but on a higher level, laws themselves can be right or wrong—a distinction that must be made outside the law rather than within it.

Not everyone who feels particular laws are unjust are going to think that the degree of injustice justifies disobedience. Some heroes, like Spider-Man at the beginning of the Civil War, had significant issues with registration but nonetheless believed that "the law was the law." (We'll see how and why he changed his mind in the next part of this book.) In the real world, someone may think that laws mandating automobile seat belts and motorcycle helmets are unjust infringements on liberty and refuse to use them, paying tickets when they get them and accepting the higher risk of injury. Others may feel the same way about these laws and choose to obey them anyway, either out of respect for law in general or simply to avoid the cost of the ticket, because they weigh and balance the relevant principles differently. In any case of conflicting principles, whether in a relatively trivial case like seatbelt laws or the much more significant context of liberty versus security, different people with the same concerns can make different choices regarding them.

~~~~~

Of course, if people have different opinions and make different judgments, it follows that there will be disagreement between them. Certainly many didn't agree with Dr. King and the civil rights movement, both in the general population as well as among government leaders—but if they had, the protests and demonstrations wouldn't have been necessary. It's easy to express a popular opinion, but it takes tremendous courage to express an unpopular one. When Spider-Man was considering joining Captain America's rebellion and asked the older hero how he stood so confidently and unwaveringly against registration despite all the voices raised against him, Cap gave one of his most eloquent speeches:

Doesn't matter what the press says. Doesn't matter what the politicians or the mobs say. Doesn't matter if the whole country decides that something wrong is something right. This nation was founded on one principle above all else: the requirement that we stand up for what we believe, no matter the odds or the consequences. When the mob and the press and the whole world tell you to move, your job is to plant yourself like a tree beside the river of truth, and tell the whole world—"no, *you* move."[45]

Cap said much the same thing more concisely to Iron Man around the same time: "What's right is what's right. If you believe it, you stand up for it."[46] Deciding what's right is a matter of judgment, and is not easy, especially in hard decisions with more than one important principle in conflict. But once you arrive at that judgment—and until you have a sufficiently good reason to reconsider it—you stand by it, despite what popular opinion or authority may say. This corresponds to Immanuel Kant's concept of autonomy, and it also speaks to an important virtue for both people and nations—*integrity*—which will be the subject of the next chapter.

---

[1] *Captain America: Sentinel of Liberty* #6 (February 1999), "Iron Will."

[2] *Civil War: The Confession* one-shot (May 2007).

[3] *New Avengers*, vol. 1, #21 (August 2006).

[4] *Iron Man/Captain America: Casualties of War* one-shot (February 2007).

[5] To scratch the surface, see Ian Carter, "Positive and Negative Liberty," *Stanford Encyclopedia of Philosophy*, March 5, 2012, at http://plato.stanford.edu/entries/liberty-positive-negative/.

[6] Kant, *The Metaphysics of Morals*, trans. and ed. Mary J. Gregor (Cambridge: Cambridge University Press, 1797/1996), p. 230.

[7] John Stuart Mill, *On Liberty* (1859), chapter 1, paragraph 9 (widely available online, such as at https://www.gutenberg.org/files/34901/34901-h/34901-h.htm).

[8] For a modern work on liberal neutrality, see Ronald Dworkin, *Sovereign Virtue: The Theory and Practice of Equality* (Cambridge, MA: Harvard University Press, 2000).

[9] *Avengers*, vol. 1, #6 (July 1964). Note the exclamation points!

[10] *Captain America*, vol. 1, #273 (September 1982).

[11] *Civil War: Front Line* #11 (April 2007). Cap said something similar when Misty Knight and the Heroes for Hire visited him and asked him to cooperate with Tony: "I'm not surrendering to a law that contradicts everything this country stands for" (*Heroes for Hire*, vol. 2, #2, November 2006).

[12] *Civil War* #1 (July 2006).

[13] *Captain America*, vol. 5, #22 (November 2006), throughout this paragraph.

[14] See also *Iron Man/Captain America: Casualties of War* one-shot, in which Cap recounts several superhero tragedies because their identities were known by their enemies, including the death of Peter Parker's girlfriend Gwen Stacy at the hands of the Green Goblin (*Amazing Spider-Man*, vol. 1, #121, June 1973).

[15] Pym was court-martialed in *Avengers*, vol. 1, #213 (November 1981), and Danvers twice, in *Avengers*, vol. 3, #7 (August 1998) and #55 (August 2002), although she was acquitted the second time.

[16] *Avengers*, vol. 1, #213. Of course, given his outsized sense of responsibility, Cap blamed himself for Pym's actions and the court martial, and had to be consoled by the Avengers' loyal butler Jarvis (*Avengers*, vol. 1, #214, December 1981). Cap later apologized to Pym for not recognizing the pressures he was under at the time and for not being a better leader (*Avengers*, vol. 1, #230, April 1983).

[17] *Civil War: Front Line* #11.

[18] *Captain America and the Falcon: Secret Empire* (2005) and *Captain America and the Falcon: Nomad* (2006).

[19] *Captain America: The Captain* (2011).

[20] The theme of electoral corruption is sprinkled through *Captain America: To Serve and Protect* (2011) and *Captain America: American Nightmare* (2011); military corruption is a theme through the entire run of *Captain America and the Falcon* #1–14 (2004–2005), written by Christopher Priest and illustrated by various artists.

[21] Dugtan Trodglen, "Remembering 'Remembrance': Stern & Byrne Take Their Turn With America's Fighting Legend," collected in *Captain America: Red, White & Blue* (2007); see also Stern's "Remembering Cap," in *Captain America: War & Remembrance* (2011).

[22] *Civil War* #1.

[23] *New Avengers*, vol. 1, #21. Cap and Tony both decried the involvement of politicians their work when they put the Avengers back together after the supervillain breakout. After Cap waxed inspirational, Tony said, "ysk, uch, the politics of it all—" to which Cap responded, "No more politics. Just us. No U.N. No governments. Just us helping people that need help. The big problems" (*New Avengers*, vol. 1, #3, March 2005).

[24] *Captain America*, vol. 5, #22.

[25] *New Avengers*, vol. 1, #21.

[26] *Iron Man/Captain America: Casualties of War*. Mind you, Tony was also well aware of these issues, which is why he took charge of registration himself, as we saw in chapter 3.

[27] *Civil War* #1.

[28] *Civil War: Front Line* #9 (February 2007), "Embedded Part 9."

[29] *New Avengers*, vol. 1, #21.

[30] *Captain America*, vol. 1, #321 (September 1986).

[31] Mill, *On Liberty*, chapter 1.

[32] At the risk of being dramatic, it also applies to Hitler and his Third Reich; when Quicksilver confronts the X-Men for remaining neutral during the Civil War, he makes an analogy to Hitler and quotes Martin Niemöller's famous poem about nonresistance, ending with "when they came for me, there was no left to speak out." When Cyclops objects to his comparison of the US government to "Hitler and his power-grabbing Nazis," Strong Guy (a mutant and member of X-Factor) responds, "as I recall… Hitler didn't grab power. He was elected" (*X-Factor*, vol. 3, #9, September 2006).

[33] This description of affairs is more than familiar to readers of the X-Men, who for years struggled against discrimination and eventually legal action: the Mutant Registration Act was passed in *Uncanny X-Men*, vol. 1, #183 (July 1984). (Quicksilver notes this similarity too in *X-Factor*, vol. 3, #9.) The analogies to the struggle for civil rights for African Americans and women is also noted by Misty Knight and Colleen Wing in *Heroes for Hire*, vol. 2, #1 (October 2006); as Wing tells Iron Man before the SHRA is passed, "making clear divisions in the civil rights of one group over another is a dangerous and familiar idea that nearly always ends in violent conflict." (Who's the futurist now, Tony?)

[34] *Captain America*, vol. 5, #22.

[35] See http://www.africa.upenn.edu/Articles_Gen/Letter_Birmingham.html (all quotes from Dr. King below are from this document). Captain America was on ice during this pivotal period in American history, but he is shown learning about it, and hearing Dr. King's "I Have a Dream" speech (also from 1963), in *Captain America: Man Out of Time* #3 (March 2011).

[36] For more on natural law, which in its modern form is not always tied to theology, see John Finnis, "Natural Law Theories," *Stanford Encyclopedia of Philosophy*, July 25, 2011, at http://plato.stanford.edu/entries/natural-law-theories/.

[37] *Thor*, vol. 1, #390 (April 1988).

[38] *Captain America*, vol. 1, #250 (October 1980).

[39] *Avengers*, vol. 3, #67 (July 2003).

[40] *Captain America*, vol. 4, #11 (May 2003).

[41] See http://www.constitution.org/fed/federa51.htm.

[42] *Avengers*, vol. 3, #70 (October 2003).

[43] *Captain America and the Falcon* #4 (August 2004).

[44] *Captain America*, vol. 5, #22.

[45] *Amazing Spider-Man* #537 (December 2006).

[46] *Iron Man/Captain America: Casualties of War* one-shot.

Chapter 7: The Integrity of a Hero and a Country

Integrity is a difficult word to define, but we can identify two significant meanings of the term, relying on the work of philosopher Lynne McFall.[1] The first meaning is in the sense of consistency, such as saying that a building has integrity, either structurally, in that it holds together well over time or during national disasters, or aesthetically, in that the design holds together as a whole. Someone who behaves consistently over time, who makes the same decisions in similar situations for the same reasons, would have integrity in this sense. But most of the time when we speak of a person having integrity, we mean something more intrinsically moral; integrity in this second, thicker sense has an important ethical dimension that goes beyond mere consistency.

In this second sense, a person with integrity holds herself up to certain values or principles and refuses to compromise them when tempted for the sake of personal pleasure or gain. (This is related to what we said in chapter 3 regarding heroic sacrifice.) Even if we can't specify what these values or principles are, we can say that they must go above and beyond the pursuit of personal benefit—if not, there would be nothing to compromise them for! Again, take your garden-variety bank robber (like many early supervillains were): his values and principles may simply be the personal acquisition of wealth, which he pursues with the utmost dedication and resolve. But he cannot be tempted away from his quest for wealth by... his quest for wealth. His "ethical" code, such as it is, is too simplistic to have integrity in this meaningful sense. But there are more principled villains, such as Doctor Doom, who adhere to higher codes of conduct, such as honesty and keeping their word, even when they are pursuing goals such as world domination and the defeat of their greatest enemies (the heroes).

Villains make strange examples for integrity, though—and there weren't many true villains in the Civil War anyway. (Well, maybe one... just kidding.) In this chapter, we'll take a closer look at Captain America's character, how he expresses his integrity, and how he has, on occasion, compromised it. We'll also consider a nation's integrity and various ways in which it can be compromised, and how a broader understanding of integrity, based on what we've discussed about judgment and conflicts of principles, can bring compromise into perspective (without excusing it entirely).

What It Takes to Have Integrity

The obvious example of a person with integrity, who both has values and principles we admire and stands by them despite temptation to compromise them for personal gain, is a hero, super or otherwise. Captain America is widely seen as a paragon of integrity; Spider-Man attests to this during the final battle of the Civil War when he thinks to himself, "He'll never sacrifice what he stands for. Not as long as he's alive."[2] This integrity is due, in large part, to role models Cap had growing up. As the narration to one story read,

> When he was a boy, heroes stood for something more than victory; more than triumph at any cost. A hero was a man of moral fiber; a man who would not see one innocent soul sacrificed if there was any alternative... and, to Captain America, there is always an alternative![3]

He also learned the importance of principles and integrity from his mother, whom the young Steve Rogers witnessed time and again withstand violent abuse from his alcoholic father, only to stand back up and face him down until he hit her again. When Steve asked her why she didn't simply stay down and avoid further beatings, she told him, "because, and you listen close, Steven... you always stand up."[4] Later, after he stole money from a local store to get rent money, his mother suspected where he got it; when he promised he would do "whatever it takes" to help support the family, she said, "Not whatever it takes, Steve. ... You promise me no matter what you'll be a good and honorable man, no matter the circumstances."[5] These early influences crafted the man Steve Rogers would later become, possessing qualities of character such as integrity that would be further enhanced by the super-soldier serum and Vita-rays (as shown in countless tellings of his origin in comics and film).[6]

As we saw in the last chapter, Captain America criticizes Iron Man's apparent lack of dedication to principles that might conflict with his goals. For instance, after his surrender at the end of the Civil War, Cap told Tony, "We maintained the principles we swore to defend and protect. You sold your principles. ... I know what freedom is. I know what it feels like to fight for it and I know what it costs to have it. You know compromise."[7] During a later episode involving alternate Earths threatening to endanger our heroes' own, Tony argued to Cap and the rest of the Illuminati, while discussing plans to counter the threat, that they should keep all their options on the table—including, implicitly, destroying the other Earths. Cap asked him, "Anthony... what the hell is wrong with you?"

and cautioned him and the others against heading down a slippery slope and justifying the unthinkable as a "necessary evil."[8] Throughout their history as Avengers, Cap's critiques of Tony for favoring results and expediency over principle are legendary, including before and after the Civil War.

But let's be fair, Tony Stark *is* a man of integrity, even though his guiding principles and how he chooses to pursue them are different than Cap's. In the end, the two heroes make different judgments for different reasons, but they both hold their principles above their own interests. While Tony's broad utilitarian goals may at times coincide with his own self-interest (and his ego), this does not mean he's compromising those goals *for* his self-interest. (As we saw in chapter 2, mixed motivations are very complicated to pull apart.) As journalists Ben Urich and Sally Floyd deduced, even his financial manipulations during the Civil War, which they initially took as an indictment of greedy warmongering, were funneled into charities to help those hurt by the conflict.[9] And earlier I listed some of the acts of extreme self-sacrifice Tony engaged in to save innocent people, which exemplify a hero with integrity. When Cap criticizes Tony's lack of principles, Cap is thinking of *his* principles, which he naturally but incorrectly holds to be the right values. Tony's principles and integrity may look very different from Cap's, but they're just as real and just as heroic.

It is not only individuals, however, who can have (or lack) integrity—groups can have it as well. Think of charities: when one is discovered to be using too few of its funds in support of its mission, instead paying its executive staff exorbitant salaries or paying for lavish trips, its integrity is questioned because the people in charge have compromised its core mission for their own gain. Companies, also, who claim to support worker's rights or the environment, but are found to be giving only lip service to them while ignoring or even actively working against them, are also said to lack integrity.

More relevant to the broader political context of this book is the idea of a nation's integrity. Captain America's disgust for politics stems from his belief that the country's elected leaders do not live up to the ideals they've sworn to uphold and further. With respect to the registration act itself, he was disappointed not only in the political leadership who passed it and signed it into law, but also the majority of American citizens who supported it. When he told Sally Floyd that "this is no longer the country I vowed to defend," we can interpret him as saying that the integrity of the United States was compromised because the registration act did not represent the principle of liberty that he held to be the essence of the nation.[10] Other opinions will differ, of course; as we saw with respect to Cap's judgment of Iron Man, people all too often ascribe integrity to someone else based on the values they hold themselves. It can be difficult to face someone with fundamentally different values and principles and, nonetheless, recognize their integrity in upholding those principles—but we must if we are to retain any measure of civility in political discussion.[11]

Back in the real world, many of the actions taken by the US government and military following 9/11 were regarded by critics as compromising the integrity of the nation. In their view, laws and policies such as the PATRIOT Act, the military actions in Iraq and Afghanistan, and especially the detention and treatment of terror suspects and enemy combatants in Guantanamo Bay and Abu Ghraib, stood in opposition to the country's self-proclaimed principles of liberty, equality, and justice. These accusations were loudest and most heated in reference to what the government called "enhanced interrogation techniques," such as waterboarding, to gain useful intelligence from terror suspects. This legal term was meant to differentiate these techniques from torture, but critics accused the government of solipsism, making arguments based on terminology rather than substance, and asserted that these techniques were torture, plain and simple.

Regardless of what we call it, it is not difficult to argue that exceptionally harsh treatment or torture compromises the ideals of liberty, justice, and equality that the United States puts forth to the world as its national identity, and therefore its integrity and reputation on the world stage. Liberty is compromised insofar as torture severely reduces a person's ability to retain control of his or her actions or responses. Questioning under harsh interrogation does not aim to convince or persuade a person into confessing information but instead coerces it using extraordinary physical or mental anguish. Justice and equality are both compromised in that the person being questioned this way is not being treated as a full person or with even the very minimal level of respect owed to human beings. (This critique extends also to detention methods and treatment, such as the dehumanization that was captured in the pictures from Abu Ghraib.) To the extent that the United States claims to stand on the principles of liberty, equality, and justice, actions such as enhanced interrogation or torture diminish the credibility of that stance in the eyes of the world.

But there is another side to the argument. Supporters of these interrogation methods may acknowledge that they're hardly ideal, and in a perfect and peaceful world we would never use them. They can even acknowledge that these practices stand in contrast with the core American principles described above. But they would argue that protecting the country and preserving the lives of its citizens and residents is also an important principle that should not always be compromised itself in favor of a strict ban on torture. If people believe that all of these principles are important—liberty, equality, justice, *and* safety—then as the threat to safety grows, it is reasonable to increase its weight compared to the others. As that happens, torture may take on the role of a necessary evil, even one that calls into question the nation's integrity. But if a threat is serious and monstrous in scale, and it is believed that torture can lead to actionable information—which is, as I said before, a serious practical objection—then the people in charge may decide that national security takes precedence over other national principles. This may lessen integrity, which many would criticize, and rightly so. But on the other hand, how far is a nation willing to go, how much are its people willing to sacrifice, to maintain integrity? If you say nothing, then by refusing to balance integrity (or some principle within it) with any other value, you are attributing an absolute value to it—and declaring one value, any value, to be of absolute priority over all others requires a very strong argument in its defense.

Broadening Integrity

Another approach to this problem is to develop a more inclusive conception of integrity that does not demand absolute fidelity to one or more values, but instead contains within it provisions for acceptable trade-offs. We have been assuming implicitly that integrity covers deontological principles like justice, equality, and liberty, but not consequentialist values such as safety and security. This implies that the latter goals have no value comparable to the former principles that are included in integrity—but is this necessarily true? This is an extreme deontological presumption, the type of "let justice be done, even if the skies fall" thinking that not many people who live under those skies would endorse. But if we include values such as security and safety in our definition of integrity as worthy goals that also express the identity of a nation—or a person—then we are free to balance them to some degree against the other principles within the concept of integrity and no longer have to regard this as necessarily compromising integrity itself.

The inclusive sense of integrity makes it easier to see Iron Man as possessing integrity, given the questionable things he has done in service of heroic and altruistic goals. When Cap faced Tony down during the episode with the Illuminati and the incursions of alternate Earths, he mocked Tony's reasoning, saying, "We're doing this for the right reasons. There's no other choice. It's the lesser of two evils. Isn't that right, brother?"[12] This doesn't sit well for a man who steadfastly puts deontological principles above consequentialist goals, which implies a lack of integrity on Tony's part. But in the context of Iron Man's own principles and goals and the way he balances them, it does represent integrity—just not Cap's kind of integrity.

At the same time, Captain America's integrity is broad enough to include some consequential reasoning as well. There's nothing that says each and every issue of concern to someone with a generally deontological code of ethics has to come down to principles, duties, and rules, always matters of right or wrong and never good or bad. Remember that Cap's belief in privacy was based not only on the right to control one's identity, but also on dangers that can come to heroes and their families when their real identities become known, as he argued to Sharon Carter, Iron Man, and Spider-Man (who learned the consequences all too well, as we'll see later in this book). He was also concerned about the likelihood of villains and criminals having a field day while the heroes were fighting amongst themselves; the Falcon expressed this concern early on, telling Cap that "after we've been fighting each other, running from each other, hiding from each other," it is likely that some villain "does something truly heinous because none of us are in a position to stop it."[13] Cap dismissively replies, "that'll have to be tomorrow's problem," but later, while he was tracking down a secret base of AIM (Advanced Idea Mechanics, a techno-terrorist group), he thought to himself, "To hell with Tony and SHIELD and all of them. I've let this conflict take me off course enough... There are other concerns, still... things that are my responsibility... my weight to carry."[14]

Most surprising of all, Cap even made a qualified endorsement of registration and accountability years before Stamford, when his 1950s replacement, William Burnside, cracked under the influence of a botched attempt to recreate the treatment that made Steve Rogers into Captain America. As the two men fought, the narration read:

> In his thoughts, he is once again a gawky youngster named Steve Rogers, wanting so desperately to fight America's enemies that he volunteered to test an unknown serum—and so became the guardian of his country. But no one knew anything about Steve Rogers—least of all himself. There had been no security checks on him, before entrusting him with his power. What if he had had the fatal flaw, that would have driven him to super-patriotism, madness, and mayhem? What if things had been just slightly different?[15]

Once again, it is not that Cap does not realize the value of training and accountability to the safety of the people heroes protect but sometimes inflict costs on. It is that, in his judgment, the principle of liberty and privacy are even more important (and superheroes can train and police themselves, as Cap and Tony did when they discovered the Young Avengers, another group of eager but inexperienced heroes).[16] Even though they take different sides in the debate, both Cap and Iron Man can see both sides of the argument—would that we all could say the same in political debates in the real world.

Does broadening the concept of integrity such as I've described, in effect, open the barn door for any decisions or behavior to be reconciled with integrity? If Captain America suddenly goes on a killing spree, would someone be justified in saying, "well, I guess he simply reached a different balance within his broad conception of integrity"? Sure, there is some danger of that if we don't use the concept correctly. But keep in mind that any concept of character or integrity must mark out what someone is likely to do from what they are unlikely to do. Just because we make these concepts more complex and nuanced does not imply that we make them loose enough to "explain" any behavior. We may find certain compromises to be consistent with a broader notion of integrity but still find others to be outside of it. Cap may disguise himself as a terrorist to infiltrate their headquarters, and he may even take a life when absolutely necessary, but he would not simply blow up the entire installation with hundreds of people in it, no matter what they may be guilty of. And if he did, his integrity would demand that he have a good reason—a *very* good reason. A broader concept of integrity doesn't provide an automatic excuse for questionable behavior; it only gives us a chance to offer one.

The Compromises of Captain America

After Captain America thought he had killed a terrorist after 9/11, he went on national TV to take full responsibility for it. A US government official told Nick Fury that by doing that, Cap had compromised the mission, and Fury just laughed. "Compromise? First time I've heard any kind of damn fool accuse Cap of that."[17]

With all due respect to Nick Fury, Captain America has indeed struggled with compromise and his personal integrity for the last several decades, including before, during, and after the Civil War. For example, he normally maintains a firm principle of fair play, refusing to lie or cheat to win a fight or defeat a foe and harshly judging others who resort to such means. During World War II he held his fellow troops to the Geneva Conventions regarding treatment of captured enemy soldiers, and also held his fellow heroes to their word, keeping them from killing enemies or breaking promises limiting violence.[18] Most dramatically, after Hawkeye rigged a bet to defeat the manipulative Grandmaster to avert an interdimensional catastrophe, Cap warned Thor during a baseball game amongst the Avengers, "watch Hawkeye—he cheats."[19]

Nonetheless, Cap has found himself in positions in which he judged it necessary to use "subterfuge and surprise," such as when he disguised himself as an ULTIMATUM terrorist to infiltrate their secret base and save hundreds of hostages they had threatened to kill. While doing it, he thought to himself, "I'm not particularly proud of having to use these terrorists' guerrilla tactics—but 110 lives are at stake! With so little time left before the deadline, I can't waste any time fighting fair!"[20] When inside the base, he threatened to break a guard's hand to get him to talk, but the guard didn't find his threat credible, saying that Cap was "far too honorable to torture for information!" Cap simply knocked the guard unconscious and thought to himself:

> These terrorists play by different rules than the average criminal I face. How am I supposed to get information out of people who'd sooner throw their life away than betray their cockamamie cause? This joker had me pegged all right. I'm not willing to stoop to their level in order to win. My code of ethics won't permit me.

Even though Cap compromised some aspects of his code of ethics, namely his dedication to fair play, he stopped at torture (even so "mild" a version, in terms of comics, as threatening to break a hand, relatively common among more street-level heroes). This shows that while Cap recognizes that some principles have to bend to others, he is careful to weigh principles according to their importance and makes sure only the less important ones are compromised, and for good reason. I should add that this episode ended (as mentioned before) with Cap fatally shooting a terrorist who was firing into a crowd of innocents in a church, an incident that left Cap racked with guilt despite acknowledging that he had no other choice. Even necessary compromises can be difficult to accept when a person values his or her integrity highly enough.

During the Civil War, Captain America certainly found himself in situations where he judged that fair play had to be compromised for the greater mission. When SHIELD tried to capture Cap in his apartment, Cap subdued all the agents and discovered that the one in charge was Dum Dum Dugan, one of the Nick Fury's Howling Commandos alongside whom Cap fought during World War II. Cap thought to himself, "They sent a friend. Three thousand agents of SHIELD on active duty, and they sent a friend. Dirty pool. I'll remember that," after which he called into SHIELD and faked Dugan's voice to throw them off his trail. "Should take them ten minutes to figure it out," he thought. "Five more to figure out which way I went. Hopefully, ten more minutes deciding if this entire trick is beneath me"—which he clearly felt it was.[21]

Later, during the first conflict between the pro-registration and anti-registration sides, Cap snuck an electron-scrambler onto Tony's armor while shaking his hand, temporarily disabling it to gain a moment's advantage in the fight.[22] To infiltrate the Negative Zone prison, Cap had Hulkling, a Young Avenger with shapeshifting abilities, knock out and replace Hank Pym to release the imprisoned unregistered heroes to help in the climactic final battle.[23] And behind the scenes, Cap conspired with Wilson Fisk, the Kingpin, to double-cross Iron Man. As Hercules and Falcon saw that Cap was torn up about this, Hercules said, "'Tis war... And at the end of the day, thy Captain is but a soldier. As such, he doth recognize that sometimes in war, hard decisions must be made to achieve thy goal. And should that cost thee a piece of thy soul? So be it."[24] Once again, even necessary compromises take their toll.

What some saw as the ultimate compromise, of course, was Captain America's surrender at the end of the Civil War.[25] As hero fought hero and, in the process, laid waste to New York City, Captain America was prevailing in his battle with Iron Man, which by now was as much personal as it was ideological. As Tony lay prone on the ground, faceplate smashed, Cap raised his shield above his head to deliver the final blow, an uncertain look in his eye...

One can only imagine what would have come next, because a half-dozen police officers, firefighters, and civilians pulled Cap off of Iron Man, yelling "Get the hell away from him!" and "Hold him down! Hold him down!" Cap implored them to "Let me go! Please, I don't want to hurt you," but while they struggled to subdue him, they asked, "Don't want to hurt us? Are you trying to be funny?" One drove the point home by saying, "It's a little late for that, man."

Cap stopped to survey the damage the heroes had caused with their fighting, then dropped his shield and shed a tear. When Falcon asked him what was wrong, Cap said "They're right. We're not fighting for the people anymore, Falcon... Look at us. We're just fighting." Spider-Man told him, "We were beating them, man. We were winning," to which Cap replied, "Everything but the argument." As he took off his mask, surrendered to the police—as Steve Rogers, not Captain

America, which he said "was a very different thing"—and was handcuffed, he told his allies, "Stand down, troops... that's an order."

Cap didn't change his mind about registration or his core principles of liberty and privacy. He did, however, come to the judgment that the cost of fighting for those principles in the circumstances he faced at the time had become too high, especially since those costs were being borne by the people of New York, not Cap or the other heroes themselves (as we discussed in chapter 4 with reference to Iron Man). Listen to how Sally Floyd described the aftermath of the final battle and the costs, both in terms of lives and ways of life (and note the close parallels to statements made in the United States after 9/11):

> This was the day America—the rest of the world, even—awoke to a new reality: things were going to be different—they *had* to be. Because if we continued this way, there was going to be nothing left for the heroes to protect.
>
> Minutes after the cease-fire, word came down that Captain America had surrendered. The big guns were silent, and half of the people in costumes melted into the night. History would tell us we dodged a bullet on that day. We were too busy putting out fires to notice.
>
> When all was said and done, the final toll was as ludicrous as it was devastating: fifty-three killed... only six of them super-powered. It was the dawn of a new age. Only time would tell if it was going to be worth getting out of bed now.
>
> Within hours, the damage control began, and it wasn't nearly enough, quickly enough. If the heroes had worked this hard to repair things in the first place, the world would already have been a better place. ...
>
> We cleared the debris, longing for the good old days. And naturally, we began to ask, "When *were* those, exactly?" Maybe these *were* the "good old days."[26]

As his former sidekick Bucky Barnes remarked to Nick Fury earlier, "Cap and Iron Man and them... they're too focused on the issues. They're forgetting why they do this in the first place," by which we can presume that he means the people those issues are supposed to represent.[27] They may have been motivated by the right reasons at the beginning, but then the fight itself took precedence, and they forgot what they were supposed to be fighting for. When Cap remembered, he stopped.

Would Tony have stopped? It's difficult to say. In a way, costs are more easily accepted in a utilitarian framework, as they're part and parcel of the decision-making framework itself, but only if they're justified by the benefits. That's a judgment call Tony would have had to make, and there's no telling which side he would have come down on. If the costs of the fight did become excessive compared to the benefits, a utilitarian is more likely to see that than a deontologist is. Assuming he's not wrapped up in the fight he's fighting at the moment—and that he doesn't let his own desires or plans interfere with the big picture, as Cap accused him of doing—we can give him the benefit of the doubt and believe that, if he found the costs to be too high, Tony would have been quicker to call an end to the battle than Cap was. That type of thought process often comes more naturally to a utilitarian, who is used to balancing benefits and costs, than a deontologist, who normally thinks in terms of right and wrong and who reluctantly considers costs only when they become catastrophically high—as Cap did before he surrendered.

We learn firsthand about Captain America's thinking behind the conflict and his surrender when Sally Floyd and Ben Urich interviewed Cap in the Raft, a maximum security installation at Ryker's Prison.[28] Just as the two journalists suspected (at one point) that Tony's self-interest influenced his choices during the Civil War, Ben suggested that pride did the same for Cap, which he denied. In explanation, he summarized the essence of his opposition to registration (portions of which we quoted previously):

> Pride was never involved. I believe what I did was right. If you know me at all, you'll know I'm a simple man at heart. I believe in the fundamental freedoms accorded us by our Constitution, Ben. I believe we have a right to bear arms, a right to defend and a right to choose. I have sworn an oath to defend America from external forces, and from within. If that means standing against my own government, rejecting a bogus law passed by my own superiors, then I suppose that's what it means. I now realize that while my intentions were correct and honorable, I could as easily have come to the table as Tony Stark or Reed Richards. I saw the possibility of a registration act as a basic violation of our rights as Americans. For that, I wish to apologize to the country I love.

It's not clear exactly what Cap is apologizing for here. Later he reiterates several times that he did what he thought—at the time—was right. At one point Sally says, "Well, bully for you. You've finally realized America wants a registration act," but I don't think that's what changed Cap's mind; he acknowledged that the voters were behind the SHRA since the beginning.

In my opinion, Captain America apologized for failing to appreciate the tremendous costs the Civil War imposed on the people on the ground until it was too late, the same costs Ben and Sally both confronted him with. Ben accepted Cap's apology but pressed him on exactly why he didn't realize his error sooner, when such a realization could have prevented millions of dollars of property damage (and saved some of the lives lost and ruined). Cap replied, "People only come to a conclusion after they examine all aspects of a problem, Ben. That's what happened here." In other words, the costs had to reach a high enough level—and he had to become aware of them, which didn't happen until the first responders pulled him off Iron Man in the final battle—before he could incorporate them into his judgment and change his mind on continuing with the fight. Until then, his judgment focused on principle first and foremost, and it wasn't until the costs became obvious to him that he stopped—and we saw that as soon as this happened, he stopped immediately. As he said, they weren't fighting for the people anymore, they were just fighting, and the people were suffering the cost—a clear violation of what Captain America stands for.

~~~~~

At this point we're about halfway through this book and we've seen each side of the story. Next, we'll look at someone who saw both sides at one time or another, and had to use judgment more than either Iron Man or Cap to decide where he was going to stand on registration. Hint: he does whatever a spider can…

---

[1] Lynne McFall, "Integrity," *Ethics* 98 (1987): 5–20.

[2] *Amazing Spider-Man* #538 (January 2007).

[3] *Captain America*, vol. 1, #268 (April 1982).

[4] *Captain America*, vol. 7, #1 (January 2013).

[5] *Captain America*, vol. 7, #4 (April 2013).

[6] For my favorite comics version of his origin, see *Captain America*, vol. 1, #255 (March 1981). As President Franklin Delano Roosevelt told him upon their first meeting, "physical strength isn't an important part of being a leader. Courage and integrity are. You have those in spades. I know the kind of life you've led, Private Rogers. You became Captain America long before they pumped you full of any chemicals" (*Captain America: Sentinel of Liberty* #7, 1999, "An Ending").

[7] *Civil War: The Confession* one-shot (May 2007).

[8] *New Avengers*, vol. 3, #2 (March 2013). When Cap calls you by your entire name, you know you're in trouble.

[9] *Civil War: Front Line* #11 (April 2007).

[10] *Civil War: Front Line* #9 (February 2007), "Embedded Part 9."

[11] I make this point in the final chapter of *The Virtues of Captain America: Modern-Day Lessons on Character from a World War II Superhero* (Hoboken, NJ: Wiley Blackwell, 2014).

[12] *New Avengers*, vol. 3, #3 (April 2013).

[13] *New Avengers*, vol. 1, #21 (August 2006).

[14] *Captain America*, vol. 5, #24 (January 2007). (Also… language.) After he dispatches the HYDRA agents trying to ambush AIM, SHIELD ambushes Cap; when they demand his surrender, Cap says, "I've had this conversation with you people a few times already… Hasn't Director Hill made you watch the tapes?"

[15] *Captain America*, vol. 1, #156 (December 1972).

[16] *Young Avengers*, vol. 1, #6 (September 2005).

[17] *Captain America*, vol. 4, #4 (September 2002).

[18] On the Geneva Conventions, see *Captain America: Theater of War: A Brother in Arms* one-shot (June 2009); for holding other Avengers to high standards, see *Avengers*, vol. 1, #216 (February 1982) and #260 (April 1985).

[19] *Avengers Annual*, vol. 1, #16 (1987). To be honest, Hawkeye would probably hold himself to a higher standard when playing baseball.

[20] All the quotes in this paragraph are from *Captain America*, vol. 1, #321 (September 1986).

[21] *New Avengers*, vol. 1, #21.

[22] *Civil War* #2 (August 2006).

[23] *Civil War* #6 (December 2006). Ironically, Hulkling is half-Skrull, and "Hank Pym" had been replaced by Skrull months prior.

[24] *Civil War: War Crimes* one-shot (February 2007). More disturbing than his violations of fair play was Captain America's gradual acceptance of killing by other heroes, inadvertent deaths caused by himself, and even torture, as seen in

stories around the time of *Civil War* and later. On that see, *The Virtues of Captain America*, pp. 122–131.

[25] Everything in the next three paragraphs is from *Civil War* #7 (January 2007).

[26] *Civil War: Front Line* #11.

[27] *Captain America*, vol. 5, #23 (December 2006).

[28] *Civil War: Front Line* #11, through the rest of this section. (Why wasn't he held in the Negative Zone prison? Good question!)

Part III: Spider-Man—Caught in the Middle

Even since his introduction in *Amazing Fantasy* #15 in August 1962, Spider-Man has been one of the most enduring and beloved superheroes of all time. Representing the everyman in the Marvel Universe—almost literally, given his mask that covers his whole face, allowing kids of any race, ethnicity, or (with some imagination) gender to imagine they could be Spidey—the webcrawler has maintained his enormous appeal for over half a century filled with spectacular adventures and amazing villains. Bitten by a radioactive spider in high school, Peter Parker first turned his sights to fame and fortune, until selfish negligence led to the death of his Uncle Ben. This tragic event steered him onto the path of heroism, driven by the classic phrase "with great power, comes great responsibility."

That ethical turn set the path for Spider-Man's moral development, as we'll explore in the next three chapters in the context of his role in the Civil War. As we've mentioned throughout this book, Spider-Man began the story supporting registration at Iron Man's side, only to switch teams to stand with Captain America against it. As an occasional point-of-view character for the reader, Spidey serves as the superhero version of the "person on the ground," watching events unfold between Iron Man and Cap while he serves with one and then the other. He also differs from the two big guns in that he has more skin in the game personally: he still has a secret identity that he values because it protects his loved ones, primarily his wife Mary Jane and his Aunt May. His role in preventing harm to the two most important people in his life is foremost in his mind when deliberating over his role in the Civil War as much as his unmasking that played such a pivotal role in it.

But at the same time, Peter also wants to do the right thing. More than perhaps any hero besides Captain America himself, Spider-Man is tormented by the possibility of crossing the line that separates heroes from villains, especially given the number of people close to him that have lost their lives to crime and criminals: starting with his Uncle Ben, but also including his first love, Gwen Stacy, and her father, Captain George Stacy. He even swears an oath, unrealistic as it may sound, that "no one dies" on his watch—not just at his hand, of course, but no one else's as well. He strives to save everyone, which is a noble goal that incorporates a

Captain America-sized level of responsibility, perhaps even more than his great power demands.

Finally, Spider-Man messes up, sometimes big. Not only did his irresponsibility lead to Uncle Ben's death, but he'll always wonder if he didn't do enough to prevent Gwen Stacy's death—or if he actually caused it. Iron Man and Captain America may argue about perfection, but Peter Parker makes no claims to it. Just like the rest of us, he makes mistakes in life and learns from them, and we learn from them at the same time, adding to his appeal as a person just like you or me. (Except he sticks to walls.)

As we will see, Spider-Man is still unformed ethically, and this is to our benefit as readers. Since he lacks the "solidified" ethical core of Iron Man and Captain America, but is still at heart a good person who always tries to do the right thing, he serves as an excellent lens through which to observe the moral conflict between Tony and Cap and put it into the context of his own situation, enabling him to see the downsides and limitations of both utilitarianism and deontology. In the next three chapters, we'll follow Peter through the Civil War storyline, starting with the time he first joined the Avengers...

Chapter 8: Peter Parker Joins the Avengers… and Iron Man

As I said in the introduction to this part of the book, Peter Parker tries to do the right thing but is not as certain he knows what that is as Iron Man and Captain America are (or think they are). For that reason and others, he can be considered a virtue ethicist-in-training. I want to be very careful, and not because the virtue ethics crowd can be ruthless (which, come to think of it, doesn't strike me as a virtue). I do not mean that Peter is a settled, dyed-in-the-wool Aristotelian or Stoic—he isn't settled or dyed in anything at this point in his life (or any point, given his perpetual youth in the comics and movies).

As we described briefly in chapter 5, a virtuous person has certain character traits or dispositions—*virtues*—that, when filtering through his or her judgment, lead to good action. Courage leads one to be courageous, honesty leads one to be honest, and so forth. Because virtues are by their nature vague, and more than one may apply in a given situation, a person needs to use judgment to decide how to act on his or her virtues at any particular time. Virtue ethics typically does not focus on rules for decision-making, such as "maximize utility" or "follow your duty," but instead relies on judgment, backed by virtuous traits, to do the heavy lifting in terms of moral behavior. As such, there is more of an emphasis on *character* in virtuous ethics, focusing on the person performing the ethical acts rather than those acts themselves.

It is mainly in this sense that I am describing Peter Parker as embodying virtue, in that he has many of the traits we desire in a hero, such as courage, honesty, kindness, responsibility, and so forth. Were he more "mature" in his virtuous character, he would have mastered the way that judgment balances the various dispositions and chooses those to act upon in any case. But he's not—in fact, he's still looking for an overall ethical approach that works in all situations, and even if he decides that virtue ethics is that approach, he's not there yet.

One reason we know he's not there yet is that he still relies on role models or, as virtue ethicists call them, *moral exemplars*. Rules can be taught; you can get the basics of how to maximize utility or use the categorical imperative from a book. (Not this book, but it's a good start.) Judgment, however, cannot be nailed down in the same way that rules can. Immanuel Kant, the primo deontologist we met earlier, was a big believer in the power of judgment and the need for it to translate general duties into action.[1] Recall Kant's statement about judgment from chapter 5:

> although the understanding is certainly capable of being instructed and equipped through rules, the power of judgment is a special talent that cannot be taught but only practiced. Thus this is also what is specific to so-called mother-wit, the lack of which cannot be made good by any school.[2]

Judgment may not be easily instructed, but it can be shown by example, which makes role models important to a moral system that stresses moral judgment—such as virtue ethics.[3]

While his Uncle Ben and Aunt May were clear role models for Peter Parker growing up—and May continues in this role to this day—he also looks up to the older, more experienced superheroes around him.[4] During the Civil War, he relied on both Iron Man and Captain America as role models in different ways and at different times. Being an unformed virtue ethicist, however, Peter was not merely seeking guidance on using judgment, but more fundamentally how to choose between advancing the good (according to Iron Man's utilitarianism) and defending the right (according to Captain America's deontology). You could say that, while he possessed the basic virtues that a hero needs to have, Peter was looking for more precise ways to put them into use, and for that reason sought out a more determinate or precise ethical system—although virtue ethicists might argue that quest is misguided, because all systems of ethics come down to judgment in the end (as we've seen).

Peter Parker, You're an Avenger Now

Spider-Man had interacted with Iron Man, Captain America, and the Avengers as a team many times before the Civil War storyline; the interconnected nature of the Marvel Universe and Spider-Man's prominence in it practically guaranteed that.[5] And while he has gone on a number of adventures with the Avengers in the past, Spidey did not become an official full-time member until the first storyline following *Avengers Disassembled*, in which a mass breakout from the Raft prison calls a number of heroes into action under the leadership of Iron Man and Cap, inspiring them to declare the team the latest iteration of the Avengers.[6] During his brief initial period as an Avenger before the Stamford tragedy, though, he received a crash course in Iron Man and Captain America's different approaches to ethics which would continue more intensely during the Civil War.

When Spider-Man rushes to the scene of the prison break, he runs into Captain America and the two go into action. Almost immediately we see Spidey's impulse to protect people as he rushes ahead, only to held back by Captain America, who says "Spider-Man, wait!! Let the SHIELD agents take position, then we'll... ." But Spidey insists, saying, "I love you like you're a really, *really* older uncle, Cap, but... I have this whole guilt thing about putting other people in harm's way."[7] Later, after he finds out that one of his foes, Electro, masterminded the breakout, he says, "That's so embarrassing. It's one of *my* bad guys. I knew somehow this would be my fault." When Luke Cage assures him, "only in your warped brain," Spidey says, "well, yeah."[8]

Eventually Captain America and Spider-Man enter the fray, along with Luke Cage, Jessica Drew (Spider-Woman), and Daredevil, to be soon thereafter joined by Iron Man. When the fight is over and 45 escaped supervillains are captured—leaving another 42 on the loose, prompting Tony to say "we officially did that half-assed"—Cap and Tony discuss putting the team back together. Cap is more enthusiastic about the idea, arguing that the team organized itself as if by fate, much as the original line-up did in the 1960s. Tony says he'll think about it, and Cap says, "Great! I'll go assemble the team."[9] (Cap is nothing if not a go-getter.)

Soon, Steve Rogers catches up with Peter Parker outside PS 108 where he teaches science. Peter assumes he's in trouble, and Steve sounds like the US Army recruiting poster he often appears in: "Last night was very inspiring, but at the same time it created a dire situation. We have a lot of work to do. So we're putting a new Avengers team together. I want you." Peter is hesitant, saying that people hate him and that he doesn't belong on a team.[10] Cap tells him, "Every time I have fought alongside you... I have been amazed," and while he has Peter stunned, he finishes with, "Come with me on this," and Peter agrees. "Who can say no to you?" he says, to which Cap replies, "Good man."[11]

The initial adventure of these new Avengers aside—including the team winding up naked and upside-down in the Savage Land, a prehistoric jungle in the Arctic—Peter settles into his role as an Avenger. Meanwhile, as mentioned previously, both the apartment he shared with his wife Mary Jane as well as the house belonging to his Aunt May were destroyed.[12] Tony Stark immediately invites the three of them to move into Avengers Tower, after which MJ and May meet the rest of the Avengers, and Captain America and the Avengers' butler Jarvis both charm Aunt May (in very different ways).[13] Here we see the bond between Peter and Tony begin to form, which we mentioned in chapter 4 as an example of Tony's penchant for manipulation.

But Peter and Captain America had their own meaningful moments early on in Peter's time in the Avengers as well. When Peter thought he had uncovered a larger conspiracy behind some apparently random and ineffective HYDRA attacks, Cap is skeptical, believing the serious danger that HYRDA represented after World War II is a thing of the past. Peter says, "You think I'm wrong," to which Cap responds,

> I'm saying you could be wrong, because I think you *are* wrong, and because—well, because the idea of going up against the HYDRA of old isn't something I like to think about. The other option... is that you're right... and ahead of the curve. Ahead of us old fogies who remember what that shadow looks like... and who keep hoping that maybe this time it's gone for good.
> But the truth is the truth, Peter. Go find it.[14]

In this short speech, Cap stresses his own shortcomings—in particular, his motivated reasoning—as well as the journalistic principle of pursuing the truth, which Peter exemplified later when he and Ben Urich investigated Tony Stark's financial dealings during the Civil War.[15] It also affected Peter in a way that foreshadows Cap's effect on him during the Civil War. As he thought to himself as he continued to investigate HYDRA,

> He talked to me the way my Uncle Ben used to talk to me. Tough as nails, but quietly idealistic and resolute. Maybe it was something to do with their generation, men who had looked into the greatest darkness in history, and came out appreciating the light more than anyone who came after them.[16]

At the end of a story that included a major newspaper saying that Mary Jane was having an affair with Tony Stark ("if anything, it'll help my reputation"), Spider-Man catches a ride on a SCUD missile loaded with chemical weapons aimed at the American Midwest.[17] In a heroic effort—what other kind is there in a superhero comic?—Spidey redirects the missile into the ocean before it explodes. He passes out and is quickly caught by Iron Man, who returns with Peter to his lab in Avengers Tower and immediately treats him with anti-toxins. When Tony tells Peter he keeps a variety of anti-toxins on hand for situations like this, Peter says that civilians might need them even more than heroes do. As Tony explains,

> What do they tell you on airplanes when the oxygen masks
> come down? "Make sure your own mask is securely in place be-
> fore attempting to assist other people." The logic of the right
> choice is cold and hard more often than it is warm and fuzzy,
> Peter.[18]

Here, Peter gets his first taste of Tony's utilitarian thinking since becoming an Avenger—and it certainly won't be his last.

When Tony decides the new Avengers team has to go public, he arranges a press conference and calls in J. Jonah Jameson, Spider-Man's true arch-nemesis, who publishes as many "Spider-Man: Menace!" headlines as Marvel Comics publishes variant covers. When Jameson sees Spider-Man lurking on a wall and asks if he's on the team, Cap affirms it and speaks up for his newest teammate:

> We know you and he have a history. I know you have your opin-
> ions about him, but I wanted to tell you, from me, that the man
> in that uniform is a true American hero. This is a fact. I've seen
> him in action with my own eyes. He's been through more than
> all of us put together, and still he perseveres.[19]

Iron Man needles Jameson by adding, "Even when the press turns the city against him, still he acts the hero." The Avengers offer Jameson exclusive press access if he backs off on Peter, to which he agrees, only to renege the next day by slandering the entire team, writing that its new recruits include "a wanted murderer, an alleged ex-member of a terrorist organization, and a convicted heroin dealer." (You can imagine Peter's surprise.) But at least it gave us a chance to hear Cap and Iron Man reveal their admiration for their friendly neighborhood Spider-Man—even as we hurtle through time towards the fateful day in Stamford.

Mr. Parker Goes to Washington

That was the name of the storyline in which Tony signed Peter up as his right-hand man, told him about registration, and took him to Washington as Tony testified in front of Congress. We focused on Tony's side of the story in Part II of this book, but here we'll see more of what was going on inside Peter's head.

Peter's involvement in the Civil War—and his close partnership with Tony Stark—begins with the "Iron Spidey" suit, which Tony designed to include much of the functionality of the Iron Man armor in a more flexible (and form-fitting) outfit, in addition to thought-controlled camouflage capabilities and four

119

mechanical arms (in case anyone thought the whole spider motif was too subtle before).[20] As we know from chapter 4, Tony also incorporated sophisticated biometric tracking equipment in the suit, which enabled him to study Peter's spider-sense in order to block it as well as simulate it, giving Peter false positive readings and granting Tony an edge in battle.[21]

Of course, Peter was suspicious and asked Tony why he was so generous with the new outfit, not accepting Tony's explanation about Peter needing suits and having "the parts lying around." Tony held his cards tight to his chest and instead flattered Peter, giving him the speech we heard in chapter 4 about having a lot in common—"both scientists, levelheaded, practical… we have similar temperaments, we speak the same language"—and needing someone he can depend on in the "potentially difficult times coming," even adding that Peter, Mary Jane, and May were "like family to me."[22] Peter remains skeptical, especially regarding Tony's request for secrecy, even from Captain America, but ultimately his gratitude, reciprocity, and loyalty—all of which can be considered virtues—win out, and he tells Tony, "I owe you a lot," "I trust you," and finally, "whatever it takes, whatever it costs, in time or in blood—I'm there. You've got your blood oath."

As we discussed earlier, Tony may have been manipulating Peter, putting him in Tony's debt by taking the Parkers in after their homes were destroyed and giving Peter the Iron Spidey suit (as well as a job with Stark Industries), in line with his ego and his utilitarian outlook. But Peter's reasons for working for Tony can be seen as purely deontological, based on duty and responsibility. While much of his decision-making later takes the form of carefully weighing the benefits and costs of registration, unmasking, and eventually switching teams, at this point Peter is acting purely out of a feeling of what's right—or, as a virtue ethicist would say, the type of person he is. (Whichever way we frame it, this is exactly what Tony was counting on.)

Soon, Tony and Peter are on a plane to Washington but, at this point in the story, Tony is still fighting registration. He makes a great case against it to Peter, expressing criticism of the legislative process while he's at it.[23] Tony and Peter focus here on the threat to heroes and their families if the secret identities get loose, with Peter very doubtful that the government will be able to effectively safeguard heroes' secrets. Tony does acknowledge that the people behind registration have a point (for reasons detailed previously), but nonetheless plans to fight it, saying ominously that "there are… other options. But I'd rather avoid that route if humanly—or superhumanly—possible."[24] (That explains hiring the

Titanium Man to attack them in the hopes of convincing the Senate committee of the necessity of free heroes.)

Peter sits quietly while Tony explains to the senators that, despite the harm to property and (more tragically) lives that has resulted from superhero activities—costs that the senators estimate at 200 billion dollars since 1946—these same activities also saved the world 47 times over and therefore have more than justified their costs (consistent with the utilitarian thinking displayed by the senators as well as Tony more generally). When the senators turn to the superhero community's responsibility and accountability for those costs, however, Tony has no reply, recognizing his own complicity in a number of foul-ups in the past.

It's here that Peter speaks up. He invokes the principle of proportionate response, that threats of a certain level should be met with responses of similar level, to explain that society needs heroes with superpowers to face villains with superpowers. Furthermore, he explains that while supervillains are usually supervillains fulltime—a questionable assertion, but we'll let that go—superheroes are superheroes only some of the time:

> They have lives, and families, and loved ones who would be at terrible risk to these very same bad guys if their identities were revealed. In those personal moments, they or their families could be harmed… because the bad guys know that if they wipe out or neutralize enough of the superheroes… there won't be anyone who can stop them the 48th time this country is in jeopardy.

One of the senators mentions police officers, prosecutors, and judges, all of whom risk retribution from wrongdoers they've arrested, convicted, or punished, but none of whom wear masks. Peter answers that those people voluntarily assumed those positions, where many superheroes came to their powers or abilities by accident and answered a calling to use them for good, even though they didn't want to do so in the open because of the risks he mentioned before. Again the senator parries, saying that registration could make it easier to carry out this calling with support from the government, rather than having to operate under the radar. (It was Peter's fault for mentioning "a system that would never allow them to operate freely.")

Round one goes to the senators. During a break in the hearings, Tony explains to Peter that he should never offer information that isn't asked for, and when Peter calls Mary Jane to let her know how it went, he says "I opened my mouth and spoke when I shouldn't have," to which she replied, "Well, that's never happened before." As we'll soon see, Peter did not learn his lesson that day.

After the hearing ends for the day, the Titanium Man just "happens to" attack Tony and Peter, spouting thinly veiled threats about the United States reining in its heroes and providing a way for America's enemies and other supervillains to get the upper hand. This gives Tony Stark the footage he needs the next day to argue to the senators that heroes must not be limited by government red tape: "If it goes wrong, as these things tend to… it could lead to a kind of unilateral disarmament of our super-powered citizens. Which is exactly what our enemies want."[25]

Even the senators are suspicious of the convenient timing of the Titanium Man's attack, and Peter takes this chance to once again chime in, this time in costume, dangling upside-down from the ceiling by a web. ("He never learns," Tony mutters to himself.) He makes a similar argument to Captain America's when he told Maria Hill that he didn't want a situation in which "Washington starts telling us who the supervillains are."[26] As Peter put it, "You're all good guys, but if you had to start deciding what sorts of things supers should get involved with, then you start eliminating the things they should not get involved with." Then he takes the argument in a different direction, explaining that many heroes (like him) fight for the people no one else notices:

> Guys like me get involved in things sometimes because no one else will… because it's not in the rule book, or it's politically in-convenient, or it's too weird, or—or simply because nobody else cares.
>
> The government, the big corporations, the money guys… they have plenty of people willing to put it all on the line to de-fend them. But somebody on the edge, somebody in trouble… the kind of guy wiser minds would say should be left to solve his own problems… who does he go to?

Peter's fear is informed by his costumed career, mostly spent battling muggers and thieves in between the flashier supervillains (many of whom started out as simple thieves themselves), not battling the galactic threats that the Avengers and Fantastic Four often face. The street-level heroes such as Spidey, Luke Cage, and Daredevil take care of the "dirty business" on the ground. As he continues to tell the senators:

> Lots of the other super-guys live in shadows because what they do is stuff you'd never, ever want to know about… because you'd never sleep well again. Leaving them alone to operate as they see fit gives you deniability, and lets them dive in where logic would say "stay away."

This is perhaps not the best rhetorical strategy when trying to convince the government representing voters afraid of uncontrolled superheroes! But Peter returns to his original point in his conclusion, suggesting, instead of registration, "a kind of good Samaritan law, like they have for drivers, where you can protect everybody when one person dives in to do something to help… while everybody else just drives by."

Unfortunately for Peter, the senators acknowledge some of his points but are not convinced by his argument, and demand that he unmask and reveal his real name and address to the committee, as anyone providing testimony must do. When Peter says he can't, one of the senators says

> that, son, is exactly why this legislation isn't going away. This is a nation of laws, and those laws are meaningless without the ability to enforce them equally. You may be above the ground, son, but you are not above the law. That super-power we allow to no one in this republic.

With that, he orders Peter's comment stricken from the record (though, luckily for us, not from the comics—only the all-powerful Editors have that ability). Tony tells Peter later that regardless of the outcome, what he said was important—"you spoke your mind about something important. Republics die when people stop doing that"—and that he gave the Senate committee something to think about. At best, he says, they may have slowed down the legislation, "we buy a year here, a year there, and sooner or later these things die of their own weight."

~~~~~

That evening, falling asleep in his apartment in front of the television, Peter misses the news report of a tragic accident in Stamford, CT, after which Tony's dreams of legislative stonewalling and delay are a thing of the past. So too are Peter's dreams of web-swinging alongside both Iron Man and Captain America, as soon he will be forced to choose sides in the ideological battle between them— and face some personal ethical choices that hit much closer to home.

[1] In this way he had much in common with the virtue ethicists, as I argue in "The Virtues of a Kantian Economics," in Jennifer A. Baker and Mark D. White, eds, *Economics and the Virtues: Building a New Moral Foundation* (Oxford: Oxford University Press, 2016), pp. 94-115.

[2] Immanuel Kant, *Critique of Pure Reason*, trans. Paul Guyer and Allen W. Wood (Cambridge: Cambridge University Press, 1998), A133/B172.

[3] Kant criticized the use of role models among "mature people," favoring autonomous reasoning instead, but approved of their use with the young who are still developing in their moral sense.

[4] This is ironic, because the introduction of Spider-Man (in August 1962) in the comics actually predates that of Iron Man (in March 1963).

[5] Spider-Man's early adventures with the Avengers are collected in *Spider-Man: Am I an Avenger?* (2011).

[6] The end of the original Avengers was chronicled in *Avengers Disassembled*, and the formation of the new team is shown in *New Avengers, Vol. 1: Breakout* (both 2006).

[7] *New Avengers*, vol. 1, #2 (February 2005).

[8] *New Avengers*, vol. 1, #4 (April 2005).

[9] *New Avengers*, vol. 1, #3 (March 2005), including the next paragraph. By the way, Reed says the number of escaped villains is 46 in *New Avengers*, vol. 1, #7 (July 2005), making the job just a little more half-assed.

[10] Never mind that he tried to join the Fantastic Four in *Amazing Spider-Man*, vol. 1, #1 (March 1963), "Spider-Man Vs. the Chameleon."

[11] Trust me that Cap was sincere; for his earlier praise of Spidey, see, for instance, *Fallen Son: The Death of Captain America* #4 (July 2007).

[12] *Amazing Spider-Man* #518 (May 2005).

[13] *Amazing Spider-Man* #519 (June 2005). Later, May puts Logan in his place, showing that she is also the best at what she does (*Amazing Spider-Man* #520, July 2005).

[14] *Amazing Spider-Man* #521 (August 2005).

[15] *Civil War: Front Line* #9 (February 2007), "Embedded Part 9."

[16] *Amazing Spider-Man* #521.

[17] Tony's comment is from *Amazing Spider-Man* #522 (September 2005).

[18] *Amazing Spider-Man* #524 (November 2005). Mary Jane sees the same side of Tony when Peter apparently dies from a superhuman beating and Tony discusses

how to make his death look more "normal" to protect her and Aunt May—cold and hard indeed, but necessary (*Marvel Knights: Spider-Man* #21, February 2006).

[19] *New Avengers*, vol. 1, #15 (March 2006), through the rest of this section.

[20] Tony mentions that he's designing a new outfit for Peter (after they destroyed his other ones during his brief "death") in *Amazing Spider-Man* #527 (February 2006), is shown making it in #528 (March 2006), and gives it to Peter to try out in #529 (April 2006)—and makes yet more improvements by #530 (May 2006), saying that "art is never finished, Peter, only abandoned." (If you're interested, Peter's first appearance in the Iron Spidey suit with the Avengers was *New Avengers*, vol. 1, #17, May 2006.)

[21] *Iron Man*, vol. 4, #14 (January 2007). The suit also filters out air-borne pathogens, protecting Peter from the Scarecrow's fear toxins, as seen as *Sensational Spider-Man*, vol. 2, #29 (October 2006). ("Wait, you have a Scarecrow villain, too?" asks Mary Jane—don't worry, you weren't the only one thinking it.)

[22] *Amazing Spider-Man* #529, through the rest of this paragraph.

[23] When Peter balks at how heavy the draft bill is, Tony says, "the bill is only the first thirty pages. The rest are riders and amendments tacked on by other senators trying to piggyback their own agendas" (*Amazing Spider-Man* #530, May 2006).

[24] *Amazing Spider-Man* #530, through Peter's phone call to Mary Jane.

[25] *Amazing Spider-Man* #531 (June 2006), for the rest of this chapter (except where noted).

[26] *Civil War* #1 (July 2006).

Chapter 9: Revealing the Man Under the Spider Mask

Tony and Peter hop on a jet as soon as they hear about Stamford and Tony gets briefed on the way. After Iron Man and Spider-Man help find those who survived and those who didn't, they stay to survey the scene and the mood. Peter is surprised how apprehensive the people are of them, but Tony isn't. "We're not responsible, but we're in the same fraternity of powers. We're the second cousins of the guys who *are* responsible for the deaths of their loved ones."[1] Then Tony directs Peter to use the enhanced vision capabilities of his new suit to look up into the sky, where he sees the president's helicopter.

After talking to the president, Tony walks out of the Oval Office and sternly tells Peter that the registration act will be passed and signed within a week. Peter asks Tony if he's going to continue to fight it, mentioning all the heroes "who have other names, real names they've worked so hard to protect," and citing Tony in particular, at which point Tony says that he revealed his identity to the president (and soon afterwards does the same to the public at a press conference).[2] He explains how registration will work, that

> those who refuse to comply will be hunted down and arrested…
> along with anyone who aided or abetted them in keeping their
> identities secret. Their assets will be frozen, their homes seized.
> And finally, they will be jailed. Imprisoned. Some, potentially,
> for a very, very long time.

Finally he says to Peter, "I have to know where you stand." When Peter says he made him a promise to stand by him and "I don't do that sort of thing lightly," Tony says that he needs everything to be "on the up-and-up" if he's going to take charge of this—by which he means that Peter will have to reveal to the world that he's Spider-Man as well.

In this chapter we'll look at some of the consequences of Peter's choice to reveal his identity, a decision that plays out well past this chapter. We'll also see his support of registration and Tony begin to slip—especially after hearing the story of Mr. Fantastic's Uncle Ted.

"My Name Is Peter Parker, and I've Been Spider-Man Since I Was Fifteen Years Old."

To say this was a huge decision for Peter would be a gross understatement. Of all the aspects of registration, the issue of his secret identity loomed the largest for him. No hero had been more diligent in guarding his or her real name than Spider-Man had. While some, such as the Fantastic Four, never kept secret identities and chose to live in the open as heroes—or, as they prefer, "adventurers"—Peter always feared what would happen to his Aunt May and other loved ones if his real name became known. After the Stamford tragedy, when many of the heroes gathered to debate registration, Sue Richards (the Invisible Woman) said operating in public has "never really been a serious concern" for the Fantastic Four, to which Peter replied, "yeah, well… not until the day I come home and find my wife impaled on an octopus arm and the woman who raised me begging for her life."[3] As mentioned before, Peter's first love Gwen Stacy was killed by the Green Goblin after he discovered who Peter really was, an incident that haunted Peter almost as much as the death of his Uncle Ben years earlier.[4]

Other heroes had also suffered from their secret identities becoming known, none perhaps more than Spider-Man's good friend Daredevil, otherwise known as Matt Murdock. Like Peter, Matt maintained his secret identity to protect those close to him, including his best friend Foggy Nelson and his love interests throughout the years (most famously his secretary, Karen Page). When the Kingpin (Wilson Fisk) discovered Matt's secret, he engaged in a very deliberate and gradual effort to destroy Matt Murdock body and soul, including going after the people Matt loved.[5] Years later, the Kingpin went even further and revealed Daredevil's secret identity to the world, which brought a new level of danger to Matt's life and loved ones from many more of his longtime enemies.[6] After struggling for years to put the genie back in the bottle, recently Matt decided to out himself again, but this time the choice was his and he controlled the process (if not the consequences).[7]

As we saw in chapter 6, even Captain America came to regard trying to maintain a secret identity as Steve Rogers as too dangerous for his friends and neighbors. While the Fantastic Four have a fortified skyscraper to shelter their children, heroes such as Daredevil, Captain America, and Spider-Man don't have the resources to protect their loved ones from the adverse consequences of their real names being known. And while it was an intensely personal decision for Peter and could easily be read as a selfish concern insomuch as it involved *his* loved ones, it must be noted that his concern was directed at others, not himself, and he did extend his concern to other members of the superhero community in similar positions. As we saw in part II in reference to Iron Man, being personally interested in an outcome does not mean it cannot also be of broader ethical importance. In many cases, overlapping motivations make it more difficult to determine moral intent, but luckily for us, Peter Parker talks—he talks a lot—making it easier to figure out what he is thinking about such things.

The person he talks to first, of course, is Tony Stark, when he drops the bomb-shell on their way back from Washington. When Tony tells him he has to unmask, Peter's initial reaction is "I can't... don't ask that of me. Anything else, but not that."[8] Tony goes a bit overboard, telling him that it's the law, although the SHRA only requires that heroes register their identities with the government, not that reveal them publicly. He lays it on even thicker when he says that if Peter refuses, Mary Jane and Aunt May will also be implicated as accomplices, and "if you turn against the law, I can't have you with me. I won't be able to protect you... or your family." Note the buttons that Tony pushes here: he invokes duty in terms of obeying the law as well as consequences in terms of concern for loved ones, two moral factors that he knows will have a large influence on Peter. (Even if we forgive Tony this subtle manipulation, his exaggeration of the requirements of the registration act—perhaps a necessary means to the end in Tony's mind—is plan deception.)

To Peter, though, the consequences from unmasking that he fears for his loved ones are likely worse than if he doesn't. As he told Sue, he fears the worst from his enemies learning the identity or whereabouts of his family, which places his concerns over his loved ones in conflict with his felt duty to comply with the law (as Tony presented it to him) as well as his loyalty to Tony (which, at this point, has yet to be tested). We see this in his conversation with journalist Sally Floyd about registration and the possibility of his unmasking.[9] "There's going to be a lot of pressure on me to reveal my identity—more than ever before," he said. "Up until now, I've always been, more or less, on the right side of the law. I don't want to be on the wrong side if the act passes, but people don't understand what they're asking of me." Then he switches to the consequences, acknowledging the recent death of Floyd's daughter, and saying,

> I've lost people too... directly as a result of what I do. People I cared about. I still have people. And now the government wants me to register my identity or go to jail. Didn't it occur to anyone what this would do to my family? ... We're husbands and wives... fathers, mothers, sons and daughters. ... If I show my

face to the world, all of the people who hate me will go after the
things I hold most dear.

He acknowledges that the people behind registration—perhaps including Tony Stark himself—"think they're doing it for a good reason—heck, they probably are—but there's a cost. That's all I want people to know: just think about it."[10] He's asking the powers that be—those with political power as well as superpowers—to think about the trade-off between the safety and security they hope to gain through registration with the safety and security heroes and their families could lose because of it, a great example of the balancing and judgment needed within utilitarianism itself (even before principles are considered).

The night he returned from Washington, Peter discussed unmasking with Mary Jane and Aunt May, a conversation that reveals a wealth of Peter's moral thinking, as well as MJ's and May's.[11] First, he and MJ trace through the different ways that events could go, including what would happen if Peter does or doesn't register or unmask. She asks him if Tony expects him to hunt down unregistered heroes, a topic we'll discuss more later, and if he'll have to "name names," which he and the reader naturally connect to the McCarthy hearings and the "Red Scare" in the 1950s, when suspected communist sympathizers were rooted out and required to name others. She also asks whether, if he doesn't go public (or register), Tony will out him anyway; Peter wants to say he wouldn't, but he can't be sure. (Peter's loyal, but he's not stupid.)

This part of the conversation provides an excellent illustration of one of the challenges of utilitarian thinking we discussed in chapter 2: how to predict the likelihood of the outcomes stemming from different choices. But Mary Jane's questions introduce a new element of the problem: accounting for what *other* people will do as well. It isn't simply how the authorities will react if Peter refuses to reveal his identity, but what Tony Stark will do as well. This puts Peter in quite a bind. On the one hand, he has sworn loyalty to this man and he has a reasonable expectation that he will receive loyalty in return. But he also knows Tony as someone who will do whatever it takes to achieve his goal, so he can't be sure that Tony will honor that loyalty when push comes to shove. (As we will see later, Peter's loyalty has its limits too.) This makes Tony's behavior even harder to predict, and therefore it's all the more difficult for Peter and Mary Jane to decide what will unfold in the various scenarios they consider. Add to that the question of what his enemies will do—although they're single-minded, vengeful supervillains, so perhaps a little easier to predict than Tony Stark is—and you have quite a mess to sort through.

Also, besides estimating the probabilities of various contingencies, there is the issue of how to compare the different outcomes themselves (also discussed in chapter 2). If Peter and Mary Jane were designing a business plan for her night-club, all of the possibilities would have benefits and costs in terms of dollars gained or lost, which are directly and easily comparable. But the various outcomes when considering registering and unmasking are hardly comparable in the same way. Helping to hunt down respected and admired colleagues such as Captain America and longtime friends such as Daredevil is horrible, but how can Peter compare it to putting MJ and Aunt May in mortal danger? Even if he only considers MJ and May, the choice is either to open them up to revenge or to turn them into wanted criminals, two different types of danger each with its own unique costs. Even if Peter could magically divine the exact probabilities of all of these things happening, comparing the different outcomes themselves is a much deeper problem, one that can't be solved simply by better estimation techniques (even if Peter were a futurist like his boss).

Of course, Mary Jane tells Peter that no matter what he decides, she and Aunt May will support him, but Peter insists that they all agree on what he's going to do because the choice affects all three of them, including both the decision over registration that threatens to turn them all into criminals, and the decision over unmasking that threatens to turn them all into targets. Having remained silent until now, Aunt May finally speaks, asking, "Can I—can I say something?" Peter says sure but that he knows where she stands, to which she says, "no, I rather suspect you don't, Peter." (Snap!) And then she lays out a different point of view, one based on deontology and a bit of virtue ethics rather than consequences and probabilities.

May told Peter that ever since she found out he was Spider-Man—years into his webcrawling career—she wasn't disappointed or upset with him for keeping the secret. Instead she was angry with other people, "because parts of the world called Spider-Man a monster, a criminal, even a criminal, even before this new law. And if I knew anything about my nephew—it's that he's not a criminal." She tells him how proud she is of him and of all the good he's done, and how she wants the world to be proud of him too, not just Spider-Man but Peter Parker as well. In a sense, she appreciates the incredible responsibility he takes on because of his power, but she wants him to take some of the credit too—not out of vanity, but out of due recognition that would counteract all of the negative press and treatment he received since he spun his first web at the age of fifteen.

Peter says he realizes and appreciates that May is proud of him, but maintains that "I have an obligation to protect you. I made a promise—." But she cuts him off, saying, "Yes, you did. At sixteen. A child's promise that has nothing to do with how the world works." She asks him why police, prosecutors, and elected officials—the same people cited by the senator in Washington—don't wear masks even though they're endangering themselves and their loved ones. When he says he doesn't know, she answers that it's because their loved ones want it that way, "because they would rather die than see the face they love, the face that gives so much to the world, covered in shame." Just as Peter and Mary Jane debated the balance amongst possible consequences, Aunt May does the same thing with deontological principles. She sees Peter's duty to keep a promise and trumps it with a duty to be true to himself: "Some things are worth the risk, Peter. You're one of them." Mary Jane, in tears, agrees, telling Peter, "She's right. Don't run. Stand your ground. Let the whole world understand why we love you—more than life itself." In the end, they chose to set aside the consequences, good or bad, and decided on principle that Peter should register and unmask. And only time would tell if the consequences would be dire enough to make them doubt that decision.

A few days later Peter was getting ready to leave for Washington to meet Tony Stark for the press conference at which his life, and the lives of Mary Jane and Aunt May, would change forever. Peter was having doubts, thinking of fleeing to "New England or Canada" (uh, only one of those is a different country, Pete), and had resolved to call the unmasking off when May brought him one of his old costumes, saying, "this way they'll know for sure it's you when they see you." Then she unwittingly pushed Peter's buttons far better than Tony could ever hope to: "Ben, and then you, always said, 'with great power comes great responsibility.' And responsibility means you don't run away when someone asks, 'who did that?'" Faced with the ultimate lesson in accountability from the woman to whom he felt the most accountable, Peter left for Washington to reveal his identity to the world.

When Peter met Tony in the White House, he reaffirmed his gratitude and loyalty:

> You took us in when we had nowhere to go. You've been good
> to MJ, and to Aunt May. You stood by us. You've been like—like
> a father to me. I made a promise that I would stand by you, no
> matter what. I keep my promises, Tony. Do what you have to.
> I'll back you up. All the way.[12]

And then he stood in front of the presidential seal, faced the cameras and reporters, introduced himself, and said the words that echoed not only through the Marvel Universe but through ours as well. (He started less than eloquently, but it picked up quickly, echoing Aunt May's words near the end.)

> Um, as most of you probably know, I've, uh, guarded my secret identity pretty carefully over the years… and it's only after a long talk with my wife and family that I've decided to take the following step.
>
> See, the registration act gives us a choice: we can continue the trend that Captain America advocates and have people with powers completely unchecked… or superheroes can go legitimate and earn back a little public trust.
>
> I'm not wearing my old mask because I'm ashamed of what I do. I'm proud of who I am, and I'm here right now to prove it…
>
> My name is Peter Parker, and I've been Spider-Man since I was fifteen years old.
>
> Any questions?[13]

And then things changed forever—and mostly for the worse.

After the Reveal

First, Peter vomited in the restroom of the White House. Then, people searching for "Peter Parker" online crashed the internet. Also, J. Jonah Jameson, the man who for years paid Peter pennies for his pictures of Spidey in action and then abused him like the son he never had (rather than the successful son he has) was understandably peeved (actually suing Peter Parker on behalf of the *Daily Bugle* for five million dollars).[14]

Now for the serious consequences. Before the storm broke, though, there were the assurances. As Tony stood outside the restroom while Peter threw up, he said, "You did the right thing, Peter. It wasn't the easy thing to do, but it was the right thing." After Peter came out, Tony continued, "For what it's worth, Peter, I know exactly what you're going through. I went through the same thing when I went public for the first time and—" but Peter cut him off, saying,

> No, Tony, you don't know what it's like. You don't know because you've never had a family to worry about. You don't have MJ and Aunt May to— Every day of my life since I was fifteen years old I've lived in absolute terror of just this moment.

Tony agrees, admitting that he doesn't have a family to protect, but Peter again cuts him off, saying he *will* have a family to protect if anything happens to him, and makes Tony promise to take care of Mary Jane and May. (This is ironic given how Tony uses their safety against him when Peter turns on him later.)

As he leaves the White House, he sees a crowd of supporters and protestors with signs proclaiming love or hate for him. In the limo Tony sent to take him to the airport, Peter receives a number of phone calls, first from MJ and May, saying how proud they are of him; then from Reed Richards, who praises Peter's courage; and finally from Sue Richards, who jumps on Reed's line to ask how Peter's holding up. (Reed and Sue start bickering, and when MJ tells May this, May demands to know why Peter started a fight between Reed and Sue: "They're such a lovely couple. I can't imagine them arguing." Um…)

Next we're shown a montage of news reports and reactions from friends, colleagues, and enemies of Peter Parker and Spider-Man. Later, as Peter and Mary Jane leave Avengers Tower—through the service entrance, as if that will fool anybody—they're mobbed by reporters and blinded by flashbulbs, until a singular man emerged from the crowd, claiming to be Captain America's #1 fan.[15] He pulls a gun, accuses Peter of being a traitor to everything [Cap] stands for, and fires. Peter webs up the barrel of his gun just in time and it explodes in the man's hand, stunning him until the crowd can subdue him. As Peter and MJ leave, the man yells, "I'll sue! You blew up my hand! I'll sue you!," to which Peter responds, "get in line." This confrontation ended without incident, but it foreshadowed events to come later in the storyline; as Cap told Peter later, "I saw that little stunt you pulled on TV. Is Mary Jane happy about the Sandman having her ZIP code now?"[16] Tony dismisses this concern, having said earlier that "certain things will change, Peter. But it's not like every deviant personality you ever crossed swords with in the past is going to start coming after you now."[17] This is a legitimate concern, however, as the Chameleon, one of Peter's earliest foes, enlisted some fellow Spider-villains to attack Peter's family after he unmasked, the Chameleon himself going after Aunt May, who proved no easy prey for even a master of disguise.[18]

But the most important news report that Peter sees features none other than Tony Stark, speaking to the heroes "who have made clear their decision not to cooperate." He says that over the last ten years, he had determined the identities of 137 heroes who decided not to register, and "starting this time tomorrow, anyone on this list who has not come forward to register, or who gives aid and comfort to those who refuse—will be hunted down, arrested and imprisoned, without exception." When asked who will do this, Tony mentioned the heroes who have registered, and particularly "a strike team consisting of Reed Richards, Hank Pym—and Spider-Man." With those words, one of the Parkers' fears came true: Peter would be forced to hunt down his former friends and colleagues, including Captain America. "He's... I mean, he was a hero to my whole generation," May says. "I can't imagine—I just can't imagine."

When Peter catches up with Iron Man, the Armored Avenger asks how his day has been, and Peter jokes, "Dandy. It's been a five-star day, starting with you... and ending with you." Then he asks Tony why he didn't get a heads up before being mentioned on the news as one of his hero hunters, and Tony said there wasn't time before invoking Peter's promise to stand by him. "I told you that things were going to get hot. You said you'd back my play, no matter what. I bet both our reputations on that. Are you changing your mind?" Peter assures him he's not, but that he wants some notice in the future, and that "I call you boss because I know it bugs you. Don't start taking it too seriously." Peter is determined to keep his word but that doesn't mean Tony has free reign over him, nicely reconciling the duty of keeping promises with the duty not to do wrong in other areas, an exercise in judgment like any other—and one that would be tested very soon. (And for the record, Tony did apologize.)

Iron Man, Spider-Man, and the other pro-registration heroes had their first battle with Captain America and rest of the resistance movement after Tony faked a news report to lure the rebels to a chemical factory, a fight during which Spider-Man faced Cap for the first time since the Civil War began, and also the fight at which the clone of Thor killed the hero Goliath.[19] When Iron Man's team regrouped and got ready to accompany the captured heroes to the Negative Zone prison, Tony tried to rally them, and in the process reflected Peter's sentiments: "It was bloody. It was painful. It was necessary. I know it was difficult for many of you. More so for some of you than others. Nonetheless, you all performed admirably. You should all be proud of what you've accomplished." Afterwards, when Tony asked why Peter was uncharacteristically quiet, he said he wasn't feeling very "court-jesterish," but that he knows "we gotta fight who we gotta fight. That's what you said." When Tony corrects him, saying it's not his choice but rather the law, Peter says, "Yeah, I know... we're all just following orders. Doesn't mean I have to like it." From this point, however, Peter does start to have doubts about whether following the law is the most important moral consideration in this Civil War.

The Law and Reed's Uncle

As he accompanies Tony on the mission to transport the captured heroes to the Negative Zone prison, Peter notices the protestors again, and thinks to himself,

> For the first time, I'm out. I'm on the side of the law, and the law's on my side. May is proud of me. MJ is proud of me. I'm on the right side of everything. So how come something so right just feels so wrong?[20]

These growing doubts, which will only worsen as the story progresses, are enhanced by the similarly increasing realization that Tony is using him. For example, Tony tells Peter he wants him riding on one of the transport vehicles because he's the only one that can sense when trouble's coming. But, Peter thinks to himself, no one knows about his spider-sense except Mary Jane and May, and "I think I need to go over this suit a little more closely… find out how much data is coming in… and more important, how much data is going out."

As that same spider-sense tells him, Captain America and some of his team are traveling through the sewers in preparation to hijack the prisoner transport, and once the teams engage each other, it's only a matter of time before Spidey runs into Cap himself.[21] Appearing after Peter yells to a fleeing unregistered hero, "the fun's just starting," Captain Literal corrects him, saying, "That's where you're wrong, Peter. There is no fun here. There's only innocent people being hurt, and arrested, and killed. And you're on the wrong side of that equation." Peter tells him he was going to say the same thing, followed by a request to surrender peacefully. Cap doesn't laugh, and instead says:

> I'm going to make this short, and to the point. I respect you, Peter, and I know you. I know your heart. I know you hate what you're doing, but you think you don't have any other choice. You're wrong. You can still do the right thing. We could use you on our side. I won't ask again.

Peter struggles, thinking that "my whole life, all I've ever really wanted is the respect of the people I admire. Aunt May. MJ. And people like him. Finally, at least, after so long… I've got it. And now I'm about to lose it forever."

And so they fight, with Peter marveling at what a fantastic fighter Cap is, until Cap realizes his allies are under attack and rushes off to join them. Peter is left with Cap's shield, and webs it high on the side of a building, thinking to himself,

I put it in a place where nobody can reach it. Correction: *almost* nobody. Because I want him to know I left it for him. When he finds it, I hope he understands. I hope he gets the message—that the shield represents the country, and the laws of the country decide who's right. Even the laws we don't like. Even the ones that suck. Cap thinks in terms of right and wrong, but this isn't a matter of right and wrong, moral or immoral, it's legal vs. illegal.

At least, that's what I tell myself in the middle of the night, when I wonder what the hell I'm doing here.

I'm legal. I'm registered. I'm authorized. And as I feel this whole situation starting to unravel all around me—I just hope to God that I'm also right.

In this passage we see the cognitive dissonance Peter is starting to experience as he experiences a conflict in his core principles. On the one hand, he's happy and relieved to finally be "right" with the law after skirting on the edge of it for so many years. He wants to believe that following the law, no matter what he thinks of the law, is the right thing to do.

On the other hand, however, Peter's starting to realize that a law being a law—passed and implemented according to the official legislative procedures—is not the same as it being a good law or a just law, and does not imply that a good citizen need follow it. This recalls our discussion of civil disobedience in chapter 6, as well as debates among legal philosophers over the status of Nazi law, in particular during the Nuremberg trials following World War II.[22] The former link is natural, as Peter starts to shift to Captain America's thinking along the lines of Dr. Martin Luther King, Jr., in his "Letter from Birmingham Jail." What's more, a law doesn't have to be unjust itself to provoke civil disobedience. A just law can be implemented or enforced unjustly, such as when harsh methods are used, whether against all citizens or only certain groups in society.[23]

Speaking of harsh methods, it was at this point in the story that Peter demanded that Tony show him the prison where they were keeping unregistered heroes.[24] Note that I didn't call it the Negative Zone prison, because at this point Peter didn't know that the prison was *in* the Negative Zone, a fact he was shocked to learn. When they meet Reed Richards at the Negative Zone portal in the Baxter Building, he says to Peter that he suggested to Tony that they bring Peter in, "being something of a scientist yourself," to which Peter replies, "Really? He never mentioned it," despite Tony's flattery early on for being a kindred scientific soul.[25] Earlier that morning Peter saw a news report about Stark Industries' windfall on the stock market, so learning that the prison was in the Negative Zone, as well as finding out how the "occupants" were treated, made him more suspicious and skeptical of Tony than ever.

But Reed Richards is the part of the story I want to focus on here, because his conversation with Peter after he finishes the prison tour reveals another view on civil disobedience. When Peter asks Reed one question—"Why?"—the patriarch of the Fantastic Four tells Peter a story about his Uncle Ted and his problems during the Red Scare in the 1950s, mentioned above. The older brother of Reed's scientist father Nathaniel, Ted was—*gasp*—a writer and "an eccentric. He was funny and colorful. And I loved him. But he was also stubborn, and didn't care for rules, and if you pushed him, he'd push back just as hard." When the House Un-American Activities Committee issued a subpoena demanding Ted testify, admitting to any communist sympathies and naming any other sympathizers he knew, he went into a wild rant—as Reed said, "I've never actually read the transcripts, but my mother used to say she was surprised the stenography machines didn't burst into flame." Whatever he might have said that offended gentler ears, Ted ended his speech with three simple words: "Go to hell."

Ted was sentenced to six months in jail for contempt, and as Reed tells it, when he got out his life was ruined: no one would hire him, his father refused to see him, and he lost his home and life savings. After a moment of silence, Reed said, "In the end, it killed him." When Peter said Reed's uncle he was brave, Reed disagreed, saying he was *wrong*. "He picked a fight he couldn't win. Whether HUAC was right or wrong wasn't the point. It was the law." He continued in a more general vein:

> Take away the law and what are we? Savages. Up to our necks in blood. That's why we give the law the authority to take every-thing away from us if we break it by murdering or kidnapping or—or simply telling powerful men to go to hell.

Reed may be a brilliant scientist but he is confused on several points regarding the law and the state. Yes, we give the state authority to enforce laws, but not to "take everything away from us" for breaking *any* law—and as we will soon see when Captain America gives his most memorable speech from the Civil War, "telling powerful men to go to hell" is an important right of each citizen in a free society, not a crime to be punished (much less by "taking everything away from us").

Reed's view represents an extreme and dangerous servility to the state, and contradicts the more important part of what he said, that *we* give the law that authority. In a democracy, the people together are the ultimate authority, and we lend some of that authority to the state to escape what Thomas Hobbes called the "state of nature," in which we would, according to Hobbes and Reed, be "savages."[26] But Reed paints this choice as one between two extremes, utter chaos and strict control, when most societies choose something in the middle. Also, Reed confuses respect for law in general—which Dr. King stressed, as we saw—with obedience to each individual law, regardless of its morality or justice. (This is an unfortunate result of the English language, which uses the word "law" for both a specific statute and for the general system of rules.[27])

However, Reed does allow for some resistance in the form of change. As he says, "The law is the law, Peter. I support it because I honestly believe we have to support it, no matter what." Peter asks, "and if the law is wrong?" to which Reed responds, "Then eventually it'll be changed, in an orderly, lawful way. We can't just obey the laws we like, or—." He was cut off by Tony, but he said enough to flesh out his earlier thoughts. We see here that Reed does not accept the law unquestionably, but simply favors official means for changing it, by repeal or revision in the legislature (or interpretation in the courts), rather than civilian resistance. In the long run this may be preferable, but right now this means that people have to obey a law that they feel is wrong, which may be, in some cases, too much to ask. Furthermore, informal resistance and formal change are not mutually exclusive, as we saw during the 1960s when civil disobedience on the part of Rosa Parks, Martin Luther King, Jr., and others put pressure on legislators and courts to change laws more quickly than they otherwise might have. Legislators and judges may do the right thing eventually, but sometimes it helps to give them a sign that things need changing, and a public act of civil disobedience can do just what is needed to do that.

~~~~~

Through this chapter, we saw Peter slowly slip away from Tony's influence and leadership, wondering if the principles Tony stood for were the ones he wanted to stand for, and if what Peter was doing was truly the best way to protect Mary Jane and Aunt May. In the next chapter, we'll see that linkage break and what happens when Spider-Man joins Captain America's side. Will that fix everything? We'll soon see.

---

1 *Amazing Spider-Man* #532 (July 2006), through the rest of this intro (except where noted).

2 *Civil War: Front Line* #1 (August 2006), "Embedded Part One."

3 *Civil War* #1 (July 2006).

4 *Amazing Spider-Man*, vol. 1, #121 (June 1973).

5 *Daredevil: Born Again* (1987).

6 *Daredevil Vol. 5: Out* (2003).

7 *Daredevil*, vol. 3, #36 (April 2014).

8 *Amazing Spider-Man* #532, for the rest of this paragraph.

9 *Civil War: Front Line* #1, "Embedded Part One," for the rest of this paragraph.

10 As Peter left her apartment, Sally said he was "kinda dorky. I like it… it's really cute," and invited him back for dinner sometime. He replied, "yeah, uh… that thing I said about family… one of those people would be my wife." If he had unmasked already, she would have known that!

11 All of this discussion is from *Amazing Spider-Man* #532. (Yes, it was a wordy issue.)

12 Yes, still *Amazing Spider-Man* #532.

13 *Amazing Spider-Man* #532—just kidding! This one was in *Civil War* #2 (August 2006), and questions were taken in *Civil War: Front Line* #2 (August 2006), "Civil War: The Program." I wasn't kidding about the real world: Spider-Man's unmasking was covered by major press here too, although I don't think his secret identity came as that much of a surprise. For example, see George Gene Gustines, "Spider-Man Unmasked," *New York Times*, June 15, 2006 (available at http://nyti.ms/1JCJTBy) and "Spider-Man Removes Mask at Last," BBC News, June 15, 2006 (available at http://news.bbc.co.uk/2/hi/entertainment/5084326.stm).

14 *Amazing Spider-Man* #533 (August 2006), through his talk with Iron Man at the end of the day (except when noted).

15 It wasn't me, I promise, although the confusion is understandable.

16 *Civil War* #3 (September 2006).

17 *Sensational Spider-Man*, vol. 2, #29 (October 2006).

18 See *Sensational Spider-Man*, vol. 2, #29–31 (October–December 2006) in particular and *Civil War: Peter Parker, Spider-Man* (2007) in general on the impact of these attacks on the people close to Peter, including not only Mary Jane and May but also the Black Cat, Liz Allen, and even the students he teaches.

[19] *Civil War* #3, shown in flashback at the beginning of *Amazing Spider-Man* #534 (September 2006).

[20] *Amazing Spider-Man* #534, through the fight with Captain America.

[21] A matter of time that includes thwarting a missile attack engineered by the Mad Thinker and Puppet Master, two of the Fantastic Four's foes, as told in *Fantastic Four* #539 (October 2006), which shows the same scene from a different view and explains why Ben Grimm, otherwise known as the ever-lovin' blue-eyed idol o' millions the Thing, becomes a conscientious objector.

[22] This was the subject of the famous debate between H.L.A. Hart and Lon Fuller in the pages of the *Harvard Law Review* in 1958, discussed by the contributors to Peter Cane (ed.), *The Hart-Fuller Debate in the Twenty-First Century* (Oxford: Hart Publishing, 2010).

[23] The proper form, dissemination, and enforcement of laws, aside from their actual content, was the subject of Lon Fuller's book *The Morality of the Law* (New Haven, CT: Yale University Press, 1964).

[24] *Amazing Spider-Man* #535 (November 2006) for the rest of this chapter.

[25] If I learned one thing from reading every Fantastic Four comic going back to issue #1 in 1961, it's this: it is not a good idea to build a portal to a chaotic and violent antimatter dimension *in your house.*

[26] Thomas Hobbes, *Leviathan* (1651), widely available online, such as at https://www.gutenberg.org/files/3207/3207-h/3207-h.htm.

[27] See George P. Fletcher, *Basic Concepts of Legal Thought* (Oxford: Oxford University Press, 1996), pp. 11–14.

Chapter 10: Whose Side Are You On, Peter?

We've seen Peter's doubts about registration, his own unmasking, and Tony Stark's role in the Civil War, build gradually from the start—remember that he was skeptical of Tony's motivation for building the Iron Spider outfit and suspected him of engineering the Titanium Man attack in Washington. As I said before, Peter may be good-natured, honorable, and a little naïve, but he's not stupid. In this chapter, we'll watch as Peter changes his mind, sides with Captain America against registration—and sees what it's like to not only skirt the edge of the law, but be hunted by it.

"I Thought You Said You Knew What You Were Doing, Tony."

The first significant crack in Peter's support for registration and Tony may have been the death of Goliath during the first major battle between the two sides in the Civil War. After the anti-registration heroes fled, leaving Tony's forces standing in disbelief in front of Goliath's fallen body, Peter flatly told Tony, "I thought you said you knew what you were doing, Tony. I thought we were doing this so no one else got hurt."[1] Back at Avengers Tower, as Reed studied the clone of Thor to try to determine went wrong, Hank Pym looked despondent. When Peter asked him if he was okay, Pym said, "No, Spider-Man, I am *not* okay. I just watched a new superhuman I helped create blow a hole through one of my oldest friends. Do you really think I'm so remote—so detached—that this wouldn't have some kind of impact on me?"[2] When Janet van Dyne (the Wasp) added that she was sorry, Peter said, "It's okay, Jan. To be honest, we're all a little freaked out. This wasn't exactly what any of us signed up for." As Hank wondered if the clone of Thor needed to be fused with a human being—as the real Thor was, in a way, with Donald Blake in his early days on Earth—Peter just asked, "Do you ever wonder if we've picked the right side here, Hank?"

Add to this the fights against former colleagues such as Captain America; the tour of the Negative Zone prison with Tony, where Peter saw firsthand the treatment of heroes held there as well as its "suddenly" permanent nature; and the conversation with Reed about his uncle Ted (all described in the last chapter). And of course, there were also his doubts about Tony's financial dealings, which he confirmed while researching with Ben Urich. When Urich expressed surprise,

141

saying that "Tony Stark was never that way" and he was "not the kind to play with people's lives for his own gain," Peter is not surprised at all: "I used to believe that, Ben. Then again, that was before he played with my life."[3]

It isn't just the reader that picks up on Peter's doubts, however. During the funeral for Goliath, while Peter huddles with Mary Jane and Aunt May, Reed—not the most emotionally perceptive guy, as his wife Sue will surely tell you—asks Doc Samson, a gamma-powered superhero therapist (really), "Is it just me or is Peter Parker acting very, very suspiciously?"[4] Tony was obviously rattled by Peter's questioning about the Negative Zone prison, a tense exchange that ended up none-too-subtle threats from Tony regarding Mary Jane's and Aunt May's safety if Peter ever turned against him.[5] And unbeknownst to Peter or Reed, Tony overheard their conversation about Reed's uncle Ted and Peter's admiration of his civil disobedience.[6]

So Tony was not surprised when Peter started to waver, and even tried to send Peter to Los Angeles to remove him from the action, saying, "I just think it would be good for you to get away from New York for a while, give you a break… help you clear your head."[7] When Peter assures him his head is clear, he asks about Mary Jane and Aunt May, and Tony assures him, "Don't worry about them. As long as they're with me, they're safe." Understandably, Peter is skeptical, decides not to go to Los Angeles, and starts taking steps himself to ensure the safety of his family. Subverting the security cameras in Avengers Tower by crawling around on the ceiling, Peter quietly wakes MJ and May and tells them they need to leave immediately because they're no longer safe. As he tells them in a cathartic (but quiet) outburst:

> I've made a terrible, terrible mistake. There's going to be a price
> to pay for that mistake and any attempt to fix it. But I have to do
> what I think is right, and right now—God help me, I realize I've
> been on the wrong side. I—

Why was Peter cut off suddenly? He heard a loud sound from inside the building, as if someone wearing armor were coming for him…

After Peter urged Mary Jane and May to get out, he armored up and ran to face Iron Man, who burst through the wall to keep him from leaving. "Thought you said… you were going out… for the night… Dad," Peter said, to which Tony replied, "and I thought you knew which side you were on."[8] As he told May and MJ minutes prior, he did—and he realized it was the wrong side. As he tells Tony, "I don't have a problem with working for SHIELD! But locking heroes in the

Negative Zone? The cyborg killing Bill Foster like that? C'mon, man! You're over your head!"[9] Tony defends his actions, saying that the cloned Thor did what he had to do (although he feels horrible about it nonetheless), normal prisons on Earth can't handle the superpower prisoners, and generally that registration is preferable to the alternative. These are all valid utilitarian arguments, and ones he's made before (as we know), but Peter has changed his mind regarding the necessity of these choices. He's come to believe that even if they do increase safety and security, these actions violate principles that he holds dear and represents things that he feels no one should do, even for the greater good. In other words, without denying the importance of what Tony is trying to do, Peter is favoring his inner deontologist as the best way to express his basically good moral character.

Of course, Tony starts pushing Peter's buttons again—and not just figurative-ly, as he triggers an override that disables the Iron Spidey suit, only to watch in surprise as Peter overrides his override.[10] As always, he touches on both Peter's duty-bound side as well as his concern for his loved ones, first by telling him, "I trusted you, Peter! I took you under my wing! Is *this* how you repay me?" and following it up soon afterwards with "Don't be a fool! You really think you can go back to your old life now that everyone knows who you are? This isn't about you anymore! What about May? What about Mary Jane?" (When Tony said "As long as they're with me, they're safe," apparently he meant "with me" in the political sense, not physically.)

None of this convinces Peter, who gets away and goes underground (literally) to hide. But he's apprehended by several of the Thunderbolts whom Tony engaged to help round up unregistered heroes, which now includes your friendly neighborhood Spider-Man.[11] The villains, B-listers at best, take advantage of Spidey's weakened condition after fighting Iron Man and nearly kill him. Frank Castle, the Punisher, kills the villains and takes the battered Spider-Man to the hideout of Captain America and the anti-registration forces. When Peter recovers, he's fully on board with Cap, who's planning the assault on the Negative Zone prison with the rest of his team. When he tells Peter that no one will judge him if he holds back because of his recent battles, Peter will hear nothing of it, telling him, "Not a chance, Cap. I need to do something to make up for all the bad moves I've made lately."[12]

Sometime between his recovery in Cap's hideout and the assault on the Nega-tive Zone prison (and the climactic battle that followed), Peter went to the school gym where Mary Jane and Aunt May are hiding. While his aunt sleeps, he checks on Mary Jane and confirms her suspicions that he has decided to fight registra-tion. "Tony's wrong. I was wrong. I have do what I can to fix this. If that means fighting Tony"—again—"then that's what I have to do."[13] Note his language: Tony is not just doing bad on the whole, but he's *wrong*, and Peter was *wrong* too. As a newly committed deontologist, he's thinking more in terms of right and wrong than good or bad, and now that he's decided he was wrong, he's taking responsibility for it, as Peter does. Furthermore, he's judged the principles that he thinks Tony violated to be more important than his duty of loyalty to Tony. This is a reminder that, just because Peter is now thinking more like a deontologist, he needs judgment just as much as ever, only in different ways (as we described in chapter 5).

Once again, Aunt May adds some valuable wisdom to the story. When Peter tells Mary Jane that he wants her and May to get far away and that "this whole mess is my responsibility and mine alone," May walks in and says, "excuse me—don't you think I should get a vote on this, Peter?" She then points out that he is not alone in this:

> You say you're responsible for this, and you are. But no more than MJ and I. You wanted to leave when this whole thing started. We talked you out of it. If you're responsible, so are we. And if we're all equally responsible for the decision, then we will all have to equally share the consequences.

Looks like Uncle Ben wasn't the only one who can teach Peter Parker about great power and great responsibility. Rather than leaving for faraway lands (or New Jersey), the Parkers three move into a motel and May gives Peter something she grabbed from Avengers Tower before they left: his original costume. She says it's because the Iron Spidey armor was compromised by Tony's spying—not to mention it was torn to shreds by the Thunderbolts in the sewers—but it's reasonable to think that his original costume also helps him feel like himself again, the Peter Parker that (eventually) does the right thing.

Let's All Make Speeches Now

Before he joins Cap and his team to break into the Negative Zone prison, Peter takes a page out of Tony Stark's playbook: he has an impromptu press conference of his own.[14] He stops at a local TV station and commandeers the camera from the weatherman, stating in no uncertain terms that he has switched sides and now stands for the principles that he believes Tony and other supporters of registration are violating.

Hello, people of New York, I've—well, I've got a confession to make. I was wrong. I made a mistake.

For the last month or so, I've been the closest person to Tony Stark—Iron Man—and I've had a chance to see his operation firsthand. I've see the very concept of justice destroyed. I've seen heroes and bad guys alike—dangerous guys, no mistake, but still born in this country for the most part, denied due process—and imprisoned, potentially for the rest of their lives, without a trial, without evidence. Held in inhumane conditions on a place called the Negative Zone.

(He goes on to make a joke about the Negative Zone being a lot like New Jersey, but I expect as much from a New Yorker.) Note that Peter not only implicates Tony for violating essential moral principles such as justice, but he also lets the public in on what's happening in the Negative Zone prison, putting the truth out there just like Captain America advised him during the HYDRA episode before the Civil War started (as we saw in chapter 8).

It is in the second part of his speech that Peter encapsulates the primary conflict at the heart of the Civil War (and, by extension, this book), as well as the climate in the United States in the real world following 9/11:

> We all want to be safe. We all want to know that we can go to bed at night and have a good chance of waking up without somebody in a costume blowing up the building. But there's a point where the end doesn't justify the means, if the means require us to give up not just our identities, but who and what we are as a country.
>
> The question isn't what does a country stand for when things are easy. The question is—what does a country stand for when standing in the hardest? When does the country we're living in stop being the country we were born in?
>
> Some people say the most important thing in the world is that we should be safe. But I was brought up to believe that some things are worth dying for. If the cost of silence is the soul of the country... if the cost of tacit support is that we lose the very things that make this nation the greatest in human history— then the price is too high.

This is an excellent statement of many of the ideas we've discussed in this book. In the first paragraph, he expertly states the criticism of utilitarian thinking that we saw back in chapter 2: it isn't that the ends *never* justify the ends, but simply that they don't *always* justify them. He also invokes national integrity, that if a country compromises its principles too easily, it risks sacrificing its very identity.

Finally, in the last paragraph, Peter deftly flips the relationship of principles and consequences that we described in chapter 5. There, we saw that maintaining one's principles may be fine until the price becomes too high—which explains why Captain America surrendered to end the final battle of the Civil War—but here, Peter explains that it can go the other way as well. If we pursue the good, such as safety and security, with no attention to what we are losing in the process, the cost in terms of sacrificed principles and integrity may itself be too high. In the end, Peter is arguing for balance, a way to secure an adequate level of security without giving up essential liberties and justice.

He wraps up his speech as he began it, speaking from the heart as Peter Parker (by now having removed his mask):

> I cannot, in good conscience, continue to support the registra-
> tion act as it has been created and enforced. I was wrong, and
> from this day on, I will do everything within my power to op-
> pose the act and anyone attempting to intimidate and arrest
> those who also oppose the act, in the cause of freedom.

Not only does he believe that the creators and supporters of registration went too far—as he told Ben Urich earlier, "this whole thing has gone far beyond where anyone thought it would go"—but he personally will no longer be a part of it, and furthermore, he will oppose anyone supporting it.[15] This, once again, is Peter Parker doing what he does best: taking responsibility, whether it's based on consequences or principles that he supports.

The next day, Captain America tries to find Peter to protect him from Tony, first by asking the Human Torch to "send up a flare"—which Johnny interprets as a huge, spider-shaped flare that says "Call me"—and then by going out himself with the Falcon. When Falcon warns him that it could be a trap, Cap agrees. When Falcon says, "but you trust him," Cap answers, "this isn't a time for trust."[16] As Cap tells his longtime partner and friend, he has no doubt that Tony would ask Peter to go on TV and pretend to have switched sides just to lure Cap and his forces out. He even supposes that Peter might try to go along with it. "But I've worked with Peter, and the thing about him is that he's the worst liar I've ever seen. He has too much respect for the truth, so when he lies, it shows. And what I saw on his face last night was the unvarnished truth." Falcon agrees, but points out that Stark knows this too, and could have maneuvered Peter into making his honest confession in order to draw Cap out. As he wisely points out, "that he's telling the truth doesn't mean he's not being used," and "if he's being used, then you're being used." Even if Cap acknowledges the truth of what the Falcon says, he chooses to believe in Peter—and perhaps, in a way, he chooses to believe in Tony as well.

When Spider-Man finds Captain America waiting for him, Cap praises his speech as brave yet foolish. When Peter says, "I had to get a message out, to the people, so they'd understand what's going on," Cap bursts his bubble, explaining that what the media took from his statement was not his revelations about the Negative Zone prison, his general points about justice, or the ends not justifying the means, but only that he's "challenging the government." This leads Peter to ask Cap, whom the media has now "pegged as a Benedict Arnold and a traitor to the American cause," how he deals with it: "How does the man who *is* the country react when the country goes a different way?" Cap starts his answer with a long quote from Mark Twain that he read as a boy, in which the classic American writer emphasizes that, in a democracy, the people are the country. The country is not the government that the people grant limited powers to—contrary to how Reed phrased it earlier—and not the media, who are merely a part of it, albeit an important part. And as such, the people must decide when the government is right or wrong and must act according to their consciences, even if they come to be labeled as traitors, because following your principles and convictions is the best way to serve the country of which you are a part.[17]

After finishing quoting Mark Twain, Captain America waxes eloquent himself, echoing what he said to Sharon Carter at the beginning of the conflict about the nation being borne of rebellion.[18] As he says to Peter,

> Doesn't matter what the press says. Doesn't matter what the politicians or the mobs say. Doesn't matter if the whole country decides that something wrong is something right. This nation was founded on one principle above all else: the requirement that we stand up for what we believe, no matter the odds or the consequences. When the mob and the press and the whole world tell you to move, your job is to plant yourself like a tree beside the river of truth, and tell the whole world—"no, you move."

This is an astonishingly powerful statement about the importance of maintaining personal principles, convictions, and integrity in face of overwhelming disapproval, an expression of the outward side of Immanuel Kant's autonomy as well as later existentialist insights about self-creation and resisting pressure from others to affect how a person defines himself or herself.[19]

Peter stares in silent awe (and then asks if he can carry Cap's books to school) before Cap says they need to back to the rest of the team. As they move, Peter thinks to himself,

> as I run toward the edge of the roof, off the edge of what I've known and into the darkness of whatever's coming, beside the one hero who will never betray his convictions, never betray those who followed him, I think—it feels good to be on the right again.

But this impression is soon tested as the two sides in the Civil War meet in the final battle, which is abruptly stopped when Captain America surrenders.

On the surface, Peter seems disappointed, telling Cap that "we were beating them, man. We were winning back there."[20] However, his inner monologue during the final battle suggests more ambivalence. For instance, he also recognizes the human impact of the Civil War; he thinks to himself, "Whether a law is right or wrong, moral or immoral, is an idea, a personal philosophy… but it always seems that fights over ideas skip over the barrier into the real world and become battles of real violence."[21] This thought moderates another one, this one about Cap: "All I know… is that now that the final battle has started, I can't stop… won't stop… until and unless he stops. And he won't. He'll never sacrifice what he stands for. Not as long as he's alive."

These two statements are consistent if we take the broader view of what Captain America stands for, especially in light of the reason for his surrender: he was reminded, by the citizens who pulled him off of Tony, of his principle of serving and protecting the people, principles that had been forgotten while he was focused on promoting the principles of liberty and justice. All of these principles are important, and as we've seen throughout this series, no one of them takes absolute priority. We have to find the optimal balance, which is what Cap and Iron Man disagree on, as well as what we disagree on in the real world regarding security and liberty in the post-9/11 world.

But we should also recognize that the conflict at the heart of the Civil War was not simply the people's safety and security on the one hand versus superheroes' liberty and privacy on the other. Ultimately, those who opposed registration, such as Cap and Spider-Man, were doing so to be able to serve the people better. This was the case Peter made to the Senate subcommittee when he appeared there with Tony before the SHRA passed, and this same idea was in his thoughts as the final battle raged. Referring to the people paying attention to the conflict and affected by the battle, he wondered to himself "if any of them realize we're not really fighting for ourselves, for our turf, for the right to wear a mask... we're fighting for *them*. For our ability to be there, without condition, when the darkness comes." You could say that, ultimately, all the characters in this story are consequentialists insofar as they want to protect people from harm, whether natural, human, or otherwise. They disagree, however, on how to best do that: by structuring their activities and institutions by consequentialist logic, or following principles that will lead to the best consequences.

This parallels Peter Parker's struggle to find the best way to protect his loved ones, by following either Tony in support of registration or Captain America in opposition to it. This can also be applied to moral theories in general: both utilitarianism and deontology are aimed at the same thing, behaving ethically. They just disagree on how to do that, but with a few exceptions on the extreme margins of normal everyday decision-making, both will lead to good decisions and often the same decisions (such as not lying and being helpful). Just like Iron Man and Captain America, good friends and fellow Avengers before *and* after the Civil War, utilitarianism and deontology are not as opposed as we might like to think (though it makes for very dramatic storytelling to pretend they are for a while).

~~~~~

Speaking of "after the Civil War," do you think everything returned to normal after Captain America surrendered? Hardly. In the next part of the book, we'll see how the choices made during the Civil War extended into the future, and the ways our three heroes benefited and suffered for them. (Mainly the latter.)

---

[1] *Civil War* #4 (November 2006), for the rest of this paragraph.
[2] Skrulls are good, aren't they?
[3] *Civil War: Front Line* #9 (February 2007), "Embedded Part 9."

[4] *Civil War* #4.

[5] *Amazing Spider-Man* #535 (November 2006).

[6] This was shown, not in *Amazing Spider-Man* #535, but in *Fantastic Four* #540 (December 2006), where the same conversation was shown but with Tony listening in.

[7] *Amazing Spider-Man* #535 for the rest of this paragraph.

[8] *Amazing Spider-Man* #535. This scene also appears in *Civil War* #5 (November 2006) but told slightly differently and with completely different dialogue (and location—oops).

[9] *Civil War* #5, throughout the rest of the battle (except where noted).

[10] As shown in *Amazing Spider-Man* #536 (November 2006).

[11] *Civil War* #5.

[12] *Civil War* #6 (December 2006).

[13] *Amazing Spider-Man* #536.

[14] *Amazing Spider-Man* #536 (for the entirety of his televised address). Somewhere in this timespan he also finds time to get thoroughly walloped by the Rhino (*Sensational Spider-Man*, vol. 2, #32, January 2007).

[15] *Civil War: Front Line* #9, "Embedded Part 9."

[16] *Amazing Spider-Man*, vol. 1, #537 (December 2006), through the end of Cap's speech and Peter's reaction (except where noted).

[17] The long passage recited by Captain America is from a fragment of an unpublished book by Mark Twain titled either *Glances at History* or *Outlines of History*, about which very little is known, but is available in Bernard A. DeVoto (ed.), *Letters from the Earth: Uncensored Writings by Mark Twain* (New York: HarperPerennial, 1962), pp. 107–109. The complete text can also be found at http://web.mit.edu/norvin/www/somethingelse/twain.html.

[18] *New Avengers*, vol. 1, #21 (August 2006).

[19] On existentialism, see Steven Crowell, "Existentialism," *Stanford Encyclopedia of Philosophy*, March 9, 2015, at http://plato.stanford.edu/entries/existentialism/.

[20] *Civil War* #7 (January 2007).

[21] *Amazing Spider-Man* #538 (January 2007) through the rest of the chapter.

Part IV: The Aftermath of the Civil War

After Captain America surrendered and told his "troops" to stand down, the Civil War was over at last. As journalist Sally Floyd described the aftermath of the final battle, countless buildings, bodies, and spirits all lay broken. As she thought, "History would tell us we dodged a bullet that day. We were too busy putting out fires to notice," and then described the massive clean-up efforts involved and wished the heroes had worked this hard to fix things before they all went to hell. In *Civil War: Front Line* #11 (April 2007), her colleague Ben Urich wrote, "We pretended to begin the rebuilding. Even though we were all just waiting for it to blow up in our faces again." And on the political front, as we hear from a TV news anchor (in *Amazing Spider-Man* #538, January 2007),

> the president is now meeting with his advisors to craft a speech he will give to the nation later tonight. Meanwhile, members of the Senate and the House of Representatives are saying that the conflict is now at an end, and that the parties on all sides should now come together in the best interest of the nation. To put our differences behind us.

After some time, things will return to a sort of "normal," but what exactly does that normal look like, and what long-term consequences of the Civil War can we see throughout the Marvel Universe?

In this final part of the book, we'll look at the fallout from the Civil War through the eyes of the three main characters we've covered so far: Spider-Man, Iron Man, and Captain America (although Cap's will be somewhat brief because he was assassinated soon after he surrendered). We'll take Spidey first because the consequences to him were the most direct and personal, touching him, Mary Jane, and his Aunt May in ways from which they manage to recover (but in a particularly unexpected fashion). Next we'll look at Iron Man, the character out of the three who felt the longest effects of the Civil War. He was appointed as director of SHIELD just in time to deal with the death of Captain America, the return of the Hulk, and the revelation of the Skrull secret invasion. The ramifications of the last incident were as monumental for Tony as the Civil War was, but again, in a very personal way. It also resulted in a change in command, replacing Tony Stark with

Norman Osborne, the former Green Goblin, who made Tony look hands-off in comparison. Defeating Norman took the one hero who could never really be replaced…

But I'm getting ahead of myself. Let's start with Peter Parker and how his life fell to pieces immediately after returning to Mary Jane and Aunt May after the final battle of the Civil War.

Chapter 11: Spider-Man, Back in Black and Out for Blood

When Spider-Man first encountered Captain America after registration began, the older hero asked him, "Is Mary Jane happy about the Sandman having her ZIP code now?"[1] Of course, that had been Peter Parker's primary concern since Tony first told him about registration and asked him to unmask in public: the safety of Mary Jane and Aunt May, the reason he worked so hard to protect his identity in the first place, especially after the Green Goblin killed his first girlfriend, Gwen Stacy, after learning his true identity.[2] Later, after he unmasked, he burst through the window of their Avengers Tower apartment to find Aunt May standing over an unconscious Chameleon (whose cookies she laced with Ambien). Peter told his beloved aunt, "I've made you and MJ targets. Taken away what little semblance of a normal life we had. God, if the Chameleon had hurt you or… or worse…." May reassures him, saying "there, there, Peter, we'll get through this. We always do…," but he ominously replies, "Not all of us, Aunt May, not always… ."[3]

This was a prophetic statement, as we'll see in this chapter when we survey Peter's experiences after the Civil War ended. His decision to reveal his identity had momentous consequences for his loved ones, and pushed him as far to the dark side as he had ever gone, and in the process risked his integrity, even considered broadly. Have far did he go? Let's see…

The Fear Is Realized

Many of Peter's foes came out of the woodwork to strike out at his family, but none was as vicious as Wilson Fisk, otherwise known as the Kingpin, who learned of Peter's unmasking from the confines of his cozy prison cell (serving as a fitting contrast to the conditions unregistered heroes suffered in Iron Man's Negative Zone prison). After Peter makes his later television appearance in opposition to registration and leaves Avengers Tower with his family to hide in a motel, the Kingpin orders his associates to find him, and gets results when a fellow motel resident sees Peter walk by holding a newspaper with his picture on the front page.[4] (Disguising himself as Dale Gribble from *King of the Hill* did not fool her.) The Kingpin then orders a hit on Peter, but as his associate tells the hitman, if he can't get "the target"… well, you know.

When Peter returns to the motel room after the final battle of the Civil War, he triggers a sensor set by the assassin, who wakes from his restful slumber to find Peter and Mary Jane standing in front of the motel room window.[5] As the assassin sets up his shot, Peter's spider-sense goes off and he pushes Mary Jane to the floor as the bullet crashes through the window. He asks MJ if she's OK, only to hear Aunt May's voice say, weakly, "P—Peter…," and when he looks up to the bed, she is bleeding from a gunshot wound to her left abdomen.

The assassin keeps firing shots, and Peter, saying the words, "no more" over and over, rushes out of the motel room and hurls a jeep in the direction of the gunshots.[6] Then he grabs May and swings to the nearest hospital while she mutters, "Peter… you shouldn't… people will see you, they'll know who you… I'm sorry… I… I made a mess of… of… so sorry…," and then passes out. Peter breaks through the window of an empty hospital room and leaves her there to be attended by the staff while he sticks to the wall outside, clenching his fists with rage while tears flow from his eyes.

When Fisk hears from a prison guard that Peter wasn't hurt but one of his companions was, he quotes the ancient Greek playwright Euripides: "Whom the gods would destroy… first they drive mad."[7] And this is exactly what happens to Peter. After he finds Mary Jane "hiding in the open" in Times Square—this is before the age of ubiquitous surveillance cameras, ironically—he tells her that May is in critical condition and it's all his fault. After making plans with MJ to register May under her maiden name and pay cash for her treatment, he leaves, telling his wife he's going "to do what I do best when I really put my mind to it, MJ… I'm going to hurt someone." As he thinks to himself later while chasing down the assassin, there's nothing he can do to save May—he can't even be at her side without risking arrest—so chasing down the people responsible is "all I can do. All I know how to do."

At this point Peter has taken leave of his principles and is driven purely by revenge—the only question, at this point, is how far he will go to avenge this wrong that, ultimately, he holds himself responsible for. As he thinks to himself while savagely beating lowlifes who he hopes can lead him to the man responsible, "on this night—the rules are gone. No jokes. No punches pulled. As of tonight, no one gets away. No one threatens my family. No one." After he gets a lead on the gun dealer who sells the unique gunsight he found at the assassin's perch, he changes into his black costume, which he stopped wearing because it "sent the wrong message."[8] Exactly what message he meant is revealed in his inner monologue, which also makes it clear that things have changed:

> Maybe I kept it because there might come a day when I'd *want* to send that message. That the rules don't apply anymore. That the gloves are off. That I won't stop, *can't* be stopped, until I find the people responsible for shooting May. I will find them. And when I do—I'm going to kill them.

This is Peter Parker with all restraint gone, all safeguards dismissed, and willing to use any means available to achieve his end—and a noble end it is not.

Step by step, Peter tracks down the assassin, apprehending him in Grand Central Station as he tries to board a train. After Peters breaks his arm while delivering dialogue straight out of the Punisher's handbook, the assassin is about to give up the person who hired him when multiple gunshots ring out, killing him. As Peter sticks to the outside of the ambulance that rushes the assassin to the hospital—the same hospital where May is being treated—he thinks to himself, "was I really prepared to kill him for shooting May? And the answer comes back. Yes."[9] Reflecting on that, he thinks, "In another time and place I would've been ashamed of that answer. But not now... not this day." This passage shows us that Peter has not lost his awareness of what he's doing. He knows he's gone over the edge, but he's justifying it to himself, excusing himself from his normally upright moral code due to his overwhelming grief and pain at the impending death of the woman who raised him. This recalls what Seneca, a Stoic philosopher, wrote about anger, cautioning that it must be resisted and, once submitted to, it cannot be controlled. As he wrote, "It is easier to exclude the forces of ruin than to govern them... once they have established possession, they prove to be more powerful than their governor, refusing to be cut back or reduced."[10]

As he holds Mary Jane outside the hospital, Peter's spider-sense picks up the tracer he tossed on the man who shot the assassin in Grand Central: he is nearby, monitoring the assassin's progress and reporting back by phone to the Kingpin. Peter quickly webs his mouth shut, takes the phone, and instantly recognizes the voice. "Hello, Mr. Fisk," he says, and when the Kingpin asks what he can do for Peter, Peter does his best Bond villain impression and says, "Just one thing, Mr. Fisk. You can die." When Fisk says he can't die—he has people to do that for him—Peter continues, "In the last 48 hours, I've broken just about every law there is, Mr. Fisk. What's one more?"[11] In his thoughts, he reaffirms that he plans to kill "anyone directly involved in the shooting," but he makes distinctions between those responsible—such as the shooter who already died and the Kingpin—and the lackey he caught outside the hospital. As far over the edge as Peter has gone in terms of his goal of murdering those responsible for May's condition, it is encouraging to see he still makes important moral distinctions regarding how he pursues that goal.

Meet the Kingpin

After frightening a punk in the subway into telling the rest of the underworld to stay away from his family, and giving a quick blood transfusion to May, hoping his radioactive-spider-enhanced blood might keep her going a bit longer, Peter breaks into the prison where the Kingpin is held. Now changed into his trademark natty white tuxedo and cane, Fisk delivers a fantastic speech about a type of person everyone held in the prison looks down on: the chump.

> A chump is someone who believes in the greater good. Who believes that good triumphs *because* it is good. Trusts the government, trusts his fellow citizen, trusts the man in the iron mask who says "Show the world your true face, Peter. It'll be okay."
>
> And we all saw that face, didn't we? The face of a chump. A chump who is now hunted by the people he believed in, spurned by the system he supported, abandoned by the friends he thought he had, his wife living in a two-bit motel and his dear, sweet aunt dying in a hospital bed because he couldn't even stand still long enough to take the bullet that was his by right.[12]

It is easy to call Peter a chump in hindsight (not to mention from behind prison walls), but all through the process, Peter had his eye on Tony Stark, a man he knew could be manipulative and self-serving. Nonetheless, Peter went along with registration and the unmasking because, at the time, he believed it was the right thing to do, both for consequentialist reasons of protecting his family, which may have been borne out had he remained with Tony, and deontological reasons of loyalty. (It was loyalty to an imperfect person, to be sure, but when you find a perfect person, be sure to let me know!)

Peter, silent in his new guise as an avenging angel, starts beating on the Kingpin, who only continues his analysis:

> Even his usual sense of humor and devil-may-care attitude seems to have abandoned him. Must be terribly distressing and unfortunate to have absolutely nothing left in life except the desire for revenge. Which is especially unfortunate since once you've made a mockery of everything you stand for and victim-

ized the women you said you loved, really, what's left *except* humor?

Kingpin realizes all too well what he has done to Peter, who was already questioning his principles and motivations after his experiences in the Civil War, and has now been reduced to his most primal desire.[13] He even touches a little bit of existentialism when he highlights the absurdity of life without meaning (and instructs us to create that meaning for ourselves).[14]

After they fight some more and the Kingpin finally goads him into speaking, Peter tells him what the black costume stands for, "a promise about all the things I said I would do—and all the things I said I would never do... all the lines I said I would never, ever cross because doing so would destroy everything this suit stands for." Then he tells Fisk that *he's* not here to kill him—meaning Spider-Man—and after unmasking he says "*I* am." This distinction is reminiscent of Captain America's surrender, in which he was careful to say that Captain America himself is not surrendering, but instead Steve Rogers—a symbolic distinction but an important one nonetheless. Peter doesn't want to sully the reputation of Spider-Man any more than it has already been, nor does he want to pretend that what he does to the Kingpin is "excused" in any way by his role as a superhero. Fisk got to him as Peter Parker, and Peter Parker will be the one to... well, we'll see.

Peter continues to thoroughly batter and mock the Kingpin and then threatens to fill Fisk's lungs with web fluid until he suffocates, slowly and painfully. He counts to three but then merely throws Fisk across the room. When Fisk demands that Peter get it over with, Peter tells him that he is going to kill him, but not today. "You see," he says, "I've learned something from you, Fisk. Something about cruelty... and timing. I've done something far worse than kill you, Fisk. I've beaten you. And every man in this room saw me beat you." Peter realizes that beating the Kingpin, who needs people to believe he cannot be beaten, is very likely for him a living hell much worse than death.

But Peter hasn't forgotten what Fisk did, or that he vowed to kill him. He tells Fisk that if his aunt dies, he will come for him, and that Fisk now knows that there is nothing he can do to stop him. More interesting is Peter's reasoning, which he explains to Fisk:

> You see, I've always tried to avoid killing anyone partly for my
> own principles and partly because I was always afraid how it
> would affect my family if I killed someone. But if my aunt is

> dead, well… that takes care of one reason, and the other… well, I can make an exception.

It's not clear what he means about his family, whether he feared what they would think of him or what would happen to them after violence escalated between him and his foes. (Not to mention, why is Aunt May his only family now?) Of more interest is the exception he claims to his principles against killing.

As we've seen throughout this book, deeply held principles can come into conflict, in which case one must be set aside momentarily in favor of one judged to be more important at the time. This extends to even the principle against killing, which Captain America had to set aside when faced with a terrorist starting to massacre innocent civilians (as we discussed in the last chapter). The question here is: on what basis is he making an exception in this case? In other words, why would he allow himself to kill the Kingpin (if May dies)? It may be as simple a reason as vengeance, rage, and grief, if Peter is not thinking rationally and instead allows his emotions to control his actions. This might not be a good reason or an ethical reason, but it would certainly be understandable as an explanation.

But something he says to the Kingpin as he prepares to leave suggests that his reasons go deeper: "You ordered her death, Fisk, so it is only appropriate that your life ends when hers does." This invokes a concept from the philosophy of punishment known as *retributivism*, which holds that punishment is owed to wrongdoers as a matter of right and justice.[15] It is often associated with the *lex talionis*, the biblical prescription of "an eye for an eye," but most modern forms of retributivism are not that simple (or brutal). Retributivism does, however, demand a certain degree of proportionality between crime and punishment, so that more serious crimes are punished more harshly (and less serious ones punished more lightly). The concept of retributivism is often defended in terms of debt, that criminals "owe" something to their victims or society at large, or annulment, that punishment in a way "cancels out" a crime (though not in a literal sense), both of which are relevant to Peter's statement that it is "appropriate" that Fisk die if May dies because he was the one who ordered the hit.

There's a hitch, though: retributivism is usually applied only to punishment carried out by an official state agency charged with such a duty, not a private citizen. One of the distinctions made between retributivist punishment and mere vengeance is the impersonal, detached nature of punishment, in which the judge, jury, and prosecutor have no connection to the case at hand and therefore are not personally vested in its resolution. Under these conditions, punishment is more likely to be imposed for reasons of right and justice, as required by retributivism, rather than out of pain and anguish on the part of loved ones of the victim. This distinction is also widely used when discussing vigilantes, a term sometimes applied to all masked superheroes, but is more accurately applied to those who assume the act of punishment itself, such as (obviously) the Punisher, or, in the current storyline, Peter Parker, if he goes through with his threat. So while Peter may justify his "exception" to himself on retributivist grounds, his sudden turn to this point of view suggests that his desire for revenge, as Fisk put it, is his true motivation.

Just Give Up

After he leaves the Kingpin, Peter has a moment to reflect on his recent behavior, and he realizes how over the line he's gone (even without killing anybody). After subduing a police detective investigating May's shooting, he thinks to himself,

> All my life, I wondered what first step some of the criminals I'd fought had taken to become what they were. Up to this moment, my criminality was a point of legal technicalities. I'd skirted illegality, done some questionable things… but this… *this*… you get sent to jail for. And they'd be right in doing so. Until now, when they said I was a criminal, I knew they were wrong. But now, for the first time, I *am* all those things.[16]

Dressed in scrubs, Peter takes May to another hospital in a stolen ambulance with a forged transfer form. By his count, he committed nine felonies in that episode alone, and thinks, "I have become the very thing I set out to fight. A criminal." One could argue that this was made necessary by the registration act that made him a criminal of conscience, and all of his resulting crimes were done to help Aunt May in the legal environment created by the registration act (and those who supported it). Peter may even realize these things, but the principle of obedience to the law remains very important to him, even when he had a very strong reason to set it aside.

But often, sticking to the right principles doesn't turn out well for the one doing the sticking, or those close to him or her. While he watched May and Mary Jane from across the street, Peter agonized over the consequences over his actions and, more interestingly, how they seemed to depend not a lick on what he did.

> I'm so sorry, Aunt May. ... I should have found a way to... to spare you this... I never should have unmasked. But... I was just trying to do the right thing. What the hell kind of life am I leading, where whether I do the right thing or wrong thing, it doesn't matter... because the people I love still suffer.[17]

It is natural to think that doing the right thing will lead to good consequences, but that's mixing two ethical systems that don't always play well together, especially at the extremes where Peter finds himself during this period. (If virtue is its own reward, that's to make us feel better for the lack of other, more obvious rewards.)

The tragic nature of the hero, whether in the comic books or real life, is that they often make great sacrifices in order to do the right thing. The plight of Peter Parker since his origin in 1961 has been that things tend not to work out for him despite the fact that he always tries to do the right thing. Furthermore, the difficulty with predicting the outcomes of choices—even for supposed "futurists" such as Tony Stark—serves as a practical argument for deontological ethics. You may not be able to predict which actions out of many will create the most good, but you may be able to determine which one is right. You may be wrong, of course, or circumstances may change what the right choice is, but at least you don't have to worry about predicting the future under a number of different contingencies. But this can be a difficult conclusion to reach but the consequences on each side of a decision are potentially catastrophic ("the sky may fall").

However, the one constant about Peter Parker is that he never gives up; what he said about Captain America during the final battle of the Civil War applies just as well to him. But even this "choice" haunts him: what if things might have been better for those he loves if he had given up? He considers this when a police officer orders him to give himself up, and he flies off the handle:

> Give up? Do you have any idea how easy that would be for me? Do you? Giving up would be a blessing! To throw my hands up! Turn myself over to you guys! Rot in some jail cell or the Negative Zone or whatever! The idea of "giving up" sits in my brain like a cancer, twenty-four/seven, just... just gnawing away at me! Maybe if I'd given up years ago, my aunt wouldn't have taken a bullet! My wife wouldn't be living in fear! Everyone I've ever loved has suffered because I wouldn't give up! Wouldn't give up helping cops or innocent people! Wouldn't give up the good fight! God in heaven... you talk to me about giving up?[18]

It's simple: his belief in the maxim that "with great power comes great responsibility" will not allow him to give up, not as long as he thinks he still has good to do in the world. This attitude he shares with both Captain America and Iron Man, as we've seen throughout this book, both in Cap's dedication to duty and principles as well as Tony's determination to make the hard decisions that need to be made.

Naturally, Peter's faith in his own purpose and usefulness was particularly shaken during this time; at one point, he did offer to turn himself in to the authorities in exchange for immunity for Mary Jane and May.[19] It's interesting that, at the end of his rant to the officer, he said "God in heaven… you talk to me about giving up?"—because that's exactly what happened next. In the most surreal Spidey comic published during this period, God appears to Peter in the form of a mysterious man in an alley and tries to restore Peter's faith in himself.[20] Peter asks if Aunt May's death is part of his grand plan, to which God responds with a question: "If I told you it were… what would you do, Peter?" Peter says, "I would beg you to save her. I would tell you I'd give up anything to save her." God asks if that includes being Spider-Man, and Peter says, "in a heartbeat," asking God to have the spider bite someone else and save him the deaths of so many close to him.

God then transports them to a beach where Peter used to go as a child with his uncle and aunt. When Peter asks what's the point of the pain, suffering, and anguish if there isn't a clear purpose or meaning—the same existential questions we all ask at some point—God points to a crowd of people on the beach and says, "well, for starters… they are. They're some of the point, Peter," an "an itsy-bitsy, teeny-weeny sampling of all the thousands upon thousands of people you've saved as Spider-Man over the years."[21] (Yes, the Almighty said "itsy-bitsy teeny-weeny"—hey, comics don't lie.) Although this shows Peter that being Spider-Man has value and why he's right to never give up, it doesn't answer his questions about suffering, such as why he can't seem to help people as Spider-Man without enduring all the pain of death among those he loves. Philosophers and theologians wondered this for centuries, and even God has no answers for that, simply telling Peter that it's his role to play—his responsibility.

One More Day

Even though Peter's belief in his role may have been salvaged, Aunt May still lay dying in a hospital bed, and her time was growing short. Luckily, the doctor taking care of May had an uncle who was one of the "thousands upon thousands," so he was willing to stall the billing department as long as possible, but said a "bottomless checkbook" would be great.[22] So Peter went after the only person he blamed as much as he blamed himself and who, coincidentally, happened to have a bottomless checkbook.

Peter breaks into Avengers Tower to find Tony, who threatens him with arrest. After a brief but intense battle, Peter covers Tony with webbing—as a spider does to his prey, of course. After he tells Tony that Aunt May is dying, he gets to the core issue between them, Tony's betrayal of Peter's trust and loyalty:

> I trusted you! I let you get close to me... you were like a father to me! I trusted you when you said I had to expose my identity! That it was the only way! I kept it secret to protect May, and MJ, but you said they'd be safe! You said—and now... now she's lying in a hospital bed... dying... and they're going to stick her in some damned charity ward... because I can't pay for it... because I'm on the run... because she was hurt when they came after me and found her.

Tony apologizes and says he didn't know, but that he can't help—he can't have any financial links to Peter or his family with the position he's now in (as director of SHIELD). "The stakes are bigger than you, or me... or even May," he says. "I'm sorry, Peter." Tony does let Peter leave, "out of respect for May," but promises that if he returns, he will take him in.

The financial situation is rectified, however, when the Avengers' butler Jarvis walks into the hospital with a two-million-dollar check to pay for the care of his "cousin May Morgan, from Blackpool." (His tears when he sees May in her room are heartbreaking.) But Peter doesn't stop with money, reaching out to everyone he knows with special knowledge or abilities, heroes and villains alike, including the famous medical specialists, Doctors Richards, Strange, and even Doom.[23] But the answer is always the same: it is May's time, and Peter should accept it and simply be with her when that time comes.

And that may have been the end of the story, had Peter not received a visit from Mephisto, the Marvel Universe's version of Satan, who suggests a bargain to save May's life.[24] He asks Peter, "You said you would do anything to save her. Is that true, or was it just a lie? Are you or are you not interested in the terms of the bargain?" Peter says he can't make the decision alone, so Mephisto transports Mary Jane to be by his side, and then makes his offer. He will change history so that Aunt May will live, but that change will also take away the one thing that, for Peter, "gives you joy, that which sustains you in your moments of greatest despair": his marriage. After one more day together, Peter and Mary Jane's marriage will be erased from reality and memory, other than "a very small part of your soul that will remember and will know what you lost. And my joy will be in listening to that part of your soul screaming throughout eternity."

This is the epitome of the choice between incommensurable options that we've seen several times in this story (and this book). There is no common scale on which one can compare a life and a marriage, both of which are of tremendous yet immeasurable value to a person. Peter and Mary Jane debate this choice, considering that May has lived a long, full life and maybe it is her time, but Peter can't forget that her situation is, to a large extent, his fault. "I'm responsible," he tells MJ. "Even if I'm not, even if we argue all the logical ways I'm not... in my heart, I am. And if that's what kills her—I couldn't live with that, MJ. I just couldn't live with myself. I'd break in two."[25]

When Mephisto returns after the one day, Mary Jane asks how they know, if he saves May, she won't just die the next day when another one of Spider-Man's enemies seeks revenge? So Mephisto sweetens the deal: when he changes history, he will also restore Peter's secret identity.[26] With that added assurance, Mary Jane immediately accepts the deal, and soon thereafter, Peter does as well. As time runs out, Mary Jane tells Peter that even though they'll have no memory of their marriage, they will find each other and be together again. And with that, Peter wakes up in his bed and finds Aunt May, hale and hearty, cooking breakfast in the kitchen. As the new status quo in the comics was called, it was a "Brand New Day" for Peter Parker and Spider-Man.[27]

To say this change was controversial with comics fans would be an understatement; to this day, it is common to hear former Spidey readers say they haven't read the title since the marriage was "forgotten." There are also significant issues behind the scenes of the comics regarding motivation for the change and whether it was consistent with Peter Parker's character for him to make a deal with the devil (literally).[28] For us, it had the unfortunate effect of abruptly altering the consequences of his decisions during the Civil War, both in terms of reversing the unmasking and saving Aunt May. The only remaining significant effect going forward would be his continued illegal status, both as a solo hero and a member of Luke Cage's underground Avengers team, and his being just friends with Mary Jane (although various stories since then have flirted with the reunion she promised him before Mephisto's spell took hold).

~~~~~

And with that, Peter's story ends. To see longer, continued, and often calamitous consequences from the Civil War, we have to look to the two heroes at the center of the battle, Captain America and Iron Man, whose fates continued to be closely linked, even after Cap's death.

---

[1] *Civil War* #3 (September 2006).

[2] *Amazing Spider-Man*, vol. 1, #121 (June 1973).

[3] *Sensational Spider-Man*, vol. 2, #31 (December 2006).

[4] *Amazing Spider-Man* #537 (December 2006). For most of this chapter, which is more chronological than we've seen to this point, these citations serve more as markers of when events described are from a new issue of the comic.

[5] *Amazing Spider-Man* #538 (January 2007).

[6] *Amazing Spider-Man* #539 (April 2007).

[7] I hesitate to question the Kingpin of Crime—especially after watching Vincent D'Onofrio's incredible performance on the Netflix series *Daredevil*—but this phrase appears even earlier, such as in the play *Antigone* by Sophocles in 442 BCE (http://classics.mit.edu/Sophocles/antigone.html).

[8] Spider-Man's black costume debuted in *Amazing Spider-Man*, vol. 1, #252 (May 1984), with its "origin" partially revealed in *Marvel Super Heroes Secret Wars* #8 (December 1984). For more, see *Spider-Man: Birth of Venom* (2007).

[9] *Amazing Spider-Man* #540 (May 2007).

[10] Seneca, "On Anger," Book I, 7(2), collected in John M. Cooper and J.F. Procopé (eds), *Seneca: Moral and Political Essays* (Cambridge: Cambridge University Press, 1995).

[11] *Amazing Spider-Man* #541 (June 2007).

[12] *Amazing Spider-Man* #542 (August 2007).

[13] By now, the Kingpin is an expert at breaking down people psychologically: see, for instance, what he did to Matt Murdock in the classic story *Daredevil: Born Again* (1987).

[14] Again, on existentialism, see Steven Crowell, "Existentialism," *Stanford Encyclopedia of Philosophy*, March 9, 2015, at http://plato.stanford.edu/entries/existentialism/.

[15] See Alec Walen, "Retributive Justice," *Stanford Encyclopedia of Philosophy*, June 18, 2014, at http://plato.stanford.edu/entries/justice-retributive/.

---

[16] *Amazing Spider-Man* #543 (October 2007).

[17] *Friendly Neighborhood Spider-Man* #20 (July 2007).

[18] *Friendly Neighborhood Spider-Man* #21 (August 2007).

[19] *Sensational Spider-Man Annual*, vol. 2, #1 (May 2007).

[20] *Sensational Spider-Man*, vol. 2, #40 (October 2007).

[21] Peter asks, "thousands upon thousands? Really?," to which God responds, "Well, I'm counting team-ups, but… yeah. At least."

[22] *Amazing Spider-Man* #544 (October 2007).

[23] *Friendly Neighborhood Spider-Man* #24 (November 2007). To be fair, Doctor Strange *is* a medical doctor as well as Sorcerer Supreme.

[24] *Sensational Spider-Man*, vol. 2, #41 (December 2007). This divine deal was foreshadowed to some extent when Mary Jane waits for Peter to return from the final battle of the Civil War, and says, "Just let him come home safe, God. I'll do anything, give up anything, if you'll just… let him come home. Please. I'll give up anything… anything… anything" (*Amazing Spider-Man* #538).

[25] *Amazing Spider-Man* #545 (January 2008).

[26] While he changed history to erase Peter and Mary Jane's marriage, he did not change the events of the Civil War and the unmasking remained. The way it worked was that everyone remembered seeing Spider-Man unmask but could not seem to remember who was under the mask. (Even YouTube videos would appear blurry to people.) Only if he revealed his identity to someone did they remember if they knew it before; for instance, see *Amazing Spider-Man* #590–591 (both June 2009), in which the Fantastic Four, some of his oldest friends in the biz, struggle to understand why they can't remember who Spidey is, and how they find out.

[27] For the details of how Mephisto changed Peter and Mary Jane's history (told in the comics several years later), see *Spider-Man: One Moment in Time* (2010), and for the beginning of Spidey's new single status, see *Spider-Man: Brand New Day Vol. 1* (2008).

[28] For more on this controversy, see my chapter "The Sound and Fury Behind 'One More Day'" in J.J. Sanford (ed.), *Spider-Man and Philosophy: The Web of Inquiry* (Hoboken, NJ: Wiley Blackwell, 2012), pp. 231–242.

Chapter 12: The Trials of Iron Man

After the Civil War ended, Tony Stark was sitting pretty, having been appointed director of SHIELD by the president of the United States. His Fifty-State Initiative was successfully launched, the Negative Zone prison was repurposed primarily for holding dangerous supervillains, and he was excited to work on the rest of the one hundred big ideas he crafted with Reed Richards and Hank Pym.[1] This was to be his zenith, however, as the next several years would prove disastrous for the man who thought he alone knew the future and how to manage it for the best.

In this chapter, we'll survey Tony Stark's tribulations following his "victory" in the Civil War. For now, let's just say things did not go smoothly, and when his term as director of SHIELD ended, they only got worse. In the end, Tony was forced to make the greatest sacrifice he could possibly make this side of his own death. We'll see if these experiences change his mind regarding which side he took on registration and what he did to support it.

Dealing with the Death of Captain America

As we'll present it here, Tony's arc after the Civil War starts and ends with Captain America. On his way into the federal courthouse in Manhattan for arraignment, in handcuffs and accompanied by a squad of federal marshals, Steve Rogers spots a small red dot on the back of the marshal in front of him. He turns his head to see a sniper in a window in a nearby building, mutters "damn it to hell," and pushes the marshal aside so he can take the bullet. Chaos ensues while several more shots ring out, and before we know it, Steve Rogers lies bleeding on the courthouse steps, Sharon Carter at his side, while the Falcon and Bucky Barnes go after the sniper, Cap's old enemy Crossbones. Soon we discover that Sharon Carter fired the extra shots at close range while under the mind control of another of Cap's foes, Dr. Faustus, working with none other than the Red Skull.[2]

That takes Steve Rogers out of our story for several years (in the real world) as the rest of the Marvel Universe tries to deal with the death of the man who had been the superhero community's moral center since his revival in 1963.[3] Of course, for many of the heroes and ordinary people in the Marvel Universe, Steve Rogers was not just a hero, Avenger, or a national symbol, but a friend and colleague, and Tony Stark was closer to Rogers than most. As he told Wolverine when his fellow Avengers snuck onto the SHIELD helicarrier to see Steve's body, "he was my friend, Logan. Maybe my best friend."[4] Many held him responsible for Cap's death—including himself, to some extent—and as we saw in chapter 4, after Steve died he questioned whether the whole conflict was worth it.

This uncertainty continues, which we see when Sharon demands to see Steve's body and Tony tries to stop her because of what she'd see: Steve's shriveled body, its condition presumably due to the deterioration of the super-soldier serum in his system after his death. Sharon asks Tony what he did to Steve, and Tony replies, "Sharon, I just told you... you can't... you can't think I would do this. You can't think I wanted any of this." Sharon says, "Can't I? You're suddenly running SHIELD while he's... he's—." Tony pleaded with her, saying "Damn it, Sharon. I was trying to do the right thing. I was trying to... save us from this... You think seeing him this way isn't killing me?," after which Sharon slapped him, saying "You don't get to say that, Stark."[5] Sharon's own pain and guilt keep her from seeing Tony's, especially when, as she says, it seems that he's done very well for himself since the Civil War ended.

One person who understood what Tony was going through after Cap's death was Clint Barton, the Avenger known as Hawkeye, who died at the hands of the Scarlet Witch when she destroyed Avengers Mansion and was later revived by her during the House of M episode (only to be killed again, although he survived... sigh, comics). When Tony offered Clint the shield and asked him to become the new Captain America, Clint refused, but only after confronting two of the Young Avengers and being taught a lesson in authenticity himself (especially after he learns one of them had taken the name Hawkeye).[6] Tony asks him why he doesn't see the value to the American people of having a Captain America again, and Clint asks him,

> "People"? Or you, Tony? You don't know how to handle it, do
> you? The grief, the pain, the loss... So you reached for the thing
> you know best—you tried to make a deal. Tried to strike a bar-
> gain that would make it all go away. And you can't. And neither
> should anyone else. Including... especially... me.

Later, at a press conference introducing the new, SHIELD-endorsed Avengers team—picked specifically by Tony and Carol Danvers, as opposed to letting the team be determined "by fate"—when someone asks if there can be an Avengers team without a Captain America, Tony says no, "there will no new Captain

America. Steve Rogers was the finest man I ever met. And it's a national tragedy that he was taken from us," and to consider his mask and shield retired.[7]

Appropriately, in light of what is to come, Cap's former sidekick Bucky Barnes doesn't trust Tony when he says there will be no new Cap, especially when he notices the shield in the Natural History Museum in Washington is a fake. But Tony seems sincere, telling a SHIELD agent later that there will no new Cap, only to receive a letter Steve prepared for Tony in event of his death, which asks him two things: to make sure Bucky doesn't sink back into the darkness, and to make sure the concept of Captain America doesn't die with him.[8] As we'll see, he finds a way to take care of both requests at the same time by asking Bucky to be the new Captain America, which he does reluctantly but successfully, albeit in his own way (carrying a gun, for instance).[9]

But let's not get ahead of ourselves—we still have Steve Rogers' funeral at Arlington National Cemetery to attend. Speaking first, Tony can't even summon words, stammering a bit before saying, simply, "It... wasn't supposed to be this way..." before walking off the podium.[10] Later, when Sam Wilson (the Falcon) gives his moving speech memorializing Cap's long service to the country and to the world, Sam talks about when the Avengers found him frozen in the ice, and Carol Danvers asks Tony how well he remembers that day, to which Tony replies, "Like it was yesterday. Greatest day of my life."

Three days later, Tony, Hank Pym, and Janet van Dyne—the three charter members of the Avengers left on Earth—flew to the Arctic with Steve's body to have Namor put it back in the ocean where they found it years ago. (The one buried in Arlington is a fake.) There, Tony regains his composure, saying "the things I wanted to stay in front of everyone at Arlington... but I couldn't bring myself to do it..."

> I know that if our roles were reversed, you could've. If, God for-bid, the funeral had been for someone else, you would have helped me through it.
>
> I wanted us all to be here today. The Hulk. Thor. The Scarlet Witch. Hawkeye. Your teammates. Your friends. They are all, one way or another, lost to us... and now I've lost you too.
>
> Maybe... maybe there was a reason you had to be on the other side of every argument. How could you be my rudder, steering me when others couldn't... I don't know if I can do it without you... I certainly won't do it as well...

This speech suggests that Cap served as Tony's "control," providing the deontological blocks he needed to reign in his utilitarian impulses, to tell him when he'd gone too far, considering means that actually weren't justified by the ends.

Tony's concern about losing his rudder was justified and, befitting his self-image as a futurist, rather prophetic. Later, when things start to go downhill, he says, "Damn it, Steve… it's all falling apart without you here. Just like I knew it would."[11] Even Spider-Man, the first time he sees Iron Man after Mephisto restored his secret identity, thinks to himself "how sad Tony looked. How heavy everything seemed." As he continues,

> The whole time I worked with him, for him—in the times I
> called him friend and the times I thought he was a total tool…
> he never seemed like he didn't know the answer. Even when he
> was wrong, you'd never know. He was confident. Always. And
> now… now he doesn't even look like he knows what day it is.
> I've never, ever seen him so… so unsure.[12]

At the time, Tony was dealing with the aftermath of a terror attack by Ezekiel Stane, son of his old foe Obadiah Stane, who modified Stark technology to create human bombs—technology that Stark disabled with a mass electromagnetic pulse, but at the price of killing four of the suicide bombers.[13] After Stane was defeated and locked away, Stark thought to himself that Stane had "shown me what kind of man I have to become—what kind of things I have to do—to keep my nightmares from coming true."[14] Even for a man who believes that the ends generally justify the means, Tony Stark is discovering his own limits as to what means are truly acceptable—even without Cap there to guide him.

With Friends Like These…

It wasn't just his enemies he had to deal with during this period, though—many of his friends and colleagues in the superhero community held grudges against him. Take, for instance, She-Hulk, his ally in support of registration who later found out that he exiled her cousin Bruce Banner to space and reacted as you might expect of a gamma-irradiated loyal family member. When she confronted him and asked who made him "my cousin's judge and jury," Tony proclaims that he's a futurist—did you know that?—and that "I could see what was coming. Chaos. Destruction. And I fixed it. Whether you know it or not, I saved the world."

It is unclear whether he was referring to the Hulk or registration when he said he "fixed it," but it's irrelevant in that both actions reflect the motivations and behavior that we looked at closely in Part II of this book. But it is She-Hulk's reaction that is more important here, as she starts to put it altogether herself. As she says to Tony in between blows:

> Oh my God. You don't see it, do you? A tin-plated tyrant... who thinks he knows more... than everyone else. Remaking the world in his own image. You know who that is? That's not Iron Man, Tony! That's Doctor Doom![15]

Tony Stark and Victor von Doom do have a lot in common, given their huge egos and confidence in their own knowledge and ability to make the world a better place. Doom takes the extra step in that he feels the world would be a better place under his rule, while we can imagine Tony being satisfied by "merely" designing the world's institutions, being the man behind the scenes.[16] Both men often lose their moorings in terms of what lines they shouldn't cross in pursuit of their goals: they're drawn to manipulation and strategy, while Doom definitely is in another league altogether in his willingness to murder those who stand in his way.[17] But as Carol Danvers thinks to herself after her first adventure with Iron Man and the rest of the SHIELD-sanctioned Avengers, "You're not king of the world, Tony. And one day, they are going to crucify you in the streets for trying to be."[18]

Tony soon encountered another longtime friend and fellow Avenger that wouldst have words with him. When Thor returned to life after the last Ragnarok that occurred about the same time as the Avengers disassembled, he encountered the fallout of the Civil War and heard news of the clone his friends made from his Asgardian DNA. When Iron Man sought him out to discuss the sudden appearance of Asgard floating above Broxton, Oklahoma, as well as registration, he said, "It's real simple, Thor. You either work with the government, for the government, or you're against the government. There's no middle ground."[19] Thor listened, silent and still, until Tony was finished, and then he literally brought down the thunder (and lightning), saying:

> You have hunted down those we once fought beside and called comrades. Killed or imprisoned those who opposed you. Regardless of their previous loyalties. Surely this would be offense enough. But you went further. Much further.
>
> You took my genetic code and, without my knowledge, used it to create an abomination—an aberration—an *insult*—and this you told the world was me. You defiled my body, desecrated my trust, violated everything that I am.

Is this how you define friendship? Is it? Is it?

After Thor beats Tony to within an inch of his life—much like Cap did in the final battle of the Civil War—Thor tells him he will take no sides in the "disagreement," and asks only that he and Asgard be left alone (which, to be honest, is taking a side, but we'll let that go because of the hammer).

It is difficult to tell where Thor stood on the ideological conflict over registration, but he clearly had strong opinions on Tony's behavior as judged against Thor's general moral position as a man of virtue.[20] He implied that Tony acted in betrayal of the virtues of loyalty and friendship by standing against those who once stood with him, as well as corrupting Thor's very person (or godhood) in helping create the murderous clone. Thor is not a grand planner, nor is he a man to follow myriad rules. But he knows what it is to be a good person, and he holds his friends and fellow heroes to nearly as high a standard as he holds himself. (Verily!)

The last of Tony's fellow heroes to judge him rather harshly after the Civil War—and who, like Thor, also missed that particular conflict altogether—was also angry about Tony's betrayal of loyalty and friendship. (And you don't want to see him when he's angry.) Ahead of his arrival on Earth, after defeating Black Bolt on the moon, the Hulk appeared as a hologram in Times Square, telling the people of Earth how the Illuminati claimed to be his friends but then exiled him into space, where he found a new home, new friends, and a new love, only for the Illuminati to send a shuttle that inadvertently killed a million inhabitants of that world, including his wife.[21] As we saw in Part I of this book, Tony blasts into space in his Hulkbuster armor to face his old friend, telling the people of the world that he takes full responsibility for the decision to exile the Hulk and for the consequences of his return.[22] This includes sending fighter jets to fire missiles at the Hulk after knocking him out and then injecting him with nanobots to dampen his strength. This only makes the Hulk angrier, and when the Hulk becomes angrier, the Hulk becomes stronger. That's bad for the world—and bad for Tony.

After fighting the heroes of Earth, the Hulk captures the members of the Illuminati and sets them against each other in gladiatorial combat—as the Hulk was subjected to when he first arrived on his new planet—and nearly made Reed Richards kill Tony Stark. But at the last minute he stopped it, saying,

> Remember this, puny humans. We came here for justice, not murder. So no one on your planet has died by our hands. And

no one will. But we'll make sure no one on Earth will ever forget
what you are. Liars. Traitors. And killers.[23]

The Hulk seems more intent on ruining the reputations of his former friends who
exiled him, revealing their "true" characters to the world, than on exacting
murderous revenge for the death of his adopted world. (Even when angry, the
Hulk does not resort to the type of "eye for an eye" thinking we described in the
last chapter.)

Finally, the Sentry, the agoraphobic and schizophrenic hero with the power of
a million exploding suns, arrives on the scene and unleashes his full power on the
Hulk.[24] It was the Sentry to whom Tony said, as we saw in chapter 4, that the
stakes are too high to do nothing, and that doing nothing is still a choice. As he
continued, "You have the responsibility, whether you want it or not. I know
you're not ready to hear this, Robert. No sane person ever really is. But it's time to
play God."[25] This time, Tony meant "playing God" in terms of unleashing his
incredible power to defeat the Hulk and save the world, but it's nonetheless
consistent with what we know about Tony and how he thinks.

When Tony told General Ross, perhaps the Hulk's oldest enemy (and one-
time father-in-law), what he said to the Sentry about playing God, Ross replied,
"You morons. Trading one monster for another."[26] This is actually an insightful
criticism of Tony's thinking, both in this case as well as his earlier choice to exile
the Hulk into space: to defeat one monster, Tony creates an even bigger one. In
his sincere attempt to solve problems, he all too often only creates bigger ones;
this applies well to his efforts to promote registration, which one can argue had
much worse consequences than the problems it was designed to prevent (as we
saw in the discussion of "was it worth it?" in chapter 4). Even though the Sentry
did defeat the Hulk, and Tony finally subdued him, massive parts of New York
City were once again destroyed as a result of something Tony was at least partially
responsible for, even if it was with the best of intentions.[27]

The Downfall

The next crisis Tony Stark would face would also come from the stars, but much
more subtly than the Jade Giant did. In a battle with a team of assassins led by
Elektra and Luke Cage's unregistered Avengers team, Elektra is killed and
transforms before their eyes to a Skrull, one of a race of shapeshifting aliens.[28] As
both Avengers teams soon discover, for years the Skrulls had methodically
infiltrated the human race, kidnapping and then impersonating select persons,
including heroes such as Spider-Woman, the Invisible Woman, Hank Pym, and

even the Avengers' butler Jarvis.[29] Now that their presence had been revealed, they announced their plans to conquer the Earth, including using a technovirus to disable all of Stark's technology (including, of course, his armor). While our heroes struggled to fight back against the Skrulls' (no longer) "Secret Invasion" while not knowing whom to trust amongst themselves, we learn that the Skrull who took the place of Hank Pym embedded a bomb inside his ex-wife Janet van Dyne, the Wasp, which was activated when she grew to giant-size during the final battle with the Skrulls. When the bomb exploded, Thor managed to contain the energies but the Wasp was killed. Adding insult to injury, it was Norman Osborn who ended the invasion by killing the Skrull queen (who had impersonated Spider-Woman since before Cap and Iron Man put the "new" Avengers together after the massive prison break).[30]

After the final battle was over and the kidnapped heroes returned to Earth—including some long thought dead, such as the Avenger Mockingbird—the Thing looked around and asked, "So, this whole Skrull thing... who's gonna take the hit for it, ya think?" Even though the Secret Invasion wasn't his fault, Tony Stark took that hit because of his failure as director of SHIELD, and a self-proclaimed futurist, to see it coming, prevent it, or counter it effectively.[31] The blame game starts with a fellow Avenger: when Tony tries to mend fences with Thor, the son of Odin will hear nothing of it, warning him,

> Don't misunderstand my intentions, Stark. I came here because
> I was needed. I told you I would never fight alongside you again.
> I told you I would never join thy ranks again. I *abhor* what thou
> hast become and I'm sure I will not be the only one who finds
> the blame in all this to fall square on thy shoulders.

Hank Pym—who been replaced by the Skrull before the Civil War even started—blamed Tony for Janet's death in particular, screaming at him during her funeral, "How could you do this? How could you let this happen? How? I really want to know! You killed Captain America! You killed Janet! But there you are! Who's next, Tony? Who's—."[32] He stopped only when Thor put a hand on his shoulder, hailed Janet as a great warrior for whose presence "the gates of Valhalla are richer today," and then flew off with Pym to mourn in private. Tony's expression reveals that, while he was not directly responsible for either Cap's or Janet's death, nonetheless he wonders how he could have prevented both and wishes he could have found a way.

As Thor predicted, the president soon announces that Tony Stark is fired, describing him as "the one who stood on the mountaintop and decided he was in charge of the world. He's the one who said he could protect us all, but he couldn't." Beyond that, SHIELD is disbanded and a new organization will be established in its place, something "far more superior and modern. And its goals will be to keep this planet safe from those who would attack it from inside *and* out." And to head this new organization, a "true hero" was called: none other than Norman Osborn, whose sudden popularity and skill at handling the press is made evident at his first post-Invasion press conference, which ends in applause.[33]

The reign of Tony Stark had ended, and here started what came to be known as the "Dark Reign," as Osborn created his own Avengers team from members of the Thunderbolts (and several former Avengers, such as Ares and the Sentry), and behind the scenes he headed the Cabal, a villainous mirror-image of the Illuminati, featuring Doctor Doom, Thor's half-brother Loki (albeit a woman at the time), and other people who you wouldn't bring home for dinner.[34]

The president may have fired him, but there was something Tony had that Osborn still wanted: the superhero registration database and all its information. This is where Tony's story gets personal and he shows his heroism like never before.

Stark Disassembled

After Norman Osborn takes Tony's place on the SHIELD helicarrier—now the HAMMER helicarrier—Tony stops by Osborn's office before leaving.[35] After asking if he stole any office supplies on his way out, Norman asks how to access the superhero registration database. Tony tells him that "it's not your personal File-o-Fax. You can't just browse it at your leisure. You need about a half-dozen warrants and probable cause and a federal judge to—," but Norman dismisses his concerns. After Tony leaves, Norman tries to access the database and finds it empty; not only was it a fake file planted by Tony, but accessing it triggered a virus Tony planted in the system, knocking out all the computer code and records on the helicarrier that weren't essential to keeping it in the air.

At their hideout, Tony tells Maria Hill (ex-director of SHIELD) and his erstwhile assistant Pepper Potts where the superhuman registration database is: in his brain, which had been enhanced by the Extremis technovirus to become "a kind of hard drive," where the records of all his friends' secret identities sit alongside all of Tony's technical knowledge, the designs for the various Iron Man suits, and more.[36] And Tony plans to wipe the hard drive, so to speak, but it can't all be done at once because of the tremendous power it takes. Traveling around the world to his various Stark Industries installations, he will use the repulsor-powered terminal stations at each one to erase, sector by sector, the information from his brain—*all* the information. "Memory, personality, all of it. Even my neural pathways and reflexes will be blanked. Wiping it all away until—well, quite frankly—brain death."

Hill asks why he doesn't simply kill himself—and hands him her gun to do it—but he says the bullet may not damage the part of his brain holding the database, leaving it for Osborn to decipher. (Later, someone else recommends jumping in a volcano; good thing Hill didn't think of that![37]) Tony describes the situation he find himself in, which sets the tone of the entire episode to follow: "I've made a lot of mistakes, and the biggest one was never, ever thinking we'd screw up so bad—that *I'd* screw up so bad—so as to turn my very life into a liability."[38] We can take this to mean that Tony is realizing that, at the very least, the concerns expressed by Captain America, Spider-Man, and others were valid, specifically that a database of their identities and other secrets could not be safe, not even locked in the head of the one person who declared himself "the greatest friend" the superhero community will ever have and who said, "do you really think I'd let anyone guard my friends' secret identities?"[39]

If only to make Tony's mission of self-lobotomization more difficult, Norman Osborn holds a press conference to announce the "discovery" of SHIELD documents revealing that Tony Stark and Maria Hill knew of the Skrull Invasion in advance and tried (unsuccessfully) to negotiate to turn the invading forces back.[40] Finally, Osborn issues a warrant for Tony's arrest "for crimes against humanity, collusion with an alien menace, flight from justice, conspiracy, criminal neglect, and treason against the planet Earth."[41] While Tony is crossing the globe from one repulsor station to another, and Maria Hill goes to down to Texas to retrieve a mysterious hard drive, they must also evade HAMMER and local authorities trying to apprehend them. (Meanwhile, Tony appointed Potts the CEO of Stark Industries, which, after Stane's physical attack and the Skrulls' virus that wiped out all Starktech, existed on paper only.)

Over the span of a dozen issues of *The Invincible Iron Man*, Tony traveled from one base to another, gradually erasing his brain while encountering a number of old friends and enemies, all while keeping one step ahead of HAMMER.[42] At each stop he gets noticeably less intelligent and more forgetful, and has to downgrade to an older model of armor because his diminishing brain power can't operate the more advanced suits. His emails look like they were written by a child, he forgets people and events—he thinks Cap is still alive—and he has to listen to audiobooks on electrical engineering to continue to maintain his armor. Pepper, now wearing the Model-1616 armor Tony designed for her earlier, finds Tony in Russia and they reminisce. He tells her that losing his intelligence is like losing his superpowers—and when she mentions Happy Hogan, her ex-husband and Tony's former best friend who was killed during the Civil War, Tony pauses and then asks, "who's Happy?"[43]

Finally, Norman Osborn, wearing his red, white, and blue "Iron Patriot" armor (later worn by James Rhodes in the film *Iron Man 3*) catches up with Tony in Afghanistan, where he's wearing the clunky armor he originally built there.[44] At this point Tony is nearly incoherent, speaking in simple one- or two-word phrases, and trying to run from Osborn rather than fight. When Tony does resist, firing his flamethrowers, Osborn says, "Yesssss. Finally. Finally! It won't feel so bad this way, Tony. You fight me back a little bit and I'm defending myself... and not just murdering you in cold blood."[45] But before Osborn delivers the final blow, both of his palms pointed at Tony's bare head and repulsors aglow, he is alerted to the fact that the battle is being broadcast around the world—courtesy of HAMMER's press corps, ironically—and it certainly looks as though he is about to execute a defeated Tony Stark. Realizing this would compromise even his tough-guy image, Osborn stands down.

After Osborn returns Tony to the HAMMER helicarrier, a doctor tells him that Tony is in a persistent vegetative state, and "any awareness, consciousness, or knowledge is lost forever." Once Norman realizes the superhuman registration database is gone, he tells the doctor to pull the plug, but the doctor shows him Tony Stark's living will, which grants power of attorney to Dr. Donald Blake of Broxton, Oklahoma—also known as Thor. It is now up to Blake, alongside Potts, Hill, and various Avengers, to figure out how to bring Tony back.

Stark Reassembled

Luckily, Tony planned ahead. After his friends take him to Broxton, Pepper's armor displays a message that Tony recorded on the day he left SHIELD.[46] In the message, Tony explained what to do if he ended up... well, exactly as he did. But first, he suggested that whoever was listening should

> ask the question—do you want me back? Can you forgive me? Because, here's the thing—I'm not apologizing. What happened, happened, and it happened because it happened and that's that. And you shouldn't apologize either. What's past is prologue.

I… okay, none of us get into this line of work because of the great 401k, right? I ran a good race—I ran a *great* race—and had a good and great life and maybe I helped out a little along the way.

Every single one of us knows there's no promise of a happy ending. We die. Heroes… die. Cap—*Bucky*—Thor—you guys know that lesson all too well. Bill Foster knew it. Janet—Clint—this is the job. This is the job. Dying is the superhero retirement plan. And lately a whole lot more of us are on it.[47]

For an unapologetic guy, however, Tony did become contrite near the end of his not-a-confession:

I never let myself believe in God, but… I don't know how to say this. Captain America and Thor were… whatever sense of a higher power I've ever had came from them. From you. And from who you thought I could be. Whenever I looked up… you were who I was looking at. For guidance, for leadership… and now, absolution.

Tony obviously wants to come back, and says that they need him together with Cap and Thor to bring Osborn down, but at the same time he understands how much he let people down and that they may not want him back—an astonishing level of self-awareness that befits his impending fate but nonetheless belies his legendary ego.

Bucky Barnes (now serving as Captain America, remember) and Donald Blake agree that they have to bring Tony back, but there is one person that has reservations, perhaps the unlikeliest one of them all. Pepper Potts runs out of the room in tears, and when Maria Hill catches up with her, Pepper tells her,

I don't understand why—after so many people got hurt—after everybody died at Stamford, and [Ezekiel] Stane and the [Skrull] invasion and—and—and after Steve and Bill and—and after Happy all died—why is it Tony gets to come back? Why is it that Tony Stark is the one that gets everything back again?

Here we see that Pepper Potts, the one person closest to Tony Stark in the world, is among those who hold him responsible for all the deaths she mentioned. And that's not all: later, she writes a letter to Tony in which she says "of course I'll do whatever you ask to help bring you back" because that's what she always does.[48] "You ask me and I come running," she writes, and then asks when it will be her turn to live, "when does heaven and earth move to help me or bring my dead husband back from the dead?"[49] Ironically, it is an Avenger recently returned from the dead who comes into the room, declares that "Iron Man is in trouble. And we're all going to bring him back," and inspires Pepper to scrunch up the letter and return to Tony's side. (More on the mystery hero soon.)

There are a few steps involved in bringing Tony Stark back, but the most important one for our purposes involves the hard drive that he had Maria Hill retrieve from Texas, which contains a brain scan that Tony made before administering the Extremis virus to himself, months before the tragedy in Stamford that led to the Civil War. "If we think of our minds as our body's operating system," Tony explained through another recording, "and Extremis was an upgrade, I did what any good geek would do before installing it. I backed myself up."[50]

It isn't easy and requires the talents of a particularly Strange doctor, but eventually Tony's mind is restored and he wakes up.[51] Twenty-four hours later, he is at a computer, archived newspapers and magazines around him, all showing headlines from the Civil War and the Skrull invasion, including the assassination of Captain America, the dissolution of SHIELD, and himself as a fugitive from the law. His only words are: "God. Oh my God."[52]

Later, Reed Richards needles Tony, one geek to another, about why he didn't back his mind up more often—he really goes on about this, to humorous effect. When Tony finally gets him to stop, he says:

> I screwed up, okay? I screwed it up. Amateur mistake number one and I made it. I made it because I didn't think it needed doing. I couldn't imagine… I couldn't imagine screwing up as bad as I did and needing it. That I'd run the show as badly as I did. Or that—or maybe I did the best I could, I don't know, I don't remember—but I thought I was above… tiny… human… things. Like making backups of my data. Or asking for help. Or saying sorry.[53]

Despite his words to Reed, however, we should be careful not to read Tony as being too apologetic; ambivalent may be a better term for it. Just as the recordings made before erasing his brain show, his feelings about the choices he made since the registration movement started are complex.

We might hope that, with some distance after "forgetting" what he did and reading about it fresh, Tony's feelings about his actions would settle a bit. As it turns out, he gives his best statement about this to one of his oldest friends who was very upset about his recent activities. As Tony helps rebuild some damaged property in Broxton, Thor approaches, speaking the ominous words that only an Asgardian can pull off: "Stark. I would have words." After some small talk, he struggles to be sensitive while asking, "Stark, you… you have… gaps… in your understanding… of what you have done. Is that correct? Of what you have done to all of us?" Tony replied,

> Regardless of what decisions I made—whether I remember making them or not—I've read about what "I" did and, Thor, I promise you—*promise you*—everything I did—I know it was because I thought it was the right thing to do *at the time* and I thought I was saving the greatest number of lives. In spite of it all and for all my sins I swear to God that's the truth.
>
> Everybody I know is pissed off at me for one reason or another and half the time I don't even remember why. I am not sorry and I'd do it again. Hopefully differently but I'd do it all again.

Thor is silent for a moment, then smiles and says, "There is the Stark I knew. There is the Stark I remember," a man who did not "yield or wilt" but maintained his convictions.

Indeed, this seems like the Stark we got to know in Part I of this book, who believes that he has a responsibility to use his gifts of brilliance and foresight to make the world a better place in the best way he knows how. But is it really the same Stark? Following Heraclitus, who famously said that you can't step in the same river twice because it is always moving and changing, some philosophers maintain that each of us is a different person at different times in our life, even second to second. Looking at it this way, the Stark who woke from the "reboot" is a duplicate of the Stark from before the Extremis storyline, who is not the same Stark who made all the consequential decisions during the Civil War, the Hulk's return, and the Skrull invasion. If so, then the current Stark should not be held morally responsible for them; we should treat him like we would a person who commits a crime while sleepwalking, under mental control, or suffering from temporary insanity. It's not just that he doesn't remember what he did—he doesn't remember it because, literally speaking, the current Stark didn't do it.[54]

Regardless of whether we hold the current Tony morally responsible for what the earlier version of Tony did, he has to live with the knowledge that, in a sense, "he" did these things, and he will continue to make amends for them. Unlike Peter Parker, who got to erase some of his mistakes through mystical means, only Tony's memories were erased, and all of his choices still ripple through the world.[55] Also, Tony realizes that he's not perfect, that all of his choices will not work out for the best, but he nonetheless believes in his responsibility to make them, to carry them out, and to bear responsibility for the consequences. As his speech to Thor implied, he does not regret what he tried to do with regard to registration and while running SHIELD, but he does wish he'd done it better. He is an imperfect man trying to pursue a perfect goal, and his success or failure must be measured not against perfection but instead against what another person could have done—just take one look at how Norman Osborn ran the world for an instructive comparison, or imagine what would have happened had he not intervened at all. Tony Stark may be sorry for what happened as a result of his choices, but he is not sorry that he made choices at all and tried to make things better. A futurist can do no less.

~~~~~

At the beginning of this chapter, I said that Tony Stark's arc following the Civil War started and ended with Captain America, so our task in the final chapter of this part of the book is set. Coming up next, we'll explain what *really* happened to Captain America on the courthouse steps that fateful day, and how he also came back, in his own way, to help Tony and the rest of the superhero community to bring down Norman Osborn, ending his Dark Reign and beginning the Age of Heroes.

---

[1] *Civil War* #7 (January 2007).

[2] *Captain America*, vol. 5, #25 (April 2007). Again, most of the citations in this chapter act as markers for the events and dialogue discussed within it.

[3] See *Fallen Son: The Death of Captain America* (2008).

[4] *Fallen Son: The Death of Captain America* #1 (June 2007).

[5] *Captain America*, vol. 5, #26 (May 2007).

[6] *Fallen Son: The Death of Captain America* #3 (July 2007).

---

[7] *Captain America*, vol. 5, #27 (August 2007). On the selection of the roster, see *Mighty Avengers*, vol. 1, #1 (May 2007).

[8] *Captain America*, vol. 5, #28 (September 2007).

[9] Tony talks Bucky into it in *Captain America*, vol. 5, #33 (February 2008) and Bucky appears in costume in *Captain America*, vol. 5, #34 (March 2008).

[10] *Fallen Son: The Death of Captain America* #5 (August 2007).

[11] *Captain America*, vol. 5, #30 (November 2007).

[12] *Invincible Iron Man* #7 (January 2009). Unbeknownst to all, Tony played an integral in restoring Peter's secret identity, led by Mephisto's meddling with history to team up with Reed Richards and Dr. Strange to make the world forget who Spider-Man is (*Amazing Spider-Man* #641, October 2010).

[13] *The Invincible Iron Man Vol. 1: The Five Nightmares* (2009), which became part of the plot of the 2013 film *Iron Man 3*.

[14] *Invincible Iron Man* #6 (December 2008).

[15] *She-Hulk*, vol. 2, #18 (June 2007). In *Incredible Hulk*, vol. 2, #106 (July 2007), she explained her support of registration based on being a lawyer, "which means I believe in truth and justice and law and order and rainbows and pretty unicorns… so I fought for the government during the superheroes Civil War." But she turned on Tony because "I believed in what I was doing. I believed in my friends. I believed in myself. And then I found out what they did," namely sending her cousin Bruce into space: "No trial. No jury. No justice."

[16] For evidence of Doom's sincerity about wanting to save humanity through his rule, see *Doomwar* (2010).

[17] As I saw it, this similarity between Stark and Doom became a problem in Marvel Comics' recent event *Avengers & X-Men: Axis* (2015), in which heroes and villains "inverted" their moral positions. Even though their basic moral orientations are very similar, after being inverted, Tony lost any deontological limits on his behavior, becoming a parody of utilitarianism, while Doom became almost a Gandhi-like figure. See my blog post "A Problem with Marvel's Axis: The Difficulty with Inverting Complex Characters," *The Comics Professor*, November 21, 2014, http://www.comicsprofessor.com/2014/11/a-problem-with-marvel-axis-the-difficulty-of-inverting-complex-characters.html.

[18] *Mighty Avengers*, vol. 1, #6 (February 2008).

[19] *Thor*, vol. 3, #3 (November 2007). Soon thereafter, on the first anniversary of Captain America's death, Thor summons the fallen hero's spirit, a very touching reunion indeed (*Thor*, vol. 3, #11, November 2008).

[20] I described him as such in my chapter "Superhero Ethics Class with the Avengers Prime" in Mark D. White (ed.), *The Avengers and Philosophy: Earth's Mightiest Thinkers* (Hoboken, NJ: Wiley Blackwell, 2012), pp. 3–17.

[21] *World War Hulk* #1 (August 2007); see *Hulk: Planet Hulk* (2007) for the background described above.

[22] *World War Hulk* #1. Tony also tells Jim Rhodes, as he works on his Hulkbuster armor, that "after all the pain and loss of the Civil War… *this* could be the one common foe, the cause that finally unites us again" (*Avengers: The Initiative* #4, September 2007). That's our Tony, always seeing the bright side.

[23] *World War Hulk* #4 (November 2007).

[24] *World War Hulk* #5 (January 2008).

[25] *World War Hulk* #4.

[26] *World War Hulk* #5.

[27] For the human impact and fallout from the battle with the Hulk, see *Hulk: WWH—Front Line* (2008).

[28] *New Avengers*, vol. 1, #31 (August 2007).

[29] *Secret Invasion* (2010) had almost as many tie-in issues as *Civil War* had, especially in *New Avengers* and *Mighty Avengers*, where much backstory of the invasion was revealed, including when Hank Pym and others had been replaced. Also, *New Avengers: Illuminati* #1 (February 2007) shows how the seeds for the Secret Invasion were planned as far back as the Kree/Skrull War, when the Illuminati themselves were captured and experimented on by the Skrulls.

[30] *Secret Invasion* #8 (January 2009), through the end of the next paragraph.

[31] The effects of the Secret Invasion, as always, were also felt by the citizens of New York; for that, see *Secret Invasion: Front Line* (2009).

[32] *Mighty Avengers*, vol. 1, #20 (February 2009).

[33] *Secret Invasion: Front Line* #5 (January 2009).

[34] See the end of *Secret Invasion* #8; *Dark Avengers*, vol. 1, #1 (March 2009); and the *Dark Reign: The Cabal* one-shot (June 2009).

[35] *Invincible Iron Man* #8 (February 2009). We never find out what HAMMER stands for—Osborn just likes the way it sounds.

[36] *Invincible Iron Man* #9 (March 2009).

[37] *Invincible Iron Man* #14 (August 2009).

[38] *Invincible Iron Man* #9.

[39] *Civil War* #7.

[40] Even though the Civil War and its parallels to post-9/11 America are behind us at this point, Osborn's press conference evokes conspiracy theories about the

tragedy, particularly if the White House and members of Congress knew anything about the impending attacks.

41 *Invincible Iron Man* #10 (April 2009).

42 See *Invincible Iron Man, Vol. 2: World's Most Wanted, Book 1* (2009) and *Invincible Iron Man, Vol. 3: World's Most Wanted, Book 2* (2010).

43 *Invincible Iron Man* #15 (September 2009).

44 In the initial origin story (*Tales of Suspense*, vol. 1, #39, March 1963, "Iron Man Is Born!"), this event took place in Vietnam, but it was updated to Afghanistan in *Iron Man*, vol. 4, #1 (January 2005) to keep Tony somewhat young.

45 *Invincible Iron Man* #19 (December 2009).

46 Unfortunately, he wasn't dressed as Princess Leia… oh, never mind.

47 *Invincible Iron Man* #20 (January 2010), through Pepper's talk with Maria Hill.

48 *Invincible Iron Man* #21 (February 2010).

49 She also asks, "When is the movie about me and not Tony Stark?" (Good question.)

50 *Invincible Iron Man* #21. Tony's analogy is not uncontroversial, and philosophers have debated the similarities between minds and computers for years; see, for instance, Steven Horst, "The Computational Theory of Mind," *Stanford Encyclopedia of Philosophy*, December 10, 2009, at http://plato.stanford.edu/entries/computational-mind/.

51 *Invincible Iron Man* #24 (May 2010).

52 In a way, this massive memory loss is reminiscent of the blackouts Tony experienced while drinking; for a poignant recap of his life including these most recent events as told at an Alcoholics Anonymous meeting, see *Invincible Iron Man* #500.1 (April 2011).

53 *Invincible Iron Man* #25 (June 2010), through the rest of this section.

54 See David Shoemaker, "Personal Identity and Ethics," *Stanford Encyclopedia of Philosophy*, February 13, 2012, at http://plato.stanford.edu/entries/identity-ethics/. This point can be taken even further to claim that, under normal circumstances, Tony shouldn't be held responsible today for something he did yesterday because today-Tony is a different person from yesterday-Tony. We might say the cases differ in terms of how much "psychological continuity" exists between the two versions of Tony; presumably, Tony before and after the self-lobotomization are far more different than Tony before and after his Monday night sleep, so we would not allow Tony today the same excuse we extended to post-reboot Tony. (But this is Tony Stark, so you never know.)

[55] When Tony asked Peter for help some time later, and Peter told him where to go, Tony said, "You know I had this brain thing, right?" Peter replied, "You got more than one brain thing, if you ask me" (*Invincible Iron Man* #500, March 2011, "The New Iron Age").

Chapter 13: Steve Rogers Returns

While Tony Stark would have to live with many of the consequences of his decision-making during the Civil War and afterwards, one of the most disastrous of them would be resolved as a much beloved hero returned. We already saw him inspire Pepper Potts to help Tony come back from his self-imposed mindwipe, and he would later help the Avengers and the other heroes to depose Norman Osborn and start to set the world right again.

Of course, I'm talking about Steve Rogers, the original Captain America, and in this chapter we'll tell his rather abbreviated story following the Civil War, which also wraps up Tony's story and sets the Marvel Universe on a new and brighter path (for a few issues, at least).

What Really Happened That Fateful Day

At the same time that Tony Stark was crisscrossing the world to gradually lobotomize himself (as detailed in the last chapter), Steve Rogers was struggling to come back to life—or, more accurately, to the present time. In the year that passed in the Marvel Universe since Steve's apparent death Sharon Carter had agonized over her role in it, even though, as we saw, she was under the mind control of Dr. Faustus at the time. But eventually she started to remember hidden details about that day, including the nature of the gun she used to shoot Steve, not a pistol but a gun straight out of a 1950s science fiction movie.[1] She also starting experiencing fragments of memories of being tied up over one of Doctor Doom's time plat-forms while the Red Skull and fellow Cap villain Arnim Zola stood around it, referring to Carter as "the constant."[2]

After Hank Pym and Reed Richards ran some tests on the gun and Carter, they realized what happened—but let's hear it from one of the men responsible. As Zola explained to Norman Osborn, the gun (also built by Doom) that Sharon fired into Steve Rogers "locked his body in time and space... and with both the platform and the constant, we were able to pluck him right out of the timestream... where he lay dormant." But when Sharon escaped and broke the machine in the middle of the process, Steve became "unstuck in time."[3] While his friends and enemies race to find a way to rescue him, Steve finds himself drifting through his past life, revisiting key moments such as his transformation into a

185

super-soldier, meeting Franklin Delano Roosevelt, watching Bucky "die," and fighting alongside the Avengers, all while being drawn to Sharon Carter, who was injected by the Red Skull with nanobytes to draw Rogers to her (hence, "the constant").[4]

When Steve Rogers finally returns to the present, he finds that the Red Skull has transferred his consciousness into Steve's body, where the two longtime foes vie for control. Needless to say, Steve wins out in the end, resumes control of his body, and is reunited with Sharon Carter and his fellow Avengers, including his former sidekick Bucky Barnes, now operating as Captain America.[5] He also returns just in time to help Tony come back from his self-lobotomization, as we saw in the last chapter, as well as to join the final battle against Norman Osborn, his "Dark Avengers," and HAMMER as they attempt to overthrow Asgard.[6]

The Siege of Asgard began with an "incident," a disaster at Soldier Field in Chicago involving Volstagg (one of the Warriors Three of Asgardian fame), engineered by Osborn and Loki to have the same effect on public sentiment toward Asgard that the tragedy at Stamford did toward superheroes and registration.[7] Using that as his justification, even against the express orders of the president to stand down, Osborn leads his forces against Asgard, which has the Avengers and the rest of Earth's heroes at its side (including Thor, who must leave Tony Stark's side as his doctor Donald Blake to face Osborn). After the television networks report that Osborn has defeated Thor, we see Steve Rogers, ready to explode with rage.[8]

At the Avengers' secret hideout in Brooklyn—all of them having been driven underground when Osborn replaced them with his HAMMER-sanctioned team of villainous imposters—Cap gave a rousing speech to the gathered heroes:

> I know I've been away for a while. But now I'm back, and I look around, and I can't stand what I see. Osborn! I don't care who put him in power and I don't care what he did to get there... All I see is a madman leading a march of troops into battle and for the life of me I can't see why. To me it looks and feels a lot like the events that made me want to be Captain America in the first place.
>
> I know not everyone here sees eye-to-eye... and I know we've had to go so far as to defend ourselves against each other... But if you came here tonight, if you chose to stand up and be counted... then I think you agree with me. It's time to take

back this country. Our friends and allies are being attacked, maybe killed. And we're going to do something about it.

All of us.

With that speech, Captain America demonstrates what has been missing since the day he was shot and "killed": a firm moral center to the superhero community, someone to balance Tony Stark's overreach that, to some extent, led to Norman Osborn's "dark reign." One doesn't have to take Cap's side in the debate over registration to see that his counsel over the years was necessary to temper Tony's utilitarian ambitions (as Tony himself admitted). Osborn's time as head of global security is an instructive example of how far over the edge someone can go when completely untethered by basic, commonsense, deontological morality based on respecting people and their rights and liberties, not only promoting their well-being and utility.[9]

Cap leads the Avengers into battle with Osborn and his Avengers—much to the delight of the White House, which waives any limitations Osborn had imposed on the heroes based on the Superhuman Registration Act. They are soon joined by a rejuvenated Iron Man, who once again faces Osborn, disabling his Iron Patriot armor and defeating him, but not in time to stop the Sentry's destruction of Asgard.[10] With their powers boosted by Loki (who's come to question his role in the Siege a bit too late), the Avengers rally to defeat the Void, the Sentry's dark side, which Osborn had held in check until his defeat. Tony commandeers the HAMMER helicarrier and drops it on the Void, causing him to revert to the Sentry. When the Sentry begs Thor to kill him, Thor refuses, so the Sentry causes the Void to return, which forces Thor to end the threat once and for all.[11] And with that, the Siege on Asgard and the Dark Reign of Norman Osborn are over... and so is our story. (Almost.)

Steve Rogers now has to consider his role in the world in two important ways. First, will he return to serving the country and the world as Captain America? Observing Bucky in action during the fight with the Red Skull and the Siege on Asgard, Steve was impressed with how his former sidekick made the role of Captain America his own, especially since, as he thinks to himself, he "never expected Tony Stark to make Bucky the next Captain America. All I did was ask him to look out for the kid. To help find his way. But Tony always was a literal thinker."[12] After they work together to defeat Mister Hyde, Bucky offers his mentor the shield and the name, but Steve refuses, telling Bucky to continue under the name Captain America, while he pursues a more official path.

When Steve visited the president after his return to the present, the president gave him a pardon for his actions during the Civil War, saying "the registration act seemed un-American to me."[13] Steve told him then that he would not be serving as Captain America again, unless the president asked him to, but the president hinted that he may soon have another role for Steve. While Steve served as Captain America (alongside Bucky) during the Siege to inspire his fellow heroes, after Norman Osborn was defeated he visited the president again, who said:

> We've seen the world according to Nick Fury... We've seen the world according to Tony Stark... And, lord in heaven, we've seen the world according to Norman Osborn. Steve Rogers, Captain... I am asking you to answer the call.

Steve accepted the new role as head of global security, but told the president, "I'm going to want to do it my way," which, based on what we know about Steve Rogers, should be distinctly different from how his predecessors performed the job. (But maybe not so different, as we'll soon see.)

The After-Aftermath

And with the fall of Norman Osborn, the "Dark Reign" ended and "The Heroic Age" began. On one of the last pages of *Siege* #4 we see a news crawl on a building in New York City that reads:

> SUPERHUMAN REGISTRATION ACT THROWN OUT
> STEVE ROGERS AKA CAPTAIN AMERICA
> REPLACES NORMAN OSBORN AS TOP COP
> WHO WILL BE THE NEW AVENGERS?

The first line puts a nice bow on the sprawling storyline that began with the tragedy in Stamford (if not the many disasters involving superheroes that preceded it). According to journalist Ben Urich, the SHRA was repealed by Congress, but Steve Rogers tells a young hero that "my first act in office was to revoke the registration act," although I question if even in his new role he has that kind of power![14] We know much of what led to the registration act being passed, but almost nothing about the motivation for its repeal, which is unfortunate. Perhaps it was Norman Osborn's use of it to suppress all superheroes other than his corrupt, murderous Avengers team, or maybe it was seeing Captain America arisen from the dead to lead his fellow heroes, whether they stood with him or against him in the Civil War, to defeat Osborn—a sight, we can imagine, with tremendous symbolism to a beleaguered public in the Marvel Universe. However it happened, it was rarely spoken of afterwards.[15]

Before Steve Rogers could assemble his new Avengers, he, Tony Stark, and Thor had a surprise dimension-hopping adventure which revealed and resolved longstanding rifts between the two heroes at the forefront of the Civil War.[16] As the three Avengers surveyed the ruins of Asgard, Tony promised that "anything can be rebuilt. Anything. Every time I've had to rebuild this armor, I made it better. Every time. Wait 'til you see my new stuff."[17] Steve simply says, "we'll see," and when Tony asks him what he meant by that, they have a conversation that flips the nature of their relationship before Cap "died":

> STEVE: I'm not convinced letting you keep that armor is in the best interests of the country, Iron Man. I haven't made up my mind.
> TONY: Oh really?
> STEVE: You knew this conversation was coming.
> TONY: Did I?
> STEVE: We'll talk about it at the appropriate time.
> TONY: Well, Captain Rogers, or whatever the hell we're supposed to call you now that you're the new Nick Fury...
> STEVE: Don't get on your high horse—
> TONY: I'll tell you something I promise is true.
> STEVE: I knew you'd be like this—
> TONY: There will never be an appropriate time to tell me that I can't have what is rightfully mine.
> STEVE: Well, look who's all for civil rights all of a sudden.
> TONY: That has nothing to do with anything—
> STEVE: Fine.
> TONY: So, what you're saying is these inalienable rights that you were willing to die for—freedom of power, all that... all of that goes out the window now that you're in charge!
> STEVE: I'm saying that it was you who put this entire country in danger when you let a maniac like Norman Osborn have the keys to your armory!

It didn't end there, but you get the idea: Steve Rogers holds Tony Stark personally responsible for Norman Osborn taking over the world and nearly destroying it, and now that he's in charge he's not sure how far to let Tony go, even if it means acting more like Iron Man than Captain America.

Over the course of their adventure together, however, Steve and Tony bonded once more, and when it was over, Steve and Tony began their reconciliation (with Thor looking on approvingly):

> STEVE: I'm sorry about the things I said before this happened. It's—it's just so hard to put away all the things that happened between us.
> TONY: All those things... all the things I said and did—I'm—I'm so, so, sorry. I know that's not enough, but I hope you will allow me the chance to earn your friendship back. I don't deserve it... I just hope you let me. I'm not half as good at—at anything as I am when I'm doing it next to you. And that's the truth.[18]

Once Steve Rogers took his position as "top cop," he set about answering the last question on the news crawl, putting together two Avengers teams: one with the big hitters like Thor, Iron Man, and Bucky (serving as Captain America), with Maria Hill in charge, and the other led by Luke Cage, including Spider-Man and Wolverine, and modeled after his underground Avengers team following the Civil War.[19] After Steve announced the teams, Tony approached him, and the two discussed how they would work together—or not.

> TONY: Steve, I don't have to be on your little team here...
> STEVE: Of course you don't *have* to. But it's the Avengers. I thought you'd *want* to.
> TONY: I'm talking about you and me.
> STEVE: I know.
> TONY: We don't agree on... just about anything anymore.
> STEVE: That's not entirely true.
> TONY: See, we don't even agree about *that*.[20]

And even though they are reconciled for now, Steve and Tony will soon butt heads again, especially after Steve discovers the existence and past activities of the Illuminati; joins them to fight the threat of incursions from parallel Earths; resists his colleague's plans to destroy them; and has his memory of the incident erased at Tony's command, only to remember later and renew the conflict between them that sees the two of them at each other's throats while the Marvel Universe is destroyed.[21] But for now, in the aftermath of the Siege and the beginning of the Heroic Age, they're friends again!

Looking at their new positions, there has been quite a reversal, as each points out to the other. Now that Steve is in charge of global security, he has gained a keener appreciation of the value of security and safety, while Tony, demoted to being one of the "little guys," comes to see the value of liberty and privacy. They haven't flipped positions completely, but rather have come to appreciate that their stances at the beginning of the Civil War were not absolute, and the other's position was more reasonable and valuable than they were able to recognize at the time.

What It Takes to Be in Charge

When Cap later discovered the existence of the Illuminati and criticized them for assuming stewardship of the all-powerful Infinity Gems, Tony invokes two of his key personality traits that he believes to be essential to the superhero profession:

> It was arrogance and it was ego. And it was absolutely right. For all this time. So, though you may think it's your job to judge me and the others for what we did here ... I think it's nothing. Nothing compared to the things we've had to do to keep the world safe. Nothing.

To this, Rogers replied, simply, "Maybe I just don't see the world the same way you do."[22] But as Cap finds out in his new job, a little arrogance is necessary to make the decisions that go with the position, and he sees that Tony was right to say decisions have to be made, and somebody has to make them. After all, in an earlier adventure with Tony, Cap himself said that "in our job, arrogance is occasionally hard to define. Some would call us arrogant to think we can make a difference in the world."[23]

Arrogance—or its milder cousin, confidence—is not a quality widely associated with most superheroes, especially Captain America, for whom humility is a central character trait.[24] Insofar as superheroes only act defensively, putting out fires and saving lives, they don't need arrogance. But if they are going to take charge and act proactively, like Tony did during the Civil War and Steve does after the Siege, it can come in handy—although, as we saw with Tony, it can go too far, to the point at which one becomes, as the She-Hulk put it, a "tyrant."[25] As in most things, the proper balance, the "right" amount of arrogance, is essential, especially if you plan to intervene in world affairs to improve the lives of people while respecting their liberty at the same time.

We expect Captain America to respect civil liberties and human rights, but leading a global security agency requires positive action as well, action with uncertain consequences and costs, sometimes in terms of the very liberties and rights he's sworn to defend. As always, such tough decisions to balance principles come down to judgment—maybe enhanced by a touch of arrogance that gives you the confidence to put that judgment into action. By balancing the consequentialist goals of safety and security with his deontological principles of liberty and privacy, maybe Steve Rogers could oversee things using the proper balance with these ethical imperatives. As it turned out, however, he soon assumed the mantle of Captain America once again in the next Earth-shattering crossover event to hit the Marvel Universe—and the cycle starts anew.

~~~~~

As they say in life as well as in comics, the more things change, the more they stay the same—and this includes the ideological conflict between Iron Man and Captain America. When Tony said to Cap long ago that "I promise you this Steve, when I have finished what I have to do, I'll look you up and we'll have a long talk about ethics," even the futurist in him could not have anticipated how true this would be![26]

---

[1] *Captain America*, vol. 5, #600 (August 2009), "One Year After."

[2] *Captain America: Reborn* #1 (September 2009).

[3] *Captain America: Reborn* #1.

[4] *Captain America: Reborn* (2010).

[5] *Captain America: Reborn* #6 (March 2010).

[6] *Siege* (2010).

[7] *Siege: The Cabal* one-shot (February 2010) and *Siege* #1 (March 2010). Osborn uses the same skill at manipulating media that he showed at his post-Invasion press conference to stir the flames of hatred against the Asgardians, as shown in *Siege: Embedded* (2010).

[8] *Siege* #1.

[9] We also saw this when Tony was "inverted" during the recent Axis event, especially in his relaunched title *Superior Iron Man*, in which he infected the entire population of San Francisco with the Extremis virus—and then charged them $100 per day to maintain it (*Superior Iron Man Volume 1: Infamous*, 2015).

[10] *Siege* #3 (May 2010).

[11] *Siege* #4 (June 2010).

[12] *Captain America: Who Will Wield the Shield?* one-shot (February 2010). Steve and Bucky continue to discuss and reminiscence over their respective roles in the *Siege: Captain America* one-shot (June 2010), which took place during the final battle of the Siege (in *Siege* #3).

[13] *Siege* #4.

[14] *Siege: Embedded* #4 (July 2010); *Age of Heroes* #4 (October 2010), "Independence Day."

[15] At least until the new *Civil War* miniseries in 2015, which imagines a world in which the conflict never ended and the United States is split in two, a bureaucratic part administered by Tony Stark and a "wild west" part overseen by Steve Rogers.

[16] *Avengers Prime* (2011).

[17] *Avengers Prime* #1 (August 2010).

[18] *Avengers Prime* #5 (March 2011).

[19] Each team had a title: see the "big guns" team's beginning in *Avengers by Brian Michael Bendis, Vol. 1* (2011), and Cage's team's start in *New Avengers by Brian Michael Bendis, Vol. 1* (2011). Rogers himself would lead the newly created Secret Avengers; see *Secret Avengers, Vol. 1: Mission to Mars* (2011).

[20] *Avengers*, vol. 4, #1 (July 2010).

[21] OK, here goes. (Deep breath.) Steve becomes aware of the Illuminati in *Avengers*, vol. 4, #8 (February 2011); he joins them in *New Avengers*, vol. 3, #1 (March 2013) and has his mind wiped in *New Avengers*, vol. 3, #3 (April 2013); he remembers in *Avengers*, vol. 5, #29 (July 2014); and they fight while the Marvel Universe dies in *Avengers*, vol. 5, #44 (June 2015).

[22] *Avengers*, vol. 4, #10 (2011).

[23] *Iron Man/Captain America Annual 1998* (January 1999).

[24] See my book *The Virtues of Captain America: Modern-Day Lessons on Character from a World War II Superhero* (Hoboken, NJ: Wiley Blackwell, 2014), pp. 51–54.

[25] *She-Hulk*, vol. 2, #18 (June 2007).

[26] *Captain America*, vol. 1, #341 (May 1988).

Conclusion

When Peter Parker undergoes a mystical transformation just before the incident in Stamford, Tony Stark runs some tests and insists that Peter "stay put" in the lab until the results come back. Captain America says, "I have to agree with Tony," and Peter mutters in reply, "Big surprise."[1]

We know now that this was the last time Tony and Cap would agree for quite a long time. As we saw at the end of the last chapter, even after Cap put Tony on his primary Avengers team, Tony said Cap, "We don't agree on… just about anything anymore." Cap replied, "That's not entirely true," which only proved Tony's point![2]

Tony and Cap do agree on the basics, however. They both place a high value on the principles of liberty and security. They also place different weights on them and, as a result, choose different means to implement them. Each wrapped himself in his preferred principle and stood up for its primary importance when they battled, but in their more level-headed moments, they realized that they were both fighting for the same things, just each in his own way.

Peter Parker internalized both sides of this ideological conflict, changing his judgments throughout the storyline as circumstances changed. From the start of his superhero career, as a fifteen-year-old boy suddenly endowed with great power that demanded great responsibility, he struggled with the conflict between his duties to do right and to protect his loved ones—a conflict that has cost him dearly over the years. To Peter, the debate at the heart of the Civil War was not just abstract or intellectual; for him, it was all personal and all too familiar.

As we in the real world face our own struggle over issues of liberty, security, and privacy, which continue in many forms even as the events of September 11, 2001, recede further into the past, we must remember these lessons also. It is not a choice between liberty and privacy on the one hand or security and safety on the other. Neither principle has any value in isolation; only together does either one have meaning. The trick is finding the proper balance to promoting both, which will not be the same from year to year, country to country, or person to person.

Will we continue to argue over this? Of course we will—in fact, we must. Democracy may thrive on a solid framework of agreement over shared principles, but it can advance only through disagreement on how to balance and implement those principles. There is a push–pull relationship between liberty and security that can never be resolved to unanimous satisfaction. We need both, but we must continually make choices about how to balance them.

The focus of this book has been on the three main characters in the Civil War storyline, and their codes of ethics and the moral judgment they made throughout have parallels to the real world that I hope I have made sufficiently clear. The best fiction helps us look at ourselves and the world around us in different ways, and the Marvel Comics Civil War, constructed out of over one hundred comic books that were written and illustrated by just as many talented comics creators, is a perfect example. It provides a way for us to step out of the real-world conflict that we know so well and instead consider a fictional version in which we can observe and consider different actions and their consequences.

One doesn't have to exaggerate or elevate the literary quality of the Civil War to do this; I have no desire to make superhero comics anything other than superhero comics. But I do think superhero comics can show us more than many people think, and hopefully I've shown a little of what they do with this book. (On that, there will surely be no disagreement.)

---

[1] *Marvel Knights Spider-Man* #22 (March 2006).
[2] *Avengers*, vol. 4, #1 (July 2010).

References

Below you will find details for every individual comic and collection I cited in this book, listed in alphabetical order by title and, in the case of individual comics, by volume and issue number. The dates given for the comics are the cover dates; the actual release date was usually two months earlier. All the comics and trade paperbacks listed below are published by Marvel Comics (except one trade collection). In terms of creators, I limited the credits to writers, pencillers, and inkers, but this is not to diminish the contributions of all the talented colorists, letterers, and editors—not to mention the artists who worked on the covers—that helped produce these great comics.

I split the references into three categories: *Civil War* collections, other collections that I cite directly (without a specific issue), and individual comics (noting when they have been reprinted in a collection, whether listed previously or not). Some of the collections will be out of print, but they are often still available at your local comic book shop, through online used book retailers, or at your local library (for free!).

For *even more* information on the comics cited in this book, I suggest the *Grand Comics Database* (http://www.comics.org), a comprehensive online archive of comics information for all publishers, emphasizing bibliographic detail, and the *Marvel Comics Database* (http://marvel.wikia.com), similar to the Grand Comics Database but (obviously) focused on Marvel Comics and featuring character profiles and links as well as story synopses and links to related comics.

Civil War collections

Black Panther: Civil War (2007), collecting Black Panther, vol. 4, #19–25 (October 2006–April 2007). Reginald Hudlin (w), Scot Eaton, Manuel Garcia, Koi Turnbull, Marcus To, and various inkers (a).

Civil War (2007), containing *Civil War* #1–7 (July 2006–January 2007). Mark Millar (w), Steve McNiven, Dexter Vines, and others (a).

Civil War: The Amazing Spider-Man (2007), collecting *Amazing Spider-Man*, vol. 1, #532–538 (July 2006–January 2007). J. Michael Straczynski (w), Ron Garney and Bill Reinhold (a).

Civil War: Captain America (2007), containing *Captain America*, vol. 5, #22–24 (November 2006–January 2007) and *Winter Soldier: Winter Kills* one-shot (February 2007). Ed Brubaker (w), Mike Perkins, Lee Weeks, Stefano Gaudiano, and Rick Hoberg (a).

Civil War Companion (2007), collecting the one-shots *Civil War Files* (September 2006), *Civil War: Battle Damage Report* (May 2007), *Marvel Spotlight #6: Mark Miller/Steve McNiven* (June 2006), *Marvel Spotlight: Civil War Aftermath* (March 2007), and *Daily Bugle: Civil War Special Edition* (September 2006). Various writers and artists.

Civil War: Fantastic Four (2007), collecting *Fantastic Four*, vol. 1, #538–543 (August 2006–May 2007). J. Michael Straczynski, Dwayne McDuffie, Stan Lee, and Paul Pope (w), Mike McKone, Nick Dragotta, Paul Pope, and others (a).

Civil War: Front Line Book 1 (2007), collecting *Civil War: Front Line* #1–6 (August–November 2006). Paul Jenkins (w), Ramon Bachs, Steve Lieber, Leandro Fernandez, Lee Weeks, and others (a).

Civil War: Front Line Book 2 (2007), collecting *Civil War: Front Line* #7–11 (December 2006–April 2007). Paul Jenkins (w), Ramon Bachs, Steve Lieber, Lee Weeks, and others (a).

Civil War: Heroes for Hire (2007), collecting *Heroes for Hire*, vol. 2, #1–5 (October 2006–February 2007). Justin Gray and Jimmy Palmiotti (w), Billy Tucci, Francis Portela, Tom Palmer, and Terry Pallot (a).

Civil War: Iron Man (2007), containing *Iron Man*, vol. 4, #13–14 (December 2006–January 2007), *Iron Man/Captain America: Casualties of War* one-shot (February 2007), and *Civil War: The Confession* one-shot (May 2007). Christos N. Gage, Daniel Knauf, Charles Knauf, and Brian Michael Bendis (w), Jeremy Haun, Patrick Zirchner, Alex Maleev, Mark Morales, and Scott Hanna (a).

Civil War: Marvel Universe (2007), collecting the one-shots *Winter Soldier: Winter Kills* (February 2007), *Civil War: Choosing Sides* (December 2006), *Civil War: The Return* (March 2007), and *She-Hulk*, vol. 2, #8 (July 2006). Various writers and artists.

Civil War: Peter Parker, Spider-Man (2007), collecting *Sensational Spider-Man* #28–34 (September 2006–March 2007). Roberto Aquirre-Sacasa (w), Clayton Crain, Angel Medina, Sean Chen, and Scott Hanna (a).

Civil War: Road to Civil War (2007), collecting *New Avengers: Illuminati* one-shot (May 2006), *Fantastic Four*, vol. 1, #536–537 (May 2006–June 2006), and *Amazing Spider-Man*, vol. 1, #529–531 (April 2006–June 2006). Brian Michel Bendis and J. Michael Straczynski (w), Alex Maleev, Mike McKone, Ron Garney, Tyler Kirkham, and others (a).

Civil War: Thunderbolts (2007), collecting *Thunderbolts*, vol. 1, #101–105 (June–October 2006). Fabian Nicieza (w), Tom Grummett, Dave Ross, Gary Erskine, and Cam Smith (a).

Civil War: War Crimes (2007), collecting *Underworld* #1–5 (April–August 2006) and *Civil War: War Crimes* one-shot (February 2007). Frank Tieri (w), Staz Johnson, Tom Palmer, and Robin Riggs (a).

Civil War: Wolverine (2007), collecting *Wolverine*, vol. 3, #42–48 (July 2006–January 2007). Marc Guggenheim (w), Humberto Ramos and Carlos Cuevas (a).

Civil War: X-Men (2007), collecting *Civil War: X-Men* #1–4 (September–December 2007). David Hine (w), Yanick Pacquette, Aaron Lopresti, Serge Lapointe, and Jay Leisten (a).

Civil War: X-Men Universe (2007), collecting *X-Factor*, vol. 3, #8–9 (August–September 2006) and *Cable & Deadpool* #30–32 (September–November 2006). Peter David and Fabian Nicieza (w), Dennis Calero, Staz Johnson, Klaus Janson, and John Stanisci (a).

Civil War: Young Avengers & Runaways (2007), collecting *Civil War: Young Avengers & Runaways* #1–4 (September–December 2006). Zeb Wells (w), Stefano Caselli (a).

Ms. Marvel Vol. 2: Civil War (2007), collecting *Ms. Marvel*, vol. 2, #6–10 (October 2006–February 2007), and *Ms. Marvel Special* #1 (March 2007). Brian Reed (w), Roberto de la Torre, Mike Wieringo, Jon Sibal, Wade von Grawbadger, and Lorenzo Ruggiero (a).

New Avengers, Vol. 5: Civil War (2007), collecting *New Avengers*, vol. 1, #21–25 (August–December 2006). Brian Michael Bendis (w), Howard Chaykin, Leinil Yu, Olivier Coipel, Pasqual Ferry, Jim Cheung, and others (a).

Punisher War Journal Vol. 1: Civil War (2007), collecting *Punisher War Journal*, vol. 2, #1–4 (January–April 2007). Matt Fraction (w), Ariel Olivetti and Mike Deodato, Jr. (a).

Other collections cited independently

Amazing Spider-Man Vol. 10: New Avengers (2005), collecting *Amazing Spider-Man* #519–524 (June–November 2005). J. Michael Straczynski (w), Mike Deodato, Jr., Joe Pimentel, and Tom Palmer (a).

Amazing Spider-Man Vol. 9: Skin Deep (2005), collecting *Amazing Spider-Man* #515–518 (February–May 2005). J. Michael Straczynski (w), Mike Deodato, Jr., Mark Brooks, and others (a).

Avengers & X-Men: Axis (2015), collecting *Avengers & X-Men: Axis* #1–9 (December 2014–February 2015). Rick Remender (w), Adam Kubert, Leinil Francis Yu, Terry Dodson, and others (a).

Avengers by Brian Michael Bendis, Vol. 1 (2011), collecting *Avengers*, vol. 4, #1–6 (July–December 2010). Brian Michael Bendis (w), John Romita, Jr., Klaus Janson, and Tom Palmer (a).

Avengers Disassembled (2006), collecting Avengers, vol. 3, #500–503 (September 2004–December 2004) and *Avengers Finale* one-shot (January 2005). Brain Michael Bendis (w), David Finch, Danny Miki, and others (a).

Avengers Disassembled: Thor (2004), collecting *Thor*, vol. 2, #80–85 (August–December 2004). Michael Avon Oeming and Daniel Berman (w), Andrea Divito (a).

Avengers Prime (2011), collecting *Avengers Prime* #1–5 (August 2010–March 2011). Brian Michael Bendis (w), Alan Davis and Mark Farmer (a).

Avengers: Kree/Skrull War (2013), collecting Avengers, vol. 1, #89–97 (June 1971–March 1972). Roy Thomas (w), Neal Adams, Sal Buscema, John Buscema, and others (a).

Avengers: The Initiative Vol. 1—Basic Training (2007), collecting *Avengers: The Initiative* #1–6 (June–November 2007). Dan Slott (w), Stefano Caselli and Steve Uy (a).

Captain America, Vol. 1: Winter Soldier Ultimate Collection (2010), collecting *Captain America*, vol. 5, #1–9 and #11–14 (January 2005–April 2006). Ed Brubaker (w), Steve Epting, Michael Lark, and others (a).

Captain America: American Nightmare (2011), collecting *Captain America*, vol. 3, #8–13 (August 1998–January 1999), *Captain America & Citizen V Annual 1998* (January 1999), and *Iron Man/Captain America Annual 1998* (January 1999). Mark Waid and others (w), Andy Kubert, Doug Braithwaite, and others (a).

Captain America and the Falcon: Nomad (2006), collecting *Captain America*, vol. 1, #177–186 (September 1974–June 1975). Steve Englehart and John Warner (w), Sal Buscema, Frank Robbins, Herb Trimpe, and others (a).

Captain America and the Falcon: Secret Empire (2005), collecting *Captain America*, vol. 1, #169–176 (January–August 1974). Steve Englehart and Mike Friedrich (w), Sal Buscema, Vincent Colletta, and Frank McLaughlin (a).

Captain America: The Captain (2011), collecting *Captain America*, vol. 1, #332–350 (August 1987–February 1989) and *Iron Man*, vol. 1, #228 (March 1988). Mark Gruenwald, David Michelinie, and Bob Layton (w), Kieron Dwyer, Tom Morgan, and others (a).

Captain America: The New Deal (2003), collecting *Captain America*, vol. 4, #1–6 (June–December 2002). John Ney Rieber (w), John Cassaday (a).

Captain America: Reborn (2010), collecting *Captain America: Reborn* #1–6 (September 2009–March 2010). Ed Brubaker (w), Bryan Hitch and Butch Guise (a).

Captain America: Red, White & Blue (2007), collecting *Captain America: Red, White & Blue* one-shot (September 2002), material from *Captain America*, vol. 3, #50

(February 2002), and *Marvel Spotlight: Captain America Remembered* (June 2007). Various writers and artists.

Captain America: To Serve and Protect (2011), collecting *Captain America*, vol. 3, #1–7 (January–July 1998). Mark Waid (w), Ron Garney, Dale Eaglesham, and others (a).

Captain America: War & Remembrance (2011), collecting *Captain America*, vol. 1, #247–255 (July 1980–March 1981). Roger Stern (w), John Byrne and Joe Rubinstein (a).

Daredevil Vol. 5: Out (2003), collecting *Daredevil*, vol. 2, #32–40 (June 2002–February 2003). Brian Michael Bendis (w), Alex Maleev, Manuel Gutierrez, Terry Dodson, and Rachel Dodson (a).

Daredevil: Born Again (1987), collecting *Daredevil*, vol. 1, #227–233 (February–August 1986). Frank Miller (w), David Mazzucchelli (a).

Decimation: The 198 (2006), collecting *X-Men: The 198* #1–5 (March–July 2006). David Hine (w), Jim Muniz and Kevin Conrad (a).

Decimation: X-Men—The Day After (2006), collecting *House of M—The Day After* one-shot (January 2006) and *X-Men*, vol. 2, #177–181 (January–March 2006). Peter Milligan and Chris Claremont (w), Salvador Larroca, Randy Green, Aaron Lopresti, Roger Cruz, and others (a).

Doomwar (2010), collecting *Doomwar* #1–6 (April–October 2010). Jonathan Maberry (w), Scot Eaton with various inkers (a).

Fallen Son: The Death of Captain America (2008), collecting *Fallen Son: The Death of Captain America* #1–5 (June–August 2007). Jeph Loeb (w), and various (a).

Fantastic Four: Foes (2005), collecting *Fantastic Four: Foes* #1–6 (March–August 2005). Robert Kirkman (w), Cliff Rathburn (a).

Fantastic Four: The New Fantastic Four (2008), collecting *Fantastic Four* #544–550 (May–November 2007). Dwayne McDuffie (w), Paul Pelletier, Rick Magyar, and Scott Hanna (a).

House of M (2006), collecting *House of M* #1–8 (August–November 2005). Brian Michael Bendis (w), Olivier Coipel and various inkers (a).

Hulk: Planet Hulk (2007), collecting *Incredible Hulk*, vol. 2, #92–105 (April 2006–June 2007). Greg Pak (w), and various (a).

Hulk: Planet Hulk Prelude (2010), collecting *Fantastic Four* #553–535 (January–April 2006) and *Incredible Hulk*, vol. 2, #88–91 (January–March 2006). J. Michael Straczynski and Daniel Way (w), Mike McKone, Keu Cha, Juan Santacruz, and various inkers (a).

Hulk: WWH—Front Line (2008), collecting *World War Hulk Prologue: World Breaker* one-shot (July 2007) and *World War Hulk: Front Line* #1–6 (August–December 2007). Peter David and Paul Jenkins (w), and various (a).

The Invincible Iron Man Vol. 1: The Five Nightmares (2009), collecting *Invincible Iron Man* #1–7 (July 2008–January 2009). Matt Fraction (w), Salvador Larroca (a).

The Invincible Iron Man Vol. 2: World's Most Wanted, Book 1 (2009), collecting *Invincible Iron Man* #8–13 (February–July 2009). Matt Fraction (w), Salvador Larroca (a).

The Invincible Iron Man Vol. 3: World's Most Wanted, Book 2 (2010), collecting *Invincible Iron Man* #14–19 (August–December 2009). Matt Fraction (w), Salvador Larroca (a).

Iron Man: Execute Program (2007), collecting *Iron Man*, vol. 4, #7–12 (June–November 2006). Daniel and Charles Knauf (w), Patrick Zircher and Scott Hanna (a).

Iron Man: Extremis (2007), collecting *Iron Man*, vol. 4, #1–6 (January 2005–April 2006). Warren Ellis (w), Adi Granov (a).

Iron Man: The Many Armors of Iron Man (2008), collecting *Iron Man*, vol. 1, #47, 142–144, 152–153, 200, and 218 (1972–1987). Various writers and artists.

JLA/Avengers (2008, published by DC Comics in association with Marvel Comics), collecting *JLA/Avengers* #1–4 (September–December 2003). Kurt Busiek (w), George Pérez (a).

Marvels (2008), collecting *Marvels* #0–4 (January–August 1994). Kurt Busiek (w), Alex Ross (a).

New Avengers by Brian Michael Bendis Vol. 1 (2011), collecting *New Avengers*, vol. 2, #1–6 (August 2010–January 2011). Brian Michael Bendis (w), Stuart Immonen and Wade von Grawbadger (a).

New Avengers Vol. 1: Breakout (2005), collecting *New Avengers*, vol. 1, #1–6 (January–June 2005). Brian Michael Bendis (w), David Finch, Danny Miki, and other inkers (a).

New Avengers Vol. 4: The Collective (2007), collecting *New Avengers*, vol. 1, #16–20 (April–August 2006). Brian Michael Bendis (w), Steve McNiven, Mike Deodato, Jr., Dexter Vines, and Joe Pimentel (a).

New Avengers: Illuminati (2008), collecting *New Avengers: Illuminati* #1–5 (February 2007–January 2008). Brian Michael Bendis and Brian Reed (w), Jim Cheung, Mark Morales, John Dell, and David Meikis (a).

Secret Avengers, Vol. 1: Mission to Mars (2011), collecting *Secret Avengers*, vol. 1, #1–5 (July–November 2010). Ed Brubaker (w), Mike Deodato, Jr. and others (a).

Secret Invasion (2010), collecting *Secret Invasion* #1–8 (June 2008–January 2009). Brian Michael Bendis (w), Leinil Francis Yu and Mark Morales (a).

Secret Invasion: Front Line (2009), collecting *Secret Invasion: Front Line* #1–5 (September 2008–January 2009). Brian Reed (w), Marco Castiello (a).

Secret War (2006), collecting *Secret War* #1–5 (April 2004–December 2005). Brian Michael Bendis (w), Gabriele Dell'otto (a).

Siege (2010), collecting *Siege: The Cabal* one-shot (February 2010) and *Siege* #1–4 (March–June 2010). Brian Michael Bendis (w), Olivier Coipel and others (a).

Siege: Embedded (2010), collecting *Siege: Embedded* #1–4 (March–July 2010). Brian Reed (w), Chris Samnee (a).

Spider-Man: Am I an Avenger? (2011), collecting *Amazing Spider-Man*, vol. 1, #348 (June 1991) and Annual #3 (November 1966), "…To Become an Avenger!"; *Avengers*, vol. 1, #236–237 (October–November 1983), #314–318 (February–June 1990), and #329 (February 1991); *New Avengers*, vol. 1, #3 (March 2005); and *Avengers*, vol. 4, #1 (July 2010). Various writers and artists.

Spider-Man: Birth of Venom (2007), collecting material from various comics from 1984–1991. Various writers and artists.

Spider-Man: Brand New Day Vol. 1 (2008), collecting *Amazing Spider-Man* #546–551 (February–April 2008). Various writers and artists.

Spider-Man: One Moment in Time (2010), collecting *Amazing Spider-Man* #638–641 (September–October 2010). Joe Quesada (w/a), Paolo Rivera, Danny Miki, and Richard Isanove (a).

Superior Iron Man Volume 1: Infamous (2015), collecting *Superior Iron Man* #1–5 (January–April 2015). Tom Taylor (w), Yildray Cinar, Laura Braga, and various inkers (a).

Thor by J. Michael Straczynski Vol. 1 (2008), collecting *Thor*, vol. 3, #1–6 (September 2007–February 2008). J. Michael Straczynski (w), Olivier Coipel and Mark Morales (a).

World War Hulk (2008), collecting *World War Hulk* #1–5 (August 2007–January 2008). Greg Pak (w), John Romita, Jr., and Klaus Janson (a).

Individual comics

Age of Heroes #4 (October 2010), "Independence Day." Dan Slott (w), Ty Templeton (a). Collected in *Age of Heroes* (2011).

Amazing Spider-Man, vol. 1, #1 (March 1963), "Spider-Man Vs. the Chameleon." Stan Lee (w), Steve Ditko (a). Collected in *Marvel Masterworks: The Amazing Spider-Man Vol. 1* (2009) and *Amazing Spider-Man Epic Collection: Great Power* (2014).

Amazing Spider-Man, vol. 1, #121 (June 1973). Gerry Conway (w), Gil Kane, John Romita, Sr., and Tony Mortellaro (a). Collected in *Spider-Man: Death of the Stacys* (2012).

Amazing Spider-Man, vol. 1, #252 (May 1984). Tom DeFalco and Roger Stern (w), Ron Frenz and Brett Breeding (a). Collected in *Spider-Man: Birth of Venom* (2007).

Amazing Spider-Man, vol. 2, #36 (December 2001). J. Michael Straczynski (w), John Romita, Jr., and Scott Hanna (a). Collected in *Amazing Spider-Man Vol. 2: Revelations* (2002).

Amazing Spider-Man #518 (May 2005). J. Michael Straczynski (w), Mike Deodato, Jr., Mark Brooks, and others (a). Collected in *Amazing Spider-Man Vol. 9: Skin Deep* (2005).

Amazing Spider-Man #519 (June 2005). J. Michael Straczynski (w), Mike Deodato, Jr. and Joe Pimentel (a). Collected in *Amazing Spider-Man Vol. 10: New Avengers* (2005).

Amazing Spider-Man #520 (July 2005). J. Michael Straczynski (w), Mike Deodato, Jr. and Joe Pimentel (a). Collected in *Amazing Spider-Man Vol. 10: New Avengers* (2005).

Amazing Spider-Man #521 (August 2005). J. Michael Straczynski (w), Mike Deodato, Jr., Joe Pimentel, and Tom Palmer (a). Collected in *Amazing Spider-Man Vol. 10: New Avengers* (2005).

Amazing Spider-Man #522 (September 2005). J. Michael Straczynski (w), Mike Deodato, Jr., Joe Pimentel, and Tom Palmer (a). Collected in *Amazing Spider-Man Vol. 10: New Avengers* (2005).

Amazing Spider-Man #524 (November 2005). J. Michael Straczynski (w), Mike Deodato, Jr., Joe Pimentel, and Tom Palmer (a). Collected in *Amazing Spider-Man Vol. 10: New Avengers* (2005).

Amazing Spider-Man #527 (February 2006). J. Michael Straczynski (w), Mike Deodato, Jr. and Joe Pimentel (a). Collected in *Spider-Man: The Other* (2007).

Amazing Spider-Man #528 (March 2006). J. Michael Straczynski (w), Mike Deodato, Jr. and Joe Pimentel (a). Collected in *Spider-Man: The Other* (2007).

Amazing Spider-Man #529 (April 2006). J. Michael Straczynski (w), Ron Garney and Bill Reinhold (a). Collected in *Civil War: Road to Civil War* (2007).

Amazing Spider-Man #530 (May 2006). J. Michael Straczynski (w), Tyler Kirkham and Jay Leisten (a). Collected in *Civil War: Road to Civil War* (2007).

Amazing Spider-Man #531 (June 2006). J. Michael Straczynski (w), Tyler Kirkham and Sal Regla (a). Collected in *Civil War: Road to Civil War* (2007).

Amazing Spider-Man #532 (July 2006). J. Michael Straczynski (w), Ron Garney and Bill Reinhold (a). Collected in *Civil War: Amazing Spider-Man* (2007).

Amazing Spider-Man #533 (August 2006). J. Michael Straczynski (w), Ron Garney and Bill Reinhold (a). Collected in *Civil War: Amazing Spider-Man* (2007).

Amazing Spider-Man #534 (September 2006). J. Michael Straczynski (w), Ron Garney and Bill Reinhold (a). Collected in *Civil War: Amazing Spider-Man* (2007).

Amazing Spider-Man #535 (November 2006). J. Michael Straczynski (w), Ron Garney and Bill Reinhold (a). Collected in *Civil War: Amazing Spider-Man* (2007).

Amazing Spider-Man #536 (November 2006). J. Michael Straczynski (w), Ron Garney and Bill Reinhold (a). Collected in *Civil War: Amazing Spider-Man* (2007).

Amazing Spider-Man #537 (December 2006). J. Michael Straczynski (w), Ron Garney and Bill Reinhold (a). Collected in *Civil War: Amazing Spider-Man* (2007).

Amazing Spider-Man #538 (January 2007). J. Michael Straczynski (w), Ron Garney and Bill Reinhold (a). Collected in *Civil War: Amazing Spider-Man* (2007).

Amazing Spider-Man #539 (April 2007). J. Michael Straczynski (w), Ron Garney and Bill Reinhold (a). Collected in *Spider-Man: Back in Black* (2008).

Amazing Spider-Man #540 (May 2007). J. Michael Straczynski (w), Ron Garney and Bill Reinhold (a). Collected in *Spider-Man: Back in Black* (2008).

Amazing Spider-Man #541 (June 2007). J. Michael Straczynski (w), Ron Garney and Bill Reinhold (a). Collected in *Spider-Man: Back in Black* (2008).

Amazing Spider-Man #542 (August 2007). J. Michael Straczynski (w), Ron Garney and Bill Reinhold (a). Collected in *Spider-Man: Back in Black* (2008).

Amazing Spider-Man #543 (October 2007). J. Michael Straczynski (w), Ron Garney and Bill Reinhold (a). Collected in *Spider-Man: Back in Black* (2008).

Amazing Spider-Man #544 (November 2007). J. Michael Straczynski (w), Joe Quesada and Danny Miki (a). Collected in *Spider-Man: One More Day* (2008).

Amazing Spider-Man #545 (January 2008). J. Michael Straczynski and Joe Quesada (w), Joe Quesada and Danny Miki (a). Collected in *Spider-Man: One More Day* (2008).

Amazing Spider-Man #590 (June 2009). Dan Slott (w), Barry Kitson and Mark Farmer (a). Collected in *Spider-Man: 24/7* (2009).

Amazing Spider-Man #591 (June 2009). Dan Slott (w), Barry Kitson, Dale Eaglesham, and Jesse Delperdang (a). Collected in *Spider-Man: 24/7* (2009).

Amazing Spider-Man #641 (October 2010). Joe Quesada (w/a), Paolo Rivera, Danny Miki, and Richrd Isanove (a). Collected in *Spider-Man: One Moment in Time* (2010).

Avengers, vol. 1, #1 (September 1963). Stan Lee (w), Jack Kirby and Dick Ayers (a). Collected in A:MM1 and A:ESS1.

Avengers, vol. 1, #4 (March 1964). Stan Lee (w), Jack Kirby and George Roussos (a). Collected in *Marvel Masterworks: Avengers, Vol. 1* (2003) and *Avengers Epic Collection: Earth's Mightiest Heroes* (2014).

Avengers, vol. 1, #6 (July 1964). Stan Lee (w), Jack Kirby and Chic Stone (a). Collected in *Marvel Masterworks: Avengers, Vol. 1* (2009) and *Avengers Epic Collection: Earth's Mightiest Heroes* (2014).

Avengers, vol. 1, #16 (May 1965). Stan Lee (w), Jack Kirby and Dick Ayers (a). Collected in *Marvel Masterworks: Avengers, Vol. 2* (2009) and *Avengers Epic Collection: Earth's Mightiest Heroes* (2014).

Avengers, vol. 1, #213 (November 1981). Jim Shooter (w), Bob Hall and Dan Green (a). Collected in *Avengers: The Trial of Yellowjacket* (2012).

Avengers, vol. 1, #214 (December 1981). Jim Shooter (w), Bob Hall and Dan Green (a). Collected in *Avengers: The Trial of Yellowjacket* (2012).

Avengers, vol. 1, #216 (February 1982). Jim Shooter (w), Alan Weiss and Dan Green (a). Collected in *Avengers: The Trial of Yellowjacket* (2012).

Avengers, vol. 1, #230 (April 1983). Roger Stern (w), Al Milgrom and Joe Sinnott (a). Collected in *Avengers: The Trial of Yellowjacket* (2012).

Avengers, vol. 1, #260 (October 1985). Roger Stern (w), John Buscema and Tom Palmer (a). Collected in *Avengers: The Legacy of Thanos* (2014).

Avengers, vol. 3, #7 (August 1998). Kurt Busiek (w), George Pérez and Al Vey (a). Collected in *Avengers Assemble Vol. 1* (2011).

Avengers, vol. 3, #9 (October 1998). Kurt Busiek (w), George Pérez and Al Vey (a). Collected in *Avengers Assemble Vol. 1* (2011).

Avengers, vol. 3, #55 (August 2002). Kurt Busiek (w), Patrick Zircher and Scott Koblish (a). Collected in *Avengers Assemble Vol. 5* (2012).

Avengers, vol. 3, #67 (July 2003). Geoff Johns (w), Olivier Coipel and Andy Lanning (a). Collected in *Avengers: Red Zone* (2010).

Avengers, vol. 3, #70 (October 2003). Geoff Johns (w), Olivier Coipel and Andy Lanning (a). Collected in *Avengers: Red Zone* (2010).

Avengers, vol. 3, #500 (September 2004). Brian Michael Bendis (w), David Finch and Danny Miki (a). Collected in *Avengers Disassembled* (2006).

Avengers, vol. 4, #1 (July 2010). Brian Michael Bendis (w), John Romita, Jr. and Klaus Janson (a). Collected in *Avengers by Brian Michael Bendis, Vol. 1* (2011).

Avengers, vol. 4, #8 (February 2011). Brian Michael Bendis (w), John Romita, Jr. and Klaus Janson (a). Collected in *Avengers by Brian Michael Bendis, Vol. 2* (2012).

Avengers, vol. 4, #10 (April 2011). Brian Michael Bendis (w), John Romita, Jr., Klaus Janson, and Tom Palmer (a). Collected in *Avengers by Brian Michael Bendis, Vol. 2* (2012).

Avengers, vol. 5, #29 (July 2014). Jonathan Hickman (w), Leinil Francis Yu and Gerry Alanguilan (a). Collected in *Avengers Volume 6: Infinite Avengers* (2014).

Avengers, vol. 5, #44 (June 2015). Jonathan Hickman (w), Stefano Caselli and Kev Walker (a). Collected in *Avengers: Time Runs Out Volume 4* (2015).

Avengers Annual, vol. 1, #16 (1987). Tom DeFalco (w), various (a). Collected in *Avengers: The Contest* (2010), *Avengers: Legion of the Unliving* (2012), and *Avengers: West Coast Avengers—Zodiac Attack* (2012).

Avengers: The Initiative #4 (September 2007). Dan Slott (w), Stefano Caselli (a). Collected in *Avengers: The Initiative Vol. 1—Basic Training* (2007) and *World War Hulk: X-Men* (2008).

Avengers Prime #1 (August 2010). Brian Michael Bendis (w), Alan Davis and Mark Farmer (a). Collected in *Avengers Prime* (2011).

Avengers Prime #5 (March 2011). Brian Michael Bendis (w), Alan Davis and Mark Farmer (a). Collected in *Avengers Prime* (2011).

Avengers & X-Men: Axis #7 (February 2015). Rick Remender (w), Adam Kubert (a). Collected in *Avengers & X-Men: Axis* (2015).

Black Panther, vol. 4, #22 (January 2007). Reginald Hudlin (w), Marcus To, Don Ho, and Jef De Los Santos (a). Collected in *Black Panther: Civil War* (2007).

Captain America, vol. 1, #156 (December 1972). Steve Englehart (w), Sal Buscema and Frank McLaughlin (a). Collected in *Captain America: Essentials, Vol. 3* (2010).

Captain America, vol. 1, #250 (October 1980). Roger Stern (w), John Byrne (w/a), Josef Rubinstein (a). Collected in *Captain America: War & Remembrance* (2011).

Captain America, vol. 1, #255 (March 1981). Roger Stern (w), John Byrne (w/a), and Josef Rubinstein (a). Collected in *Captain America: War & Remembrance* (2011).

Captain America, vol. 1, #268 (April 1982). J.M. DeMatteis (w), Mike Zeck and John Beatty (a).

Captain America, vol. 1, #273 (September 1982). David Anthony Kraft (w), Mike Zeck and John Beatty (a).

Captain America, vol. 1, #321 (September 1986). Mark Gruenwald (w), Paul Neary and Dennis Janke (a).

Captain America, vol. 1, #339 (March 1988). Mark Gruenwald (w), Kieron Dwyer and Tony DeZuniga (a). Collected in *Captain America: The Captain* (2011).

Captain America, vol. 1, #340 (April 1988). Mark Gruenwald (w), Kieron Dwyer and Al Milgrom (a). Collected in *Captain America: The Captain* (2011).

Captain America, vol. 1, #341 (May 1988). Mark Gruenwald (w), Kieron Dwyer and Al Milgrom (a). Collected in *Captain America: The Captain* (2011).

Captain America, vol. 1, #401 (June 1992). Mark Gruenwald (w), Rik Levins and Danny Bulanadi (a). Collected in *Avengers: Galactic Storm, Vol. 2* (2006).

Captain America, vol. 4, #4 (September 2002). John Ney Reiber (w), John Cassaday (a). Collected in *Captain America: The New Deal* (2003).

Captain America, vol. 4, #11 (May 2003). Chuck Austen (w), Jae Lee (a). Collected in *Captain America: The Extremists* (2003).

Captain America, vol. 5, #6 (June 2005). Ed Brubaker (w), Steve Epting (a). Collected in *Captain America: Winter Soldier, Vol. 1* (2006).

Captain America, vol. 5, #22 (November 2006). Ed Brubaker (w), Mike Perkins (a). Collected in *Civil War: Captain America* (2007).

Captain America, vol. 5, #23 (December 2006). Ed Brubaker (w), Mike Perkins (a). Collected in *Civil War: Captain America* (2007).

Captain America, vol. 5, #24 (January 2007). Ed Brubaker (w), Mike Perkins (a). Collected in *Civil War: Captain America* (2007).

Captain America, vol. 5, #25 (April 2007). Ed Brubaker (w), Steve Epting (a). Collected in *The Death of Captain America, Vol. 1: The Death of a Dream* (2008).

Captain America, vol. 5, #26 (May 2007). Ed Brubaker (w), Steve Epting (a). Collected in *The Death of Captain America, Vol. 1: The Death of a Dream* (2008).

Captain America, vol. 5, #27 (August 2007). Ed Brubaker (w), Steve Epting and Mike Perkins (a). Collected in *The Death of Captain America, Vol. 1: The Death of a Dream* (2008).

Captain America, vol. 5, #28 (September 2007). Ed Brubaker (w), Steve Epting and Mike Perkins (a). Collected in *The Death of Captain America, Vol. 1: The Death of a Dream* (2008).

Captain America, vol. 5, #30 (November 2007). Ed Brubaker (w), Steve Epting and Mike Perkins (a). Collected in *The Death of Captain America, Vol. 1: The Death of a Dream* (2008).

Captain America, vol. 5, #33 (February 2008). Ed Brubaker (w), Steve Epting and Butch Guise (a). Collected in *The Death of Captain America, Vol. 2: The Burden of Dreams* (2008).

Captain America, vol. 5, #34 (March 2008). Ed Brubaker (w), Steve Epting and Butch Guise (a). Collected in *The Death of Captain America, Vol. 2: The Burden of Dreams* (2008).

Captain America, vol. 5, #600 (August 2009), "One Year After." Ed Brubaker (w), Butch Guice and many other artists (a). Collected in *Captain America: The Road to Reborn* (2010).

Captain America, vol. 7, #1 (January 2013). Rick Remender (w), John Romita, Jr. and Klaus Janson (a). Collected in *Captain America, Vol. 1: Castaway in Dimension Z, Book 1* (2013).

Captain America, vol. 7, #4 (April 2013). Rick Remender (w), John Romita, Jr. and Klaus Janson (a). Collected in *Captain America, Vol. 1: Castaway in Dimension Z, Book 1* (2013).

Captain America and the Falcon #4 (August 2004). Christopher Priest (w), Bart Sears and Rob Hunter (a). Collected in *Captain America and the Falcon, Vol. 1: Two Americas* (2004).

Captain America Comics #1 (March 1941). Various stories. Joe Simon, Jack Kirby, and Ed Herron (w), Joe Simon, Jack Kirby, and Al Liederman (a). Collected in *Marvel Masterworks: Golden Age Captain America Vol. 1* (2012).

Captain America: Man Out of Time #3 (March 2011). Mark Waid (w), Jorge Molina, Karl Kesel, and Scott Hanna (a). Collected in *Captain America: Man Out of Time* (2011).

Captain America: Reborn #1 (September 2009). Ed Brubaker (w), Bryan Hitch and Butch Guice (a). Collected in *Captain America: Reborn* (2010).

Captain America: Reborn #6 (March 2010). Ed Brubaker (w), Bryan Hitch and Butch Guice (a). Collected in *Captain America: Reborn* (2010).

Captain America: Sentinel of Liberty #6 (February 1999), "Iron Will." Mark Waid (w), Ron Garney (w/a), and Dan Green (w). Collected in *Captain America: Sentinel of Liberty* (2011).

Captain America: Sentinel of Liberty #7 (March 1999), "An Ending." Brian Vaughan (w), Steve Harris and Rodney Ramos (a). Collected in *Captain America: Sentinel of Liberty* (2011).

Captain America Theater of War: A Brother in Arms one-shot (June 2009). Paul Jenkins (w), John McCrea and various inkers (a). Collected in *Captain America: Theatre of War* (2010).

Captain America: Who Will Wield the Shield? one-shot (February 2010). Ed Brubaker (w), Butch Guice and Luke Ross (a). Collected in *Captain America: Two Americas* (2010).

Civil War #1 (July 2006). Mark Millar (w), Steve McNiven and Dexter Vines (a). Collected in *Civil War* (2007).

Civil War #2 (August 2006). Mark Millar (w), Steve McNiven and Dexter Vines (a). Collected in *Civil War* (2007).

Civil War #3 (September 2006). Mark Millar (w), Steve McNiven, Dexter Vines, and Mark Morales (a). Collected in *Civil War* (2007).

Civil War #4 (November 2006). Mark Millar (w), Steve McNiven and Dexter Vines (a). Collected in *Civil War* (2007).

Civil War #5 (November 2006). Mark Millar (w), Steve McNiven and Dexter Vines (a). Collected in *Civil War* (2007).

Civil War #6 (December 2006). Mark Millar (w), Steve McNiven and Dexter Vines (a). Collected in *Civil War* (2007).

Civil War #7 (January 2007). Mark Millar (w), Steve McNiven, Dexter Vines, John Dell, and Tim Townsend (a). Collected in *Civil War* (2007).

Civil War: Choosing Sides one-shot (December 2006), "Choosing Sides." Ed Brubaker and Matt Fraction (w), David Aja (a). Collected in *Civil War: Marvel Universe* (2007) and *Immortal Iron Fist Vol. 1: The Last Iron Fist Story* (2007).

Civil War Files one-shot (September 2006). Various writers and artists. Collected in *Civil War Companion* (2007).

Civil War: The Confession one-shot (May 2007). Brian Michael Bendis (w), Alex Maleev (a). Collected in *Civil War: Iron Man* (2007).

Civil War: Front Line #1 (August 2006), "Embedded Part One." Paul Jenkins (w), Ramon Bachs and John Lucas (a). Collected in *Civil War: Front Line Book 1* (2007).

Civil War: Front Line #2 (August 2006), "Embedded Part Two." Paul Jenkins (w), Ramon Bachs and John Lucas (a). Collected in *Civil War: Front Line Book 1* (2007).

Civil War: Front Line #2 (August 2006), "Civil War: The Program." Paul Jenkins (w), Leandro Fernandez (a). Collected in *Civil War: Front Line Book 1* (2007).

Civil War: Front Line #3 (September 2006), "Sleeper Cell Part One." Paul Jenkins (w), Lee Weeks and Rob Campanella (a). Collected in *Civil War: Front Line Book 1* (2007).

Civil War: Front Line #7 (December 2006), "Embedded Part Seven." Paul Jenkins (w), Ramon Bachs and John Lucas (a). Collected in *Civil War: Front Line Book 2* (2007).

Civil War: Front Line #8 (January 2007), "Sleeper Cell Part Six." Paul Jenkins (w), Lee Weeks and Nelson (a). Collected in *Civil War: Front Line Book 2* (2007).

Civil War: Front Line #9 (February 2007), "Embedded Part 9." Paul Jenkins (w), Ramon Bachs and John Lucas (a). Collected in *Civil War: Front Line Book 2* (2007).

Civil War: Front Line #10 (March 2007), "Embedded Part 10." Paul Jenkins (w), Ramon Bachs and John Lucas (a). Collected in *Civil War: Front Line Book 2* (2007).

Civil War: Front Line #11 (April 2007). Paul Jenkins (w), Ramon Bachs and John Lucas (a). Collected in *Civil War: Front Line Book 2* (2007).

Civil War: War Crimes one-shot (February 2007). Frank Tieri (w), Staz Johnson, Tom Palmer, and Robin Riggs (a). Collected in *Civil War: War Crimes* (2007).

Civil War: X-Men #1 (September 2007). David Hine (w), Yanick Pacquette and Serge Lapointe (a).

Daredevil, vol. 3, #36 (April 2014). Mark Waid (w), Chris Samnee (a). Collected in *Daredevil by Mark Waid Volume 7* (2015).

Dark Avengers, vol. 1, #1 (March 2009). Brian Michael Bendis (w), Mike Deodato, Jr. (a). Collected in *Dark Avengers* (2011).

Dark Reign: The Cabal one-shot (June 2009). Various stories, writers, artists. Collected in *Siege Prelude* (2010).

Fallen Son: The Death of Captain America #1 (June 2007). Jeph Loeb (w), Leinil Yu and Dave McCaig (a). Collected in *Fallen Son: The Death of Captain America* (2008).

Fallen Son: The Death of Captain America #3 (July 2007). Jeph Loeb (w), John Romita, Jr. and Klaus Janson (a). Collected in *Fallen Son: The Death of Captain America* (2008).

Fallen Son: The Death of Captain America #4 (July 2007). Jeph Loeb (w), David Finch and Danny Miki (a). Collected in *Fallen Son: The Death of Captain America* (2008).

Fallen Son: The Death of Captain America #5 (August 2007). Jeph Loeb (w), John Cassaday (a). Collected in *Fallen Son: The Death of Captain America* (2008).

Fantastic Four, vol. 1, #1 (November 1961). Stan Lee (w), Jack Kirby, George Klein, and Christopher Rule (a). Collected in *Marvel Masterworks: Fantastic Four, Vol. 1* (2009) and *Fantastic Four Epic Collection: The World's Greatest Comic Magazine* (2014).

Fantastic Four, vol. 1, #4 (May 1962). Stan Lee (w), Jack Kirby and Sal Brodsky (a). Collected in *Marvel Masterworks: Fantastic Four, Vol. 1* (2009) and *Fantastic Four Epic Collection: The World's Greatest Comic Magazine* (2014).

Fantastic Four, vol. 1, #533 (January 2006). J. Michael Straczynski (w), Mike McKone and Andy Lanning (a). Collected in *Fantastic Four: The Life Fantastic* (2006) and *Hulk: Planet Hulk Prelude* (2010).

Fantastic Four, vol. 1, #534 (March 2006). J. Michael Straczynski (w), Mike McKone, Simon Coleby, and Andy Lanning (a). Collected in *Fantastic Four: The Life Fantastic* (2006) and *Hulk: Planet Hulk Prelude* (2010).

Fantastic Four, vol. 1, #535 (April 2006). J. Michael Straczynski (w), Mike McKone, Andy Lanning, and Cam Smith (a). Collected in *Fantastic Four: The Life Fantastic* (2006) and *Hulk: Planet Hulk Prelude* (2010).

Fantastic Four, vol. 1, #536 (May 2006). J. Michael Straczynski (w), Mike McKone and various inkers (a). Collected in *Civil War: The Road to Civil War* (2007).

Fantastic Four, vol. 1, #537 (June 2006). J. Michael Straczynski (w), Mike McKone and various inkers (a). Collected in *Civil War: The Road to Civil War* (2007).

Fantastic Four, vol. 1, #539 (October 2006). J. Michael Straczynski (w), Mike McKone and various inkers (a). Collected in *Civil War: Fantastic Four* (2007).

Fantastic Four, vol. 1, #540 (December 2006). J. Michael Straczynski (w), Mike McKone, Andy Lanning, and Cam Smith (a). Collected in *Civil War: Fantastic Four* (2007).

Fantastic Four, vol. 1, #542 (March 2007). J. Michael Straczynski (w), Mike McKone, Andy Lanning, and Cam Smith (a). Collected in *Civil War: Fantastic Four* (2007).

Fantastic Four: Foes #2 (April 2005). Robert Kirkman (w), Cliff Rathburn (a). Collected in *Fantastic Four: Foes* (2005).

Friendly Neighborhood Spider-Man #20 (July 2007). Peter David (w), Todd Nauck and Robert Campanella (a). Collected in *Spider-Man: Back in Black* (2008).

Friendly Neighborhood Spider-Man #21 (August 2007). Peter David (w), Todd Nauck and Robert Campanella (a). Collected in *Spider-Man: Back in Black* (2008).

Friendly Neighborhood Spider-Man #24 (November 2007). J. Michael Straczynski (w), Joe Quesada and Danny Miki (a). Collected in *Spider-Man: One More Day* (2008).

Heroes for Hire, vol. 2, #1 (October 2006). Justin Gray and Jimmy Palmiotti (w), Billy Tucci and Tom Palmer (a). Collected in *Civil War: Heroes for Hire* (2007).

Heroes for Hire, vol. 2, #2 (November 2006). Justin Gray and Jimmy Palmiotti (w), Billy Tucci, Francis Portela, and Tom Palmer (a). Collected in *Civil War: Heroes for Hire* (2007).

Incredible Hulk, vol. 2, #106 (July 2007). Greg Pak (w), Gary Frank and Jon Sibal (a). Collected in *World War Hulk: The Incredible Hercules* (2008).

Invincible Iron Man #6 (December 2008). Matt Fraction (w), Salvador Larroca (a). Collected in *The Invincible Iron Man Vol. 1: The Five Nightmares* (2009).

Invincible Iron Man #7 (January 2009). Matt Fraction (w), Salvador Larroca (a). Collected in *The Invincible Iron Man Vol. 1: The Five Nightmares* (2009).

Invincible Iron Man #8 (February 2009). Matt Fraction (w), Salvador Larroca (a). Collected in *The Invincible Iron Man Vol. 2: World's Most Wanted, Book 1* (2009).

Invincible Iron Man #9 (March 2009). Matt Fraction (w), Salvador Larroca (a). Collected in *The Invincible Iron Man Vol. 2: World's Most Wanted, Book 1* (2009).

Invincible Iron Man #10 (April 2009). Matt Fraction (w), Salvador Larroca (a). Collected in *The Invincible Iron Man Vol. 2: World's Most Wanted, Book 1* (2009).

Invincible Iron Man #14 (August 2009). Matt Fraction (w), Salvador Larroca (a). Collected in *The Invincible Iron Man Vol. 3: World's Most Wanted, Book 2* (2010).

Invincible Iron Man #15 (September 2009). Matt Fraction (w), Salvador Larroca (a). Collected in *The Invincible Iron Man Vol. 3: World's Most Wanted, Book 2* (2010).

Invincible Iron Man #19 (December 2009). Matt Fraction (w), Salvador Larroca (a). Collected in *The Invincible Iron Man Vol. 3: World's Most Wanted, Book 2* (2010).

Invincible Iron Man #20 (January 2010). Matt Fraction (w), Salvador Larroca (a). Collected in *The Invincible Iron Man Vol. 4: Stark Disassembled* (2010).

Invincible Iron Man #21 (February 2010). Matt Fraction (w), Salvador Larroca (a). Collected in *The Invincible Iron Man Vol. 4: Stark Disassembled* (2010).

Invincible Iron Man #24 (May 2010). Matt Fraction (w), Salvador Larroca (a). Collected in *The Invincible Iron Man Vol. 4: Stark Disassembled* (2010).

Invincible Iron Man #25 (June 2010). Matt Fraction (w), Salvador Larroca (a). Collected in *The Invincible Iron Man Vol. 5: Stark Resilient, Book 1* (2010).

Invincible Iron Man #500 (March 2011), "The New Iron Age." Matt Fraction (w), Salvador Larroca and many other artists (a). Collected in *The Invincible Iron Man Vol. 7: My Monsters* (2011).

Invincible Iron Man #500.1 (April 2011) Matt Fraction (w), Salvador Larroca and many other artists (a). Collected in *The Invincible Iron Man Vol. 7: My Monsters* (2011).

Iron Man, vol. 1, #149 (August 1981). David Michelinie and Bob Layton (w), John Romita, Jr. and Bob Layton (a). Collected in *Iron Man Vs. Doctor Doom: Doomquest* (2008).

Iron Man, vol. 1, #150 (September 1981). David Michelinie and Bob Layton (w), John Romita, Jr. and Bob Layton (a). Collected in *Iron Man Vs. Doctor Doom: Doomquest* (2008).

Iron Man, vol. 1, #168 (March 1983). Denny O'Neil (w), Luke McDonnell and Steve Mitchell (a). Collected in *Iron Man Epic Collection: The Enemy Within* (2013).

Iron Man, vol. 1, #172 (July 1983). Denny O'Neil (w), Luke McDonnell and Steve Mitchell (a). Collected in *Iron Man Epic Collection: The Enemy Within* (2013).

Iron Man, vol. 1, #228 (March 1988). David Michelinie and Bob Layton (w), Mark Bright and Bob Layton (a). Collected in *Iron Man: Armor Wars* (2007), *Captain America: The Captain* (2011), and *Iron Man Epic Collection: Stark Wars* (2015).

Iron Man, vol. 4, #1 (January 2005). Warren Ellis (w), Adi Granov (a). Collected in *Iron Man: Extremis* (2007).

Iron Man, vol. 4, #7 (June 2006). Daniel Knauf and Charles Knauf (w), Patrick Zircher and Scott Hanna (a). Collected in *Iron Man: Execute Program* (2007).

Iron Man, vol. 4, #12 (November 2006). Daniel and Charles Knauf (w), Patrick Zircher and Scott Hanna (a). Collected in *Iron Man: Execute Program* (2007).

Iron Man, vol. 4, #13 (December 2006). Daniel and Charles Knauf (w), Patrick Zircher and Scott Hanna (a). Collected in *Civil War: Iron Man* (2007).

Iron Man, vol. 4, #14 (January 2007). Daniel and Charles Knauf (w), Patrick Zircher and Scott Hanna (a). Collected in *Civil War: Iron Man* (2007).

Iron Man, vol. 4, #18 (July 2007). Daniel and Charles Knauf (w), Roberto De La Torre and Jon Sibal (a). Collected in *Iron Man: Director of SHIELD* (2007).

Iron Man, vol. 4, #19 (August 2007). Christos N. Gage (w), Butch Guise (a). Collected (seriously) in *World War Hulk: X-Men* (2008).

Iron Man, vol. 5, #18 (January 2014). Kieron Gillen (w), Joe Bennett and Scott Hanna (a). Collected in *Iron Man: Iron Metropolitan* (2014).

Iron Man/Captain America Annual 1998 (January 1999). Kurt Busiek (w), Patrick Zircher and Randy Emberlin (a). Collected in *Iron Man: Revenge of the Mandarin* (2012).

Iron Man/Captain America: Casualties of War one-shot (February 2007). Christos Gage (w), Jeremy Haun and Mark Morales (a). Collected in *Civil War: Iron Man* (2007).

Marvel Knights: Spider-Man #21 (February 2006). J. Michael Straczynski (w), Pat Lee and Dream Engine (a). Collected in *Spider-Man: The Other* (2007).

Marvel Knights Spider-Man #22 (March 2006). Reginald Hudlin (w), Pat Lee and Dream Engine (a). Collected in *Spider-Man: The Other* (2007).

Marvel Super Heroes Secret Wars #8 (December 1984). Jim Shooter (w), Mike Zeck, John Beatty, Jack Abel, and Mike Esposito (a). Collected in *Secret Wars* (2011).

Mighty Avengers, vol. 1, #1 (May 2007). Brian Michael Bendis (w), Frank Cho (a). Collected in *Mighty Avengers Vol. 1: The Ultron Initiative* (2008).

Mighty Avengers, vol. 1, #6 (February 2008). Brian Michael Bendis (w), Frank Cho (a). Collected in *Mighty Avengers Vol. 1: The Ultron Initiative* (2008).

Mighty Avengers, vol. 1, #15 (August 2008). Brian Michael Bendis (w), John Romita, Jr., Klaus Janson, and Tom Palmer (a). Collected in *Mighty Avengers Vol. 3: Secret Invasion, Book 1* (2008).

Mighty Avengers, vol. 1, #20 (February 2009). Brian Michael Bendis (w), Lee Weeks, Jim Cheung, Carlo Pagulayan, and Jeffrey Huet (a). Collected in *Mighty Avengers Vol. 4: Secret Invasion, Book 2* (2009).

New Avengers, vol. 1, #2 (February 2005). Brian Michael Bendis (w), David Finch, Danny Miki, and Mark Morales (a). Collected in *New Avengers Vol. 1: Breakout* (2005).

New Avengers, vol. 1, #3 (March 2005). Brian Michael Bendis (w), David Finch, Danny Miki and others (a). Collected in *New Avengers Vol. 1: Breakout* (2005).

New Avengers, vol. 1, #4 (April 2005). Brian Michael Bendis (w), David Finch and Danny Miki (a). Collected in *New Avengers Vol. 1: Breakout* (2005).

New Avengers, vol. 1, #7 (July 2005). Brian Michael Bendis (w), Steve McNiven and Mark Morales (a). Collected in *New Avengers Vol. 2: The Sentry* (2005).

New Avengers, vol. 1, #15 (March 2006). Brian Michael Bendis (w), Frank Cho (a). Collected in *New Avengers Vol. 3: Secrets & Lies* (2006).

New Avengers, vol. 1, #17 (May 2006). Brian Michael Bendis (w), Mike Deodato, Jr. and Joe Pimentel (a). Collected in *New Avengers Vol. 4: The Collective* (2007).

New Avengers, vol. 1, #21 (August 2006). Brian Michael Bendis (w), Howard Chaykin (a). Collected in *Civil War: New Avengers* (2007).

New Avengers, vol. 1, #31 (August 2007). Brian Michael Bendis (w), Leinil Yu (a). Collected in *New Avengers Vol. 6: Revolution* (2007).

New Avengers, vol. 3, #1 (March 2013). Jonathan Hickman (w), Steve Epting and Rick Magyar (a). Collected in *New Avengers, Vol. 1: Everything Dies* (2013).

New Avengers, vol. 3, #2 (March 2013). Jonathan Hickman (w), Steve Epting and Rick Magyar (a). Collected in *New Avengers, Vol. 1: Everything Dies* (2013).

New Avengers, vol. 3, #3 (April 2013). Jonathan Hickman (w), Steve Epting and Rick Magyar (a). Collected in *New Avengers, Vol. 1: Everything Dies* (2013).

New Avengers: Illuminati one-shot (May 2006). Brian Michael Bendis (w), Alex Meleev (a). Collected in *Road to Civil War* (2007).

New Avengers: Illuminati #1 (February 2007). Brian Michael Bendis and Brian Reed (w), Jim Cheung and Mark Morales (a). Collected in *New Avengers: Illuminati* (2008).

New X-Men, vol. 1, #115 (August 2001). Grant Morrison (w), Frank Quitely, Tim Townsend, and Mark Morales (a). Collected in *New X-Men Vol. 1: E Is for Extinction* (2002).

Secret Invasion #8 (January 2009). Brian Michael Bendis (w), Leinil Yu and Mark Morales (a). Collected in *Secret Invasion* (2010).

Secret Invasion: Front Line #5 (January 2009). Brian Reed (w), Marco Castiello (a). Collected in *Secret Invasion: Front Line* (2009).

Sensational Spider-Man, vol. 2, #29 (October 2006). Roberto Aquirre-Sacasa (w), Angel Medina and Scott Hanna (a). Collected in *Civil War: Peter Parker, Spider-Man* (2007).

Sensational Spider-Man, vol. 2, #30 (November 2006). Roberto Aquirre-Sacasa (w), Angel Medina and Scott Hanna (a). Collected in *Civil War: Peter Parker, Spider-Man* (2007).

Sensational Spider-Man, vol. 2, #31 (December 2006). Roberto Aquirre-Sacasa (w), Angel Medina and Scott Hanna (a). Collected in *Civil War: Peter Parker, Spider-Man* (2007).

Sensational Spider-Man, vol. 2, #32 (January 2007). Roberto Aquirre-Sacasa (w), Sean Chen and Scott Hanna (a). Collected in *Civil War: Peter Parker, Spider-Man* (2007).

Sensational Spider-Man, vol. 2, #40 (October 2007). Roberto Aquirre-Sacasa (w), Clayton Crain (a). Collected in *Spider-Man, Peter Parker: Back in Black* (2008).

Sensational Spider-Man, vol. 2, #41 (December 2007). J. Michael Straczynski (w), Joe Quesada and Danny Miki (a). Collected in *Spider-Man: One More Day* (2008).

Sensational Spider-Man Annual, vol. 2, #1 (July 2007). Matt Fraction (w), Salvador Larroca (a). Collected in *Spider-Man, Peter Parker: Back in Black* (2008).

She-Hulk, vol. 2, #8 (July 2006). Dan Slott (w), Paul Smith (a). Collected in *She-Hulk Vol. 4: Laws of Attraction* (2007).

She-Hulk, vol. 2, #18 (June 2007). Dan Slott (w), Rick Burchett and Cliff Rathburn (a). Collected in *She-Hulk Vol. 5: Planet Without a Hulk* (2007).

Siege #1 (March 2010). Brian Michael Bendis (w), Olivier Coipel and Mark Morales (a). Collected in *Siege* (2010).

Siege #3 (May 2010). Brian Michael Bendis (w), Olivier Coipel and Mark Morales (a). Collected in *Siege* (2010).

Siege #4 (June 2010). Brian Michael Bendis (w), Olivier Coipel and Mark Morales (a). Collected in *Siege* (2010).

Siege: Embedded #4 (July 2010). Brian Reed (w), Chris Samnee (a). Collected in *Siege: Embedded* (2010).

Siege: The Cabal one-shot (February 2010). Brian Michael Bendis (w), Michael Lark and Stefano Gaudiano (a). Collected in *Siege* (2010).

Siege: Captain America one-shot (June 2010). Christos N. Gage (w), Federico Dallocchio (a). Collected in *Siege: Battlefield* (2010).

Tales of Suspense, vol. 1, #39 (March 1963). "Iron Man Is Born!" Stan Lee and Larry Lieber (w), Don Heck (a). Collected in *Marvel Masterworks: Iron Man, Vol. 1* (2010) and *Iron Man Epic Collection: The Golden Avenger* (2014).

Thor, vol. 1, #390 (April 1988). Tom DeFalco (w), Ron Frenz and Brett Breeding (a). Collected in *Thor Epic Collection: War of the Pantheons* (2013).

Thor, vol. 3, #3 (November 2007). J. Michael Straczynski (w), Olivier Coipel and Mark Morales (a). Collected in *Thor by J. Michael Straczynski Vol. 1* (2008).

Thor, vol. 3, #11 (November 2008). J. Michael Straczynski (w), Olivier Coipel and various inkers (a). Collected in *Thor by J. Michael Straczynski Vol. 2* (2009).

Thor, vol. 4, #1 (December 2014). Jason Aaron (w), Russell Dauterman (a). Collected in *Thor Volume 1: Goddess of Thunder* (2015).

Thunderbolts, vol. 1, #21 (December 1998). Kurt Busiek (w), Mark Bagley and Scott Hanna (a).

Uncanny X-Men, vol. 1, #183 (July 1984). Chris Claremont (w), John Romita, Jr. and Dan Green (a). Collected in *Essential X-Men Vol. 5* (2011).

What If?, vol. 1, #3 (June 1977). Jim Shooter and Gil Kane (w), Gil Kane and Klaus Janson (a). Collected in *What If? Classic Volume 1* (2005).

What If?, vol. 1, #10 (August 1978). Don Glut (w), Rick Hoberg and Dave Hunt (a). Collected in *What If? Classic Volume 2* (2006).

What If? Civil War one-shot (February 2008), "The Stranger." Ed Brubaker (w), Marko Djurdjevic (a). Collected in *What If?: Civil War* (2008).

What If? Civil War one-shot (February 2008), "What If Captain America Led All the Heroes Against Registration?" Kevin Grevioux (w), Gustavo and various inkers (a). Collected in *What If?: Civil War* (2008).

What If? Civil War one-shot (February 2008), "What If Iron Man Lost the Civil War?" Christos Gage (w), Harvey Tolibao (a). Collected in *What If?: Civil War* (2008).

What If? Fallen Son (February 2009), "What If... Iron Man Had Died?" Marc Sumerak (w), Trevor Goring (a). Collected in *What If?: Secret Wars* (2009).

Wolverine, vol. 3, #43 (August 2006). Marc Guggenheim (w), Humberto Ramos and Carlos Cuevas (a). Collected in *Civil War: Wolverine* (2007).

World War Hulk #1 (August 2007). Greg Pak (w), John Romita, Jr. and Klaus Janson (a). Collected in *World War Hulk* (2008).

World War Hulk #4 (November 2007). Greg Pak (w), John Romita, Jr. and Klaus Janson (a). Collected in *World War Hulk* (2008).

World War Hulk #5 (January 2008). Greg Pak (w), John Romita, Jr. and Klaus Janson (a). Collected in *World War Hulk* (2008).

X-Factor, vol. 3, #9 (September 2006). Peter David (w), Dennis Calero (a). Collected in *Civil War: X-Men Universe* (2007).

Young Avengers, vol. 1, #6 (September 2005). Allan Heinberg (w), Jim Cheung and various inkers (a). Collected in *Young Avengers* (2010).

Notes